Of A Tree Called Life

The Irish Holocaust in New Orleans

Michael Pumphrey

Copyright © 2017 by Michael Pumphrey
All rights reserved

ISBN   978-0-9828700-3-7

Published by
LITERARIAN PUBLICATONS

Manufactured in the United States of America

For each of the Irish lives lost too soon

digging the New Basin Canal

and

for Aunt Dorothy who encouraged me

to write this book

AUTHOR'S NOTE

U.S. Army Corps of Engineers Photo c. 1941

At the Jefferson/Orleans Parish line, Interstate 10 takes a sharp right turn as it enters New Orleans proper. Few speeding down the highway today are aware that this section of the interstate was built over what had once been the course of the New Basin Canal. Fewer still are aware of the role poor Irish immigrants played in constructing that waterway, nor of the price they paid in doing so. Accordingly, this book is a work of fiction based on an historical fact. The stories of the Irishmen who dug the canal have been all but lost to history, the only acknowledgment of their existence being a small monument at the foot of West End Boulevard overlooking Lake Pontchartrain. It reads: In memory of the Irish immigrants who dug the New Basin Canal, 1832-1838, this Celtic cross carved in Ireland has been erected by the Irish Cultural Society of New Orleans.

Names, characters, places and incidents portrayed in this book are purely the product of my imagination or are used fictitiously. Any resemblance to actual persons living or dead, businesses, companies, events or locales is entirely coincidental..

ACKNOWLEDGEMENTS

Special thanks goes out to those who have given of their time, talents and encouragement in helping this book to be written, this story to be told. It is with a little prayer offered up that I might not have left anyone out whose contributions should be acknowledged, that I declare a debt of gratitude to Paige Peyton, Chip Sandifer, Marc Schrenker, Terry O'Donnell, Bill Pumphrey, Carrol Delano, and Dorothy Teague Hudson.

OF A TREE CALLED LIFE

History, despite its wrenching pain, cannot be unlived; but if it is faced with courage, need not be lived again.

Maya Angelou

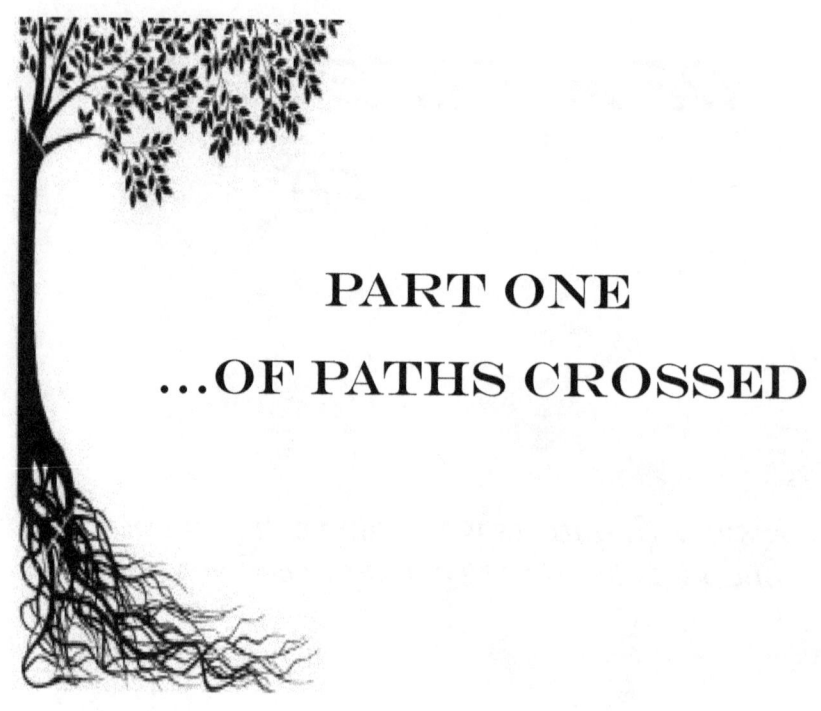

PART ONE
...OF PATHS CROSSED

ONE

There was a time before the world knew Katrina; a time before the towers fell; a time before storms racked the deserts; a time when this venerable, vulnerable old city seemed to sleep more peacefully. There was that night of the Odyssey Ball, when for a brief while the elegant crowd gathered at the museum of art to make merry and toast another major acquisition. And there was that night T. K. Issacson and I spent reading words set down 175 years ago, on pages now yellowed, in ink now faded, while old New Orleans danced and slumbered and sang and cried and breathed and died outside the shuttered windows of that old house on Carondelet Street.

In my time, there have been other memorable moments. This is but one of several, and yet it is a story worth the telling; it is a story worth the reading. It is the story of two families as disparate as Frost's two roads diverging in that yellow wood; two families whose paths once again converged for a brief moment in time after the passage of so many decades.

Every once in a blue moon there are blue skies in old New Orleans. Mostly it happens in the month of October when, for a few short weeks, the shroud of humidity lifts, the temperature moderates and pleasant breezes venture down from the north. It was just such an October weekend that they rode the wind on rented wings in order to arrive at the ball on time: chartered jets were never the Issacson family's mode of transportation. To the contrary, demanding careers necessitated that T.K. and his new bride, Susan, travel in such ostentatious style. Even in the Big Apple, where displays of the almighty dollar are taken to the level of sport, no one in the Issacson family ever indulges in extravagance. Ever. Calling attention to their good fortunes would be as alien to The Family as wearing their Jewishness on their sleeves.

Let me expound on this: his full name is Thomas Kelly Issacson V, but even as a second-grader it seemed terribly pretentious to him, and pretense was something not fostered within the family. At the dinner table one evening, he announced that he wished to be known simply as T.K. His playground buddies took to the name right away, and over time the entire family did too, to the extent that ever after he has been simply T.K., to family, friends and confrères alike.

Now T.K.'s paternal grandmother, Lillian, was the unquestioned matriarch of The Family, and on her eightieth birthday she announced her Forrest Hills Tudor took up too much of what little time she had left. She downsized into a condo in The Pinnacle on Forrest Hills' Prospect Avenue, and spacious as it was for a condominium, the move still necessitated culling through half a century of accumulations, among which treasures was no less than the Catherine Issacson portrait.

It had been in the family for as long as anyone could remember, hanging at the top of the stairs in her foyer. It had essentially gone unheeded for the decades until, quite by chance, Susan noted the signature and insisted the painting had to be an original O'Bannion. No less than three experts authenticated it as the only known example of a society portrait done by the gentleman famous for poignant portraits of Native Americans of the desert southwest. It was worth a small fortune, but then Isaacson money is so old it is mildewed, and money, in and of itself, never impresses anyone in The Family. Perhaps that was why they took such a casual attitude toward it. At a scale slightly larger than life, however, it was not well-suited to Grandmother Lillian's new apartment, and since Catherine had originally hailed from New Orleans, the old girl decided to donate it to the New Orleans Museum of Art.

In the end, she almost pulled the plug on the gift when the museum pressured her to be the guest of honor at the portrait's unveiling at its annual Odyssey Ball. Calling attention to herself like that ran counter to her every instinct, but ultimately it was decided that it was too late to pull out of the transaction, that T.K. and Susan would make the trip to New Orleans to represent the family and insure undue attention was not focused on their generosity.

That was how our paths crossed, how two family lines briefly came together once again, one fine October evening in old New Orleans. Like two gnarled branches from the same old oak, reaching out to the sun in different directions, time and history caused our limbs to cross once again.

It's really as simple as that.

TWO

We were the Walkers and they the Isaacsons, so perhaps it was fate or perhaps it was divine intervention that caused our family paths to intersect again after so many years. It would have been much easier for us to pass one another like the proverbial two ships in the dark, rather than meeting up the way we did. Allow me to explain. My wife and I are avid supporters of NOMA, but with two young boys in private school and an underfunded college tuition plan, our support was not sufficient to score tickets to the patron's reception immediately prior to the ball itself. That particular evening we arrived a little late, even by New Orleans standards. Had we missed a red light or two; or had I fumbled with my black tie a little longer; or had my wife decided to change shoes for the tenth time, we might never have met the young couple from New York.

As it turned out, however, we stood admiring the Catherine Isaacson portrait presiding over the landing of the museum's grand staircase, just as T.K. and Susan paused to bid it farewell. As we stood side-by-side, strangers, Susan noticed my wife's gaze darting from the locket Catherine wore in the portrait to the one dangling from her neck that evening. She lifted it up and held it out for Pamela to admire.

"Yes, it's the same one. A gift from my husband's grandmother."

Pamela politely described it as magnificent. I, in turn, inquired of T.K., "So she would have been your..."

"My great...great...great grandmother. I think I got the 'greats' in there."

"And Hiam Isaacson would have been her husband?" I asked, receiving a curious nod in return. I introduced Pamela and myself to the couple and casually commented that I felt like Mr. Isaacson was almost family. "I practically grew up in the Isaacson mansion. It's been in our family for over 150 years now. My aunt lives in it today."

T.K. Isaacson's eyes opened wide. "Really? You mean it's still standing? After all these years?"

"Absolutely. Probably the most intact antebellum in the city."

"Would it difficult to find? I'd like to take a drive by and see it while we're here. Get a picture of it, if possible."

"Very easy if you know where the Pontchartrain Hotel is. On St. Charles Avenue."

The Isaacson's shared a glance. "That's where we're staying!"

"Well, then, it's directly behind the hotel. On the uptown, lakeside corner of Carondelet. Can't miss it."

"Oh, we'll definitely have to check it out tomorrow. We wouldn't want to miss that."

It was at that point that I said something that would, unbeknownst to either of us, be a defining incidence in both our lives. "I can do you one better than that," I told my new acquaintance. "How would you like a private tour?"

THREE

After some finessing, I convinced my Aunt Alice Monroe to open the house to the descendants of the gentleman who built it, and the following afternoon they came calling. Beneath a canopy of pungent sweet olive trees flanking the front gate they paused to read the historical marker.

THE H. ISAACSON MANSION
C. 1823
THIS FINE EXAMPLE OF ANTEBELLUM NEW ORLEANS ARCHITECTURE WAS BUILT BY HIAM M. ISAACSON, A WEALTHY SUGAR CANE PLANTER, BANKER AND COTTON BROKER. IT REMAINS TO THIS DAY THE MOST IMPORTANT RESIDENCE BUILT IN THE OLD JEWISH SECTION OF THE AMERICAN SECTOR. TRAGEDY STRUCK IN 1837 WHEN ISAACSON'S YOUNG FIANCÉE WAS BRUTALLY MURDERED IN THE HOME. IN 1838 THE HOUSE WAS ACQUIRED BY MLLE. AMANDA MANEAU, A FREE WOMAN OF COLOR AND CONSORT TO ETIENNE, MARQUIS DUBOISBLANC.

Looking up from the medallion Susan mused, "Somehow, I just can't see anyone from your family living in something this..." she searched the sky for the right word, "Opulent. Is that it?"

"It is a little grandiose." T.K. nodded toward the marker. "Interesting, this business about his having a fiancée who was murdered. Maybe that's why he left New Orleans for New York."

"No one in your family ever said anything about it?"

"Nobody ever said much about him at all. At least that I recall. I asked grandmother about Catherine once but she was a little cryptic. You could tell she didn't want to talk about her. I asked dad why, but he just said my grandfather had been the same way. He seemed to think he might have been a slave owner, or something like that."

Susan studied the house for a moment, taking in the harmonic proportions of its geometry and the ironwork on the deep porches, or galleries, as intricate as fine Belgian lace. "You think?"

"Well, he came from England originally. Maybe he stole the crown jewels or something. I wonder, though, if this is how the

Isaacson family came to America? In such high style? Mother's family came through Ellis Island and shared a three-room, cold-water flat in the Bronx with another couple. Amazing when you think about it."

Susan prodded him on. "Come on. I can't wait to see what's inside."

And hesitant though she had been to open her house to strangers, Aunt Alice dutifully gave them the grand tour with all the grace and charm of a quintessential southern doyenne. She proudly pointed out all the original furnishings and details in the double parlors, the dining room, and the six bedchambers. She explained how the carpets would be rolled up in the grand hall and musicians would be stationed on the staircase landing so New Orleans' elite could while the night away waltzing across the wide plank pine floors, beneath the massive candle-lit chandeliers. When the tour was completed we settled in the cypress paneled library where Aunt Alice ordered a pitcher of mint juleps from Gaston, her faithful *major domo* of heaven only knows how many years. It was then that T.K. said how unfortunate it was that the only known portrait of Hiam Issacson is a tiny one in Susan's locket. She slipped it from around her neck, gingerly opened the case and presented it to Aunt Alice for her inspection. Peering over her bifocals, she suddenly blurted out, "Why sugar, that's not Hiam Isaacson! That's that pitiful Irish boy."

T.K. and Susan seemed dumbfounded; indeed, we all did. "What do you mean, Irish boy?" I challenged her.

"I mean just what I said. And y'all keep going on about that picture being Catherine Issacson. That girl was never married to Hiam. He was an old bachelor man the whole time he lived in this house. Might have been married after he moved to New York, I couldn't say. I don't know anything about him after he left here."

"Now Aunt Alice, what makes you think that?" I asked her, completely confused as to the course the conversation had taken.

"Hell's bells, Bodie," she responded, calling me by the pet name she had given me years ago. "I read the <u>Picayune</u> this morning. They had a big picture of that painting right there in the Living Section. The woman was wearing this very same necklace!" She waved the locket in the air before passing it back to Susan.

T.K. allowed a nervous clearing of his throat. "So wouldn't that just substantiate that she was my great-great-great grandfather's wife? I mean, everyone in my family for generations has said she was. I'm pretty sure that she's buried right beside him in one of the cemeteries in Brooklyn. I've never been there, but that's what I've always understood."

"No honey, that's not right," Aunt Alice insisted. "I'm sorry, but that girl's buried right here in New Orleans. In the old Lafayette No. One. Whoever's buried beside him in Brooklyn may be his wife all right, but it certainly isn't that Dunnigan girl."

My Aunt Alice was getting up in years by that time, and I must confess I wondered if perhaps her mind had begun to play tricks on her. "Why do you say that?" I pressed.

"That damned locket, that's why! You've been to Lafayette Cemetery. You know which tomb I'm talking about. It's the biggest one there. Right when you're coming in the front gate across from Commander's Palace. The Mary Katherine Dunnigan one. Y'all go out there and see for yourselves if you don't believe me. Isaacson had the thing built for her. That's a fact. Stuck her in the wall, first, then hauled a bunch of fancy marble and sculptors from over in Italy to build the damned thing! Probably cost a million dollars to build something like that today. Go on and see for yourselves. There's even a statue of her right there on the monument. And she's wearing that very same locket. Standing in the same pose as in that picture y'all gave the museum." Then, without taking a breath, she bellowed, "Gaston where the hell is my mint julep!"

A muffled "It's coming, Miss Alice. It's coming," came from down the hall.

It was obvious Alice was getting worked up, so we let things settle for a moment before we pried further. "Aunt Alice, how'd you find all this out, anyway?" I eventually asked.

She pointed a bony finger with blood red nail polish at me. "Go slide the ladder down to the far left side of the bookcase. Go on! Climb on up there to the top shelf. Just don't fall off and break your silly neck."

I did as she said, seeing that she was still agitated. "Up there on the top row. Reach behind the books and you'll find another book. Not very thick."

I fumbled around, but found nothing. "No, there's nothing up here."

"Yes there is! Look! It's up there I tell you!"

I fumbled around some more. "No, there's nothing—no wait!" I pulled a slender volume bound in cracked alligator leather from behind a row of books and held it up. "Is this it?"

"That's it. Now get on down and bring it to me."

I managed to back down the ladder without falling and deposited the book into her waiting hands. "You see, y'all think when hair gets as white as mine that we have all the answers to life. Well guess what? We don't! Life's just as gray when you're eighty as when you're eighteen." She dusted the volume with one of her ubiquitous monogrammed hankies, treating it with all the reverence of a sacred relic.

"I don't know whether this is the right thing to do or not, but y'all have lots of questions and this book has most of the answers. Records what went on in this house when Hiam Isaacson owned it. Now it can't ever, ever be taken out of this house. You understand that, Bodie? When this house is handed down to you, y'all can't ever allow this book outside these walls."

"Why not?" Pamela wanted to know.

"'Cause almighty hell will break lose if you do! Now boys, y'all can sit here and read over this book if you want to. It's like a diary or a journal. It was written by a woman named Amanda Maneau. She ran this house the whole-time Isaacson lived here. And a good while after. Read it if you like. You'll see. It'll answer just about all the questions either one of you have about your families. But I warn you!" Once again the bony finger with the blood red polish pointed, first at me, then at T.K., as she looked hard and deep into each of our eyes, "You may not like what you find out."

Aunt Alice Monroe held the book out toward us. I was so confused I hesitated a moment. T.K., however, did not. He reached forward and took it, leaned back in the chesterfield and opened it. He perused it for just a bit before looking over at me, a mischievous smile on his face. "What do you think? I'm game."

I shrugged and nodded, and Aunt Alice said, "I believe I'll retire to the upstairs gallery. Enjoy all this fine weather while we have it. In New Orleans, you take pleasant weather like this whenever you can get it." We waited as she waddled her way out into the grand hall. "Gaston! I'm going up on the front gallery. You've got five minutes to get me my mint julep or you're fired!"

And from inside the kitchen we heard the familiar refrain, "It's coming," then the sound of Aunt Alice's chair lift squeaking up the staircase.

"Lying bastard," she could be heard mumbling just loud enough to be heard out in the butler's pantry. "Knows I won't fire him. Whole damned bunch probably huddled around the T.V. out in the kitchen watching Days of Our Lives. Just can't get decent help anymore."

I apologized again for my Aunt's earthy language, but noticed T.K. was engrossed with the alligator-bound book with the initials AM embossed on the cover. "What do you think?" I asked him. "Shall we take turns reading? You start and I'll take over when you want."

With that, T.K. Isaacson opened the book to the first page of flowing script.

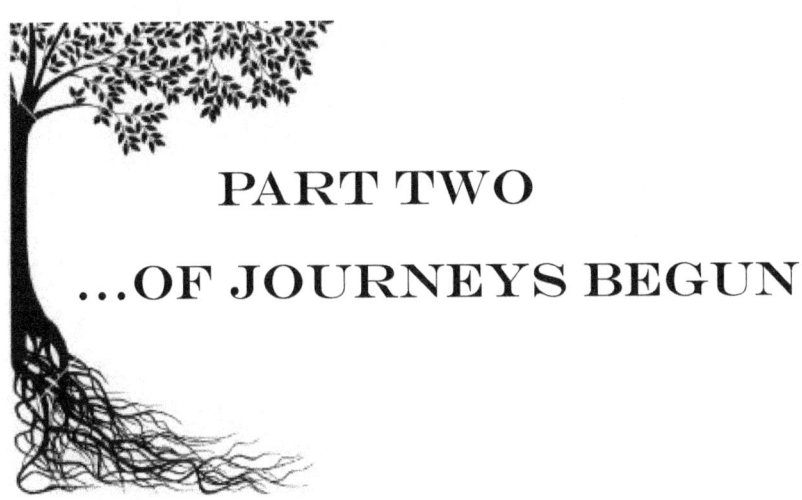

PART TWO
...OF JOURNEYS BEGUN

Thursday, 22 June 1837

Mon Dieu, mon Dieu! It is a duppy that hangs over this house—a curse even the garde of a mambo so powerful as Mme. Laveau cannot send back to the bowels of hell. Mon Dieu, mon Dieu! How did we come to such a sad state? Our master walks the halls of this mansion, wailing and crying like a woman. Shameful he is. He crushes to his bosom the little child, till I tink he shall squeeze its little soul from out its very body. No one can console him. All day and all night long the Jews come, trying to ease his burden with their swaying prayers and chants. But all is to no avail. Our master is inconsolable, a cadaver astral—one of the living dead, I fear. What will become of this great house and those who dwell within it? Shall we be lost as well?

Three times have I summoned Mme. Laveau—"Mamaloi"—to this house, and three times has her power failed us. The Dessounin Ritual does not separate the gros-bon-ange—the energy of the soul—from those now dead so soon. They even refuse the sacred Mange' Morts offering. Even on the Nine-Night when we pour the lines of the crossroads in water up to the ve-ve and join hands to chant ko-bo-ni-jo; ko-bo-ni-jo; ko-bo-ni-jo, our master's Z'e'toile—his star of destiny—remains darkened. Now comes word from Mme. Laveau by messenger that she has had a dream; that in her dream I am to write down in this book all that has transpired beneath this roof. Do this, she assures me, and peace will once again reign over this house, for as long as this book shall remain within its walls. Will this magic work? I know not. I know only I must try. I have hope I can save all with my writing, that this dream she has points to the magic to rid us of such bad luck as we now endure.

How did such ill-fortune come to fall upon this fine house and the master who lords over it? 'Twas those Irish womens who brought it with them, all the way across from the great ocean, I tinks. They brought it with them and now it takes this house and all within it as its own. Mme. Laveau says "No." It is that canal and Mon.Isaacson's money made in building on it that brings the bad luck." Mme. Laveau says too great's the corps cadavers lying buried at the bottom of that canal for any good to ever come of it. Mme. Laveau says the only way to break the bad luck—to send the Tonton Macoute back to Duvalier—is to put to ink all that has happened in this house. This and only this will quiet the cries of those lying beneath the dark waters of the canal. And so do I take pen in hand and begin the task.

But where to start, I ask myself. So much has happened in so little time. Yet can there ever be a place to start but at the beginning? I tink no. I will start there, at the beginning—with that fair young man with the big brown eyes and hair the color of the dark cherries of August; the one with his face all painted up with the freckles. There is the start, and I shall prevail upon his ally, that skinny wisp of mon who sits under the big oak tree across the back street, staring endlessly at this house, crying like a woman, himself. He will know his friend's true story. I will pick the memories from his mind, like a vulture picking the flesh from off his dead friend's bones, until the story is mine, until the story is written down for all who read my letters to know. And then, may he and all his Irish kind forever burn in hell for all the misery they have wrought upon this fine house and the good people who now weep and wail within its walls.

T.K. peeked at me over the top of the open book. He laid it—dropped it, really—in his lap. "Stunned" was the only word to describe us at that moment in time. Both of our mouths hung wide open and we were unable to break our gawk. At length, grins overtook us both and we began to hoot out loud, we could not help ourselves.

"What in heaven's name has your aunt found here?" I was asked.

"No idea. I think I understand why she doesn't want the thing taken out of this house, though."

"Well, who do you suppose this Mme. Laveau person is? Some sort of a witch?"

"Has to be Marie Laveau, the famous voodoo priestess. Her or her daughter. They'd have been carrying on their shenanigans about then. Funny, though, I've heard about Marie Laveau all my life—she's big in New Orleans lore. I've just never run up against a real person writing about her before. This could be important, you know. Historically at least."

"You mean she would have been an actual Voodoo person?" T.K. asked, not quite sure whether he should believe me or not.

"Without a doubt. She's a historical figure all right. She was a quadroon. You know, she had African grandparents. But she was what they called a free woman of color. Lived to a ripe old age, but she's been dead probably a hundred fifty years now. She's supposed to be buried in a tomb in St. Louis No. 1. Big tourist attraction. She was one powerful woman in her time. Still is, as a matter of fact. People sneak into the cemetery after dark all the time and perform rituals at her tomb."

"Rituals? Voodoo rituals?

"Sure. They are supposed to knock on the door of the tomb three times. Scratch three crosses on it and leave some offering."

"I had no idea people still did things like that. Whatever for?"

"Cheap thrills, most likely. Supposedly, if she likes your offering, she'll grant you some favor. That sort of stuff's always been appealing to some people."

"Sounds rather like what this Amanda Maneau was looking for, herself. Someone to come along and 'hocus-pocus,' make everything right again."

I furrowed my chin and nodded slightly. "To an extent, it probably was. But consider the timeframe when all this was happening. This was the early nineteenth century, not the twenty-first. People could be very superstitious back then."

"Well, if this is any glimpse of what's to come, it's going to be a long, long night reading this stuff. Let's get at it, what do you say?"

Friday, 23 June 1837

I am told it has stood for over one-hundred years now, that oak tree across the back street; the one a bolt of lightning split nearly in half in its younger years. Down through time, it has managed to survive, however, its once single trunk now two discernible ones. In spite of the trauma, it thrives spreading a healthy umbrella over much of the streetscape.

There he stood near sundown, beside that tree across the back street, all caked in mud from head to toe from digging on that God-forsaken canal. He made the blood run cold in my veins, just standing there, staring at this house the way he did. I tell you, I'd have rather approached a moccasin-snake, but I knew what I must do. So a little plate of food I made him up. A nice roll, not too hard. A fine piece of fish, fried up fresh that morning. A dab of mirleton. The boy is nothing but skin and bones as it is. Many of his kind are at the bottom of that canal what's still got more meat on them than this one.

I took the plate out to the coach house where I could stand in the carriageway out of the rain, already starting to drizzle. "Come. Eat," I called out loud to him, holding out the plate to tempt him over, but he just made to walk away. After him I called even louder, "You be hungry, I can tell from your looks. Besides, I need to make the talk with you, jeune homme veuillez." He stopped; he pivoted; he looked at me for a goodly while. I was about to give up, to lay the plate down for him to find, like some stray dog, and go back into the house, when he crossed the street and stood full in front of me. Not scared of the devil himself was this one who stood there in the falling mist.

"And what might ye be wantin' of me?" he scowled.

My heart leapt up inside myself, but I managed to hold up the plate to him. "Look, I've brought you food." He looked at that plate of food like I've seen men fresh off the sailing boats look at women-folks walking down the street, but he stood his ground.

"And what might I be wantin' with the food from this house?"

"You need the food, mon," I insisted, "I can see you do. Go now. To the well in the courtyard there and wash your muddy hands and face, then come and eat."

Still he moved not the least, until, with one fell swoop, his hand struck out and snatched the roll from off the plate so fast my eyes could scarcely follow. "This'll do me," he said. The mist was washing the mud from out his hair. Muddy like the Mississippi, it ran down his face, down the sleeves of his shirt, across his hands and over the roll, but he gnawed at it anyway. "Now, what is it you're needed to be talkin' to the likes o' me about?"

"If you won't finish the food I fixed you, then come in out of the rain. Nobody will be minding you being here in the carriageway," I implored of the boy. He looked me cold in the eye and I did fear for my very life, but he stepped in out of the drizzle. "How old are you?" I asked him.

"Me age?" he says. "You made up that fine platter of food and lured me in here out o' the rain to ask me bloody age? What's it to you?"

"You must be about the same age as he was. Your friend. The one that..." I couldn't finish my own sentence.

"The one that your fine lord, there," he tossed his head up at the mansion, "killed, just as sure as if he'd put a gun to his heart. Ain't that what you meant?" His very words took the wind from out of my lungs. I could barely protest.

"You blame Mon. Isaacson for your friend's death?" I managed to gasp.

"As surely as I stand here. And his name was Rory, me friend. Rory O'Kelley. He was nineteen when he died. Same age as me. Now, if you'll be excusing me..." He turned to leave, but again I protested.

"Hold it! Sit for a while. Finish some more of the food or it will just go to the dogs." Dead in his tracks he stopped, I tell you, and I feared he would finish me off for sure this time. Slowly, slowly he turned 'round to me.

Leave it to them, then," he growled. "American dogs live better than Irishmen in America do anyway."

I knew not what more to do. In a fit of standing my ground, I tossed the plate out into the street where it shattered, the rain washing the food down the muddy road. "Fine! If you don't want the food, won't you sit a spell and make the talk with me, mon? I mean you no harm. Surely you must know that." And with that I hiked up my skirt and sat myself down on a fresh bale of hay. "Go on. Sit. The hay is clean." Not for a moment was it that those cold eyes left me, as he squatted down across from me, ever so slowly.

The boy tossed his head up at the house yet another time. "Ye got whiskey in that fancy house of yers?"

"Monsieur keeps spirits," I replied. "What's it to you?"

"Ye want to talk to me, woman, it'll cost ye a drink of whiskey," he bargained and in my head, I recalled all the talk I had heard before, how all the Irish digging that canal loved their strong drink and their public rows. But if it took strong drink to get the story out of him, he would have it. Just in case he had any notions about a brawl with me, though, I resolved to bring protection—maybe a kitchen knife or one of the boys—back with me when I returned.

"You may have your drink, if that's what you want," I told him. Wait here until I return." And off I went to the house, to pilfer monsieur's choice whiskey for a story from this skinny Irish boy.

He was sitting right where I had left him when I returned, but his eyes quickly grew wide and he rose to his feet when he saw I brought with me a footman bearing a whole decanter full of whiskey and a fine crystal goblet. I stopped short. "Sit," I told him, and he obliged obediently. I motioned for the footman to set the intoxicant on the hay bale and wait at the other end of the carriageway. It had grown dark, so I lit a lantern to see to the pouring of the boy's drink. In the faint yellow light, I handed the glass to him and he examined it closely before he drank it all down. He wiped his mouth on his dirty sleeve and held up the goblet to the lantern's light, watching the crystal facets dance in the dim glow. "The likes of me ain't fit to wash a glass as fine as this," he said as he handed it back to me. "So I've been told."

"I tink you do feel sorry for yourself, monsieur. You would be welcome to wash my dishes any time you feel like taking the trouble from off my hands."

"Patrick. Me name's Patrick O'Bannion. I would appreciate yer calling me by me bloody name," he snapped.

T.K. Isaacson suddenly became very animated. "There it is, Susan! Patrick O'Bannion. He must be the one! The guy who painted the Catherine Isaacson portrait—or whomever is in that picture. Maybe we can find out for once and for all if he's the same Patrick O'Bannion who was the famous painter out west."

"I was an art history major," Susan explained. "I recognized the name the first time I looked at the signature. I asked a friend who's a curator at MOMA to look at it and he seemed convinced it. They seemed to think it was the same artist. T.K.'s grandmother had a couple of other experts evaluate it and they thought it was an original O'Bannion, too. Others aren't so convinced, however: there's just not any record of his doing society portraits. Or of his ever having been in New Orleans. It's been documented that he came from Ireland to Galveston, Texas. And that he lived there for a short while before going out west. Out to the New Mexico territory. That's where he made his name painting Indians and western landscapes."

It would have been interesting to find out a little more about this mysterious artist I had never heard of, but T.K. had grown excited and he quickly continued with the reading.

"Very well, Patrick. Now, my name is Amanda Maneau, but since I am older than you, you may call me Mlle. Maneau." He nodded in consent. "And now that you have enjoyed your drink of whiskey, please tell me the story of your friend Rory O'Kelley."

"Rory O'Kelley was as good a man as ever walked the face o' the earth, that much I'll tell ye. So why do ye want to know about him?"

"I have my reasons. Important reasons. Besides which, you've had your drink. You made me a bargain. Need I remind you of that? Or, are you not a mon of your word?" It was with the tiniest of a smile sneaking over his face that he answered me, a twinkling in his eyes adding emphasis to his words.

"Aye. A man 'o me word I am, at that. I may not be much more, but I am a man o' me word. So where would ye have me to begin?"

"At the beginning would be fine," I told him. And as I continued to ply him with the whiskey, the story of Mr. Rory O'Kelley poured out of the boy's soul, like spirits out of a fine crystal decanter.

They were like two old warriors from opposite sides waiting out a final truce—Rory O'Kelley and his daddy were. At the end, they had thrown down their weapons of self-defense and cast off their mantles of self-interest, only to marvel at that tiny glimmer of humanity they found in each other's eyes. In peace they embraced one another, in time to turn and leave in opposite directions, the one to the west, the other to the east; off toward an unknown tomorrow, never to see one another again. The night his father died, Rory sat up with him from the wee hours of the morning the day before, holding his hand and stroking his hair, trying to weigh the good times against the bad, in hopes the latter would be greater than the former. Hard it is, being the son of a father; too much politics be involved, too much struggle for the power. Now they waited out the inevitable together.

An only child was this Rory O'Kelley. His mother almost died giving him the birth, and never would her health be the same afterwards. But she did manage to live on fourteen more years, before her lungs finally gave out on her and she died of the winter fever. Rory, there in the back of his mind, did always feel his daddy blamed him that his mother was so frail. It just seemed the weaker his mother got, the less and less his father had to do with him. Sure, it was hard on the boy too. All at the same time he had to help care for his poor mother and help his father with the coaxing of a pitiful crop of potatoes out of the rocky soil, year after year.

Ragged he nearly ran himself, but his father never gave him a bit of the credit. When work was done, night after night the old man would disappear down the road, to one of the taverns where the surroundings would be cheerful and he could dull the pain that would be waiting for him back home with a pint or two of stout.

Times were, when he was but a youngster, that his father would take him to the pub, proudly sit him up on the bar and tell him to tell the house about the smart pills. "This Englishman asks this li'l Irish boy what he's got in his jar," little Rory would always start out. "Them's smart pills he tells 'em. 'Smart pills? Let me have one o' them pills then, lad,' the Englishman tells the boy. 'O' no sir. One o' these pills will be a costin' ye a full crown,' the boy tells him. 'A full crown!' the Englishman hollers. But still he gives the boy a crown and the boy gives him a pill. He eats the pill, but the Englishman says, 'For the sakes o' me, lad, I don't feel no smarter.' 'No?' asks the little boy. 'Here, give me another crown and take another one.' So the Englishman gives the boy another crown and eats another one o' the pills, but he says he still don't feel no smarter. 'I fear ye must be very foolish, sir', says the boy. 'But give me one last crown and take yet another o' the pills.' The Englishman pays the lad and chews another o' the pills. 'Say,' he says to the boy. 'These pills 'o yers taste like rat pills!' And with that the little Irish boy tells the Englishman, 'See there! You're getting' smarter already!'"

Always the pub would erupt in laughter at the little Rory's tale, no one laughing harder than his own father would. His daddy would tassel the boy's hair and buy him a pickled egg, and Rory was not to remember another time so warm with his own dear papa. But as Rory got older and his mother got sicker, his father took to leaving him at home when he would go to the pub each night. And when he would at last come back home, Rory would try to see to it his father's plate of food was warm but not dried out. Then he'd retreat to the corner by the fire and try to make himself invisible, so as not to incur his papa's wrath. Life had not been kind to the old man, and he took to lashing out in his frustration at the nearest thing at hand, that usually being his only son. And the more he lashed out at the lad, the more Rory came to believe the only time he could count on his father's attention was for an upbraiding or a beating.

And so it was that by the time they had the cold Irish sod spread over his mother's remains, the two had retreated into their own corners of disdain for each other, there to sulk like a couple of boxers condemned to go the distance. They stood opposite one another, that sad morning, contemplating the little mound of dirt before them—the pitiful grief a father and his son shared for the same woman. "Now, what with your mother gone, I expect you'll be a wantin' to move along, won't you?" his father finally spoke.

Rory thought for a moment before answering. "That I will, I suppose." And the two turned and went home together without so much as another word between them. And yet, it would be three more years Rory was to stay on at the home place. He always intended to leave, it just seemed there was never anywhere much for him to go. Now, at last, with his papa on his deathbed, he was glad he had stayed around.

After his mother's death, the anger inside his father seemed not to spill over as frequently as before. For true, it was an uneasy peace between the two of them, but now with the old man about to pass on, Rory was glad he was to be there with him at the end. Better this, than him running off somewhere and his own flesh-and-blood dead in that house for days and months on end, before anyone would find him. There toward the end, it was a cold sweat that was to overtake his father. Rory fetched a moist rag and made to wipe the sweat from the old man's face, but the cool of the moisture did bring him suddenly around. He looked up into his son's eyes with a start. "Twas your own dear mother I was a dreamin' about there, son," he whispered. "She reminded me to tell ye somethin'."

What's that, da?" Rory asked.

"Ye know where me pocket watch is, don ye?"

"That I do."

"Good. And in the fireplace ye'll be a findin' a loose stone. If ye'll take that out, there ye'll find where I hid your mother's weddin' band. It's these two things that's all of value I have to leave ye, lad. But these ain't fer hoardin' up, mind ye. Take and sell 'em quick. Use the money to help get yerself away from Ireland. Go to America, why don't ye, me son? Make yer future there, where there's a future to be made." And then the old man just gave up the ghost and died. Rory was only seventeen years and already he had no mama, no papa, no one but himself. He stayed on, on the craggy old home place just long enough to see his father buried in the ground beside the wife he loved. Long enough to round up their three laying hens and one unreliable milk cow and sell them for a pittance. And then he lingered a little longer, just long enough to break up all the furniture in the house and smash out the window glass: the landlord had never given the O'Kelley's anything but trouble, and now it was time the O'Kelley's gave him some trouble in return.

Needle and thread did Rory take into his own hands, where after a long piece he managed to sew a pouch into his under drawers, there to bank his mama's ring, his daddy's watch, and the two-quid four he got for the cow and hens. And then he left for Belfast, never looking back as he walked barefoot down the rocky, muddy road, his shoes tied by their strings and swung over his shoulder so as not to wear out the flimsy soles more than they already were. His papa had had a much nicer pair of shoes, with good thick soles still on them, but it would not have been right to bury the old man with bare feet, so he set out with his own old shoes slung over his shoulders.

It was four days and three nights the journey took him. Always he walked close to the edge of the road. Always he looked ahead for some big rock or shrub he could hide behind if anyone approached, for times were hard in Catholic Ireland and highwaymen roaming the back roads were known to prey on their own, poor kind just as quickly as they would a fat, rich Protestant. At nights he would stop to measure himself off a portion of the bread roll that was his only food. Somewhere far away from the road, he would eat his bread, pray to the saints for safe passage, and sleep fitfully on the cold and damp ground. It was a hard journey for a lad who had just lost his own father, but on he ventured, until at last he came to the great river valley where the city he had heard so much about suddenly appeared before him. Like one of the "wee ones" he had so feared as a child, one moment nothing was there; the next moment there was Belfast.

A lad less intelligent than Rory O'Kelley might have made straight away for the waterfront, where he would have begged, pled, and bargained—to no avail—for passage on one of the tall ships. A lad less intelligent might have, but not Rory O'Kelley. A keen observer was he, and soon he noticed the looks he drew from the fancy city dwellers he met on the street. He looked down upon himself and saw how his clothes were soiled, his hands were filthy and mud was caked between his toes. No it wouldn't do for him to venture deeper into the heart of the city, in such a sad state of dishevelment. Abruptly he turned and hurried out of the city. If only he had a mite of soap, he could find some secluded place on the river where he could wash the grime from his clothes and his body. But where to get hands on a piece of soap? On he walked, retracing the steps that had brought him into the city. His mind pondered his predicament with every step he took, until at last his gaze fell upon the fine old manor house beside the road, and the rather plump house wench he could see boiling up a batch of laundry in the back yard.

Soap! Surely he could buy a mite of soap off this lass, he thought. But no. Surely the very sight of him would send her running to the manor house, screaming bloody murder. No, he would need to show her the price of that bit of soap first. But then his money was sewn into his drawers, and it wouldn't do for him to be seen standing in the middle of the road with his hand down his own pants, trying to fish a coin from out his drawers. He thought better of it and determined to take cover behind the manor's big stone barn. There, surely, he would find privacy enough to tear a pence or two from out his pants. He swung wide in an arc, trying to keep low, always keeping his eye on the laundress poking with a paddle at the clothes boiling in the cauldron. Thanks he gave to the saints that she was too busy with her laundering to notice the dirty boy creeping 'round behind the barn.

Once he got to the back of the barn, he leaned up against the hard stone wall and breathed a sign of relief, then went about doing what he had to do, knowing full-well the longer he did linger, the more likely he'd get caught. He dropped his shoes to the ground, undid his pants and hastily stepped out of them. He reached his hand inside his under drawers and fidgeted with the pouch, swearing under his breath when he could not pull even the smallest of the coins through his stitching. Quickly, he slipped off his drawers, flipped them inside out and bit at his fine stitch-work, as he stood naked from the waist down, shivering in the cold Irish wind. He struggled and struggled before he finally was able to extract a penny coin, which he quickly held between his teeth as he inspected the pouch to see that the rest of his money wouldn't fall out. Then, suddenly! A voice did come from out the blue!

"And what might you think you'd be a doin' there, lad?" It was the laundress standing before him, the paddle stuck out like a bayonet in front of her. Jumped Rory did, like he had never jumped in his life. Without so much as an aforethought, he dropped his drawers and flung his arms up in the air. Surely the wench would be beating him to death with that paddle any instant now, he thought. He closed his eyes and prayed. Hard. So hard that when he again opened them he found the laundress, by then, to be leaning on the paddle and smiling, all the while staring at that private area betwixt his legs that was fully exposed to God and all. "Well now, seems like I found me somethin' to do besides the laundry on this fine specimen of an afternoon, doesn't it laddie-boy?" she teased him. Panic almost strangled Rory; never had he been so ashamed in his entire life. He quickly spun around and threw himself up against the barn, trying to shield his personal area from her prying eyes. "And don't the view just keep a getting' grander," she taunted him on.

Poor Rory, he glanced over his shoulder only to find the wench with her pretty face cocked, staring and grinning at his rear part. He tried to pull his shirt down over his backside, but it was too short. Finally, he gained sufficient presence of mind to swoop down and scoop up his pants. He clutched them up against his groin and turned to stand his ground against the rude lass. "I'll thank ye to be turning yer head," he demanded though teeth still clenching the coin.

"I'll be a turnin' me head whenever I'm good and ready. Now tell me, what are you doin' out here behind the barn, all naked from the waist on down? I've a mind to call the authorities on you."

Panic welled up in him again. He adjusted his grip on his pants to use his right hand to take the coin from between his teeth. He thrust it out to her with a trembling hand. "Here, take it. It's for a wee bit o' soap. Nothin' more, miss."

The wench took his coin and looked it over carefully. She bit down on it before looking back up to Rory. "And what might you be wantin' with a bit 'o soap now?"

"To go down to the river and clean me self," he told her. "I've been on the road these four days now. I aim to go into town and look for work to get me passage on one of them boats to America. Wouldn't do for me to show up all dirty and grimy, now, would it?" The laundress fairly laughed in poor Rory's face.

"So, you think you'll just be a wandering' into town and there'll be ship captains just waitin' in line to give you a job on their boat, so you can work off the price of your passage to America. You and how many hundred others like you?" she asked, as Rory dropped his head.

"You have my coin, there, miss. Will you be givin' me that portion of soap now, or no?"

She eyed him up and down for a bit. "O' I aim to clean you up before I send you into town. Maybe even see to it you have a decent set o' clothes on your back when you go. But it's goin' to cost you more than this, boy," she said as she showed him the coin. "His lordship and his family are in London for the rest of the month. You know what that means? That means I've the house all to meself. That means you're goin' to be showin' me a good time if you expect me to do all these nice things for you. Now follow me."

Rory struggled to get his drawers on as the wench walked away. She turned back to him and laughed. "Don't worry a puttin' on your finery there. No one's about to see you but me anyways. And you'll just be a pullin' 'em off again so's I can boil 'em for you, won't you?" He thought about her words, then followed her to the big bubbling cauldron. There, the laundress took his pants from him and dumped them in. "Give me your shirt too," she demanded.

"Woman!" Rory protested, "I don't aim to stand here butt naked in the big middle of some lordship's yard."

"You want your shirt washed for you, you have to take it off. Or would you be a thinkin' you might just jump in that boilin' water, shirt and all?" Rory thought it over for a moment. He already was naked where it counted most, so he kept his drawers clutched up against his middle and managed to unbutton his shirt with one hand. The wench helped him slip his arms out and tossed the shirt in the pot with the rest of the clothes.

"You goin' to pitch your drawers in there or no?" she asked, but the look on Rory's face told her he was not about to surrender them. "O' fine. They probably need to be burnt anyway. Come on in out o' the cold with me, boy. I'll fix you a bath in the kitchen." And Rory followed her into the house, his head bowed and his shoulders slumped in shame.

There in the kitchen, he thought about his father. How many times had he heard the old man say how good for the soul is a little dose of humility. It seemed to Rory he was getting an extra helping of humility, sitting there in some stranger's kitchen, naked as a jaybird, while the wench went about heating water for his bath. He sat with his legs tightly crossed, his under-drawers strategically placed atop his lap. "And what might your name be?" the wench asked him.

"Rory. Rory Thomas O'Kelley, miss," he replied. "And you?"

"Maggie. You can call me Maggie, Rory Thomas O'Kelley." She lifted a pot of boiling water from the fire and dumped it into the tub, then tested the water with her elbow. "Aye. Water's fine. In you go, boy."

Rory looked up at her in surprise, "Aren't you goin' to turn your back?"

"Whatever for? I've already seen everything you have there, now. haven't I?" She was right, of course; he knew it, but still it was embarrassing. As quick as he could, he leapt from his chair and jumped into the tub, splashing water out and over the floor, as he did. "And look what you have done there," Maggie complained. "It's you who'll be mopping that up." She took a metal bowl and dipped it into the tub and poured water over Rory's head, and as he shook the water from his eyes, she lathered up a brush and began to scrub at his back.

"I'm perfectly capable of washing me own self, ye know."

"I'm sure you are. But you wouldn't be havin' near as much fun washing yourself as me doin' it, now, would you? So it's America you want to go to, is it? Fine place, that America. So I've heard. But I wouldn't be getting' any of me hopes up about findin' no work aboard a ship to pay your passage over, though. Even if you did, you wouldn't like the kinda things they'd be expectin' of you. You must trust me on this, Rory." She rinsed his back, then gently rubbed it to take away some of the sting of the brush. Rory tilted his head back and closed his eyes. The warm bath and Maggie's gentle touch made him feel snugger that he had felt in a very long time. "Me friend that used to work here in this house with me, she and her girlfriend got their passage paid to a place called New Orleans. Was recruited by a nun, they was. Can you imagine that, a nun! Come all the way from New Orleans to recruit girls to go back with her and go into the service in them fancy homes in America. Can you imagine that, Rory O'Kelley?" Maggie sighed and stared off into space. "I shoulda gone with 'em too, but I didn't.

"They work off the price o' their tickets in some fine house there, getting' paid half again what a girl gets paid o'er here!" She grabbed Rory by the foot, almost ducking him under the water as she did, and began scrubbing at his filthy toes. "I got a letter from her not long ago. I think she said she works for a Jew. I've never seen a Jew, have you?" Rory just shook his head and Maggie dropped his poor foot and began working with the brush on his hands. "She says he's a nice man, her employer. Not nothin' like his lordship." She stopped the brushing of his hand in mid-swipe. "Come to think of it, now, she said her employer was sending a ship to Ireland to pick up men who would work off their fare digging some sort of ditch. Said a lot of businessmen were sending o'er here for workers. They need diggers that bad in America." Maggie dropped Rory's hands and lifted his arm by the elbow. "I've seen you got good strong legs, now make a muscle for me," she demanded as she cupped her hand around his upper arm. "Sure, you're used to good hard work. I can feel that arm muscle big as a gourd. That's what you should do. Find yourself one of them boats taking men back to New Orleans. That's goin' to be the best way for the likes of you to ever make it to America." Maggie took up the soap and began to lather up the boy's chest.

"And where might a man be findin' one o' these ships, taking folks to jobs in America, free and clear?"

"You ask around, silly boy. You go into town and ask around, down by the waterfront. Or were you thinking I would be doin' all that for you?" she asked as she plunged the soap down between his legs. It didn't take long for her answer, "O' my yes. That is a good boy there, isn't it?" she said as she felt the extent of Rory's response. She would take the boy into town if need be—crawl through hell with her back broke if need be. Whatever it took to get him on his way to America she would do. Only not too soon. Not before his lordship was due to return.

And so it was near eleven days Rory O'Kelley stayed on with the pretty-faced wench in that manor house. There, Maggie saw to it he was fed and groomed and even given a pilfered set of his young lordship's castoff clothes to wear—boots and all. And in return, timid though he was at first, he proved to be an eager student of the lessons of manhood the soft, plump Maggie imparted to him. Upon that lordship's property he had first wandered a dirty, lost and lonely boy. Eleven days later when Maggie accompanied him to the wharves he would be a man.

They had visited the waterfront—Maggie and Rory—several times over the course of the eleven days. Each time she had boldly approached any ship's officer she could find, demanding if they knew what ships might be taking men to New Orleans for the digging of some waterway—free of charge, of course. Each time the answer had been the same. "Ballast passage," that's what they were looking for; cheap passage on empty ships returning to America, where the passengers themselves acted as the ballast for the ship. But no. There were no such ships leaving from Belfast. Try Dublin, maybe. Even Londonderrey.

"And how am I to get this lad to Dublin?" Maggie would always implore. "Abandon his lordship's estate and carry him on me back?" It was a question to which there would be no satisfactory answer, she knew before she even asked it. But then, by act of God it seemed, the morning came when the cutter ship Troth sailed into Belfast Harbor, to drop anchor, briefly, before sailing on for America. In her solicitations on young Rory's behalf, Maggie soon found out the ship's destination: to New Orleans would it sail. Her hopes would soon be dashed, however, as she would learn there was not a single free space aboard. There, in her exasperation, Maggie did resolve that Rory would indeed get to America—to New Orleans, where she would write a letter of introduction to her friend, so as to get him gainful employment once he got there. She would have far preferred to have kept him by her side a while longer, but his lordship would be back soon and he would only send them both packing if he found the lad on his property. So it was, on the morning of the eleventh day of his stay, she woke Rory early, bathed him thoroughly, dressed him in the young lordship's clothes, and took him to the wharf. There, she handed him the letter of introduction to her friend, and a ticket of passage on the Troth, bound for a city called New Orleans, in a place called Louisiana. What Rory would only find out later was that Maggie, in her desperation to get him out of Ireland, to a better future in a far off land, had looted a mismatched selection of her ladyship's extensive collection of silver tableware. Just enough from each set that would not be missed, she hoped. The selection she had taken to the old barmaid at the Bull and Boar, and sold for just enough to buy Rory's passage, not a penny more.

Rory accepted the ticket, but stared at it for the longest of time. Then it was that he looked up to Maggie with tears stinging his puppy-like eyes and pled with her not to send him away, to let him stay on with her. "I'll hear nothing of it!" she scolded him. "To think I worked me fingers to the bone to get you that ticket," she lied, "and here you stand for all the world to see cryin' like you was a baby. You big 'stand-up-in-the-corner-and-bawl-for-buttermilk-when-you-know-we-don't-have-a-drop-in-the-house!' She took him by the shoulders and spun him around. "Go on. Be a getting' yerself aboard that boat before I'm out the price of that ticket." She gave him a little shove, and off he dragged himself, up the gangway to the Troth. Maggie watched him for the briefest time, then quickly spun and made her way up the road to the grand old manor house. She could not bring herself to look back at the tall ship easing its way out of the harbor, bound for the new world and the promise of a better way of life.

It would be aboard the sailing ship Troth, bound for this city, that skinny Patrick O'Bannion would first meet Rory O'Kelley. Two young men of the Irish soil, they were, braving the treachery of the Atlantic in spring, in search of a destiny they could not foresee. Unbeknownst to either of them, it had indeed been Mon. Isaacson and his confederation of Canal Street merchants who had chartered that very ship to carry their cotton to England. And for the return trip, they did advance the ship's owners payment for thirty spaces, thirty spaces for thirty fresh laborers, ready and eager to help with the digging of what was to be called the New Basin Canal. Also, unbeknownst to Rory and Patrick—and to monsieur and his confederates for that matter—was the fact that the ship's captain had demanded tribute from both Rory and Patrick before he would consent to take them on the run. Already were the spaces filled with men bound for digging in the canal, but two more spaces could he squeeze in, provided the price of regular passage found its way into his pocket. Poor Maggie would plead innocent to the misdeed of stealing from her ladyship's silver closet, but would be tried and convicted nonetheless. It would be from languishing too long in a cold, wet prison that she would die, all for the crime of stealing to pay a thief's tribute to send Rory O'Kelley on to a better life in a curious new world.

The passage was hard. An angry Atlantic fought them every inch of the way, threatening time and time again to send them to the bottom of sea, all for the crime of seeking to improve their lot—or so it seemed to the young men. More likely, I tink, it was the ocean what was trying to turn them back, away from the trials that would await them on the swampy shores of this other world. But their captain was experienced and a wise seaman (even if he was a thief) and he prevailed over the sea. The two young men persevered, swinging in their hammocks as the old ship tossed and rolled upon the sea, creaking and cracking like it would break apart at any minute. Waves of homesickness would sweep over them, like the sea washing over the deck of that ship, and they would turn to one another for courage.

A cutter ship built for speed, but modified to carry the cargo flowing out of America back to the Old World, had the Troth been. There were no first class compartments; there really wasn't even a steerage, in any proper sense of the word. What there was, the two young men soon found out, was a hold full of salt bound for New York, above and around which hammocks had been strung for the sleeping. It was the salt that absorbed the moisture always seeping in through the hull, which made the hold as cold and wet as the prison Maggie was to waste away in. And the wrathful Atlantic tossed and pitched the ship so that all were obliged to stay below lest they be washed overboard. Down below, the constant motion gave way to seasickness, till the smell of stale vomit lingered throughout the hold. And no sooner was the seasickness conquered, than the lack of decent conditions was to give way to bouts of diarrhea, making matters all the worse. It was a trying time for all packed down in that cold, dark cargo hold, like swine off to the slaughter. So trying was it, that it often seemed the bother was not worth the promise of tomorrow, no matter how bright it appeared in their dreams.

It would not be until the salt had been unloaded on the New York wharf they were forbidden to set foot upon, and the Troth had sailed on down the Atlantic Coast, out on into the warm waters of the Gulf Stream, that Rory O'Kelley and Patrick O'Bannion were to become fast friends. Before, their association had been built upon that youthful age they shared; that and, at times, the need to keep each other from jumping over the side of the ship to end their anguish. Now they could bask in the sunshine of the ship's deck, where they could engage in the friendly sports of penny pitching, or can kicking or roughhousing or other such competition men require if they are to form friendships among themselves. Free of the stench of the cargo hold, the physical attributes of the small band of spinsters aboard opened up a whole new range of conversations. Free of the horrible hell below, they were at last at liberty to get to know one another. And they laughed, they sang, they sparred, they shared their life-stories, even as the Troth rounded the Florida Peninsula and sailed straight away, off in the direction of the setting sun.

It was with some amusement that Rory did watch his new-found friend work his way into the affections—if not the pocketbooks—of the maidservants sailing with them. For the most part, they had kept to themselves out of paranoia, a line of blankets being the only separation between their part of the hold and the rest. Up on the deck, it would be little they would say to the me folk aboard the vessel, until Patrick would procure a sliver of paper that is. Carefully he would select his subject, then with charcoal pencils from the kit of paints he carried, he would set about sketching the image of one of the ladies. So exceptional were Patrick's sketches, that once presented to the subject the drawing would set off a round of giggles and gab among the womenfolk and Patrick would soon find himself the center of their attention. Later, Rory would learn that it was this talent at drawing the likeness of others that paid for Patrick's fare, and that left him feeling low that he relied on a woman's wits to get him passage. Somehow, in his eyes that made his friend a better man than he. Still, those days in the sun proved to be good ones, the stuff of memories.

But then came the day the ship Troth turned and sailed its way into the mouth of the great Mississippi. The river's current was strong and the wind was weak, so it took them a great while to make the winding journey upriver. Mostly, all loitered on the deck—the passengers—contemplating with silent tongues and squinting eyes the chocolate waters of the Mississippi; the broad expanse of salt marshes teeming with the monstrous alligators; the great stands of Cypress trees farther on upriver. A most inhospitable view was it that greeted these wayfarers for mile after mile of their journey up the great river. Yet when at last the cutter rounded English Turn, they could see the spires of St. Louis Cathedral towering over the city. Gathered together out on the open deck, they hung off the rails trying to fill their heads with the sights, sounds and smells of this new life unfolding before them for the first time.

While they waited for the captain to dock the ship at the St. Peter Street Wharf, a farmer aboard the vessel took out his bagpipe and began to play. By Patrick O'Bannion's reckoning, there were more women aboard the ship than men, which is not surprising since the Irish womens are known to immigrate in greater numbers than do the menfolk.

All the maiden women gathered themselves together in their usual protective assembly, huddled around the stern mast and jabbering with much expectation about this new and mysterious world they had heard so much about, but were only now laying eyes upon. It was the two boys who first broke ranks, once the piping began, and approached the school of women for dancing partners. By the time the captain had the ship docked, it seemed everyone was dancing around and celebrating, carrying on so in their merriment they were oblivious to the company of nuns marching aboard like a platoon of occupying soldiers. On and on the rag-tag band of pilgrims celebrated; on they danced, until Rory was grabbed by the collar and pulled apart from his dancing partner by one of the nuns—the Mother Superior. It would take the odd flock of veiled women little time to gain control of the frivolous bunch of dancing womens and get them into a disciplined rank to disembark.

It had been young Father O'Donnell who had come aboard with the nuns, whom the boys spied working the crowd of men passengers. As soon as he spotted them he rushed to the boys' side, putting his arms around their shoulders and pulling their heads in close to his, that his words might not be overheard by the captain or crew. "Be yer names on the manifest, lads?" he asked of them in all earnestness.

They weren't sure they told the Father. "Think, then, men. This is important. When ye first came aboard and they asked yer name, did Captain write it down in his book?" Neither boy remembered him doing so. "Were ye asked to sign a scrap of paper, then? A contract with an outfit called the New Basin Canal Association?" he petitioned them. No. Of that they were sure; neither had put his mark upon a paper. The priest did ponder the situation a bit, which gave alarm to the two boys. Then he acted bravely, decisively. "Go below and get yer belongings and come back up to me without delay," he ordered.

Rory owned nothing more than his old set of clothes tied up in a piece of sackcloth; Patrick nothing more than his art kit, so they were back atop before the priest barely had time to know they were gone. He snatched both by the arms and led them to the gangway where the captain waited as the womenfolk were being organized to vacate the horrid Troth, at long last. "Captain, I ask ye," Fr. O'Donnell called out over the women's' chatter, "Be so kind as to show me these lads names in your manifest journal, if you will."

"You go straight to hell, sir!" the captain roared at the priest. "I'll do nothing of the kind! These men are the property of the New Basin Canal Association. Their passage was paid for by the association, and I aim to see they are delivered to 'em." Patrick cowered, terrified by the exchange. The captain had profaned a priest, no less; and in front of womenfolk, at that. To be sure, the fine Fr. O'Donnell showed no cowardice in the face of a foe as formidable as the captain and Rory did speak up, taking his strength, as he did, from the example set by the priest.

"Twas me friend Maggie what paid for me passage, Captain. Ye know full well she did, and I'll thank ye to refrain from lying to the good Father here about it. If ye know what's good for ye, that is."

Again Fr. O'Donnell challenged the Captain. "Show me where these lads signed servitude papers then, or I shall have no choice but to escort these two from off yer ship."

"You have no authority on board my vessel. These lads are the property of the New Basin Canal Association, I tell you. Now take your hands off them, and get your arse off this ship before I have you arrested!"

"I need no authority on board yer ship, sir. My authority comes from the Lord Jesus Christ. And if you cannot show me the names of these two lads in yer manifest, then I have no choice but to assume ye have been cheating the ship's owners again, and I shall take them with me. But if ye can show me their passage was paid by the association, by virtue of their names being duly signed to a binding contract, then I will be only too happy to remand them to ye, sir. And offer ye my apologies in the doin'."

The captain scowled down at the young priest like he would have taken his head off. Of course, the young men's names were not on the manifest for the company auditors to see and question why their fares were not to be found in the lock-box. That money was his by right, the captain rationalized. That money and the reward he would receive from the New Basin Canal Association for bringing them two diggers more than they had bought passage for. The captain wheeled around to stare down the two boys.

"Is this what you want, then, men? To go off with your pantywaist priest there. Go then, if you will. He'll have you buildin' churches for the measly portion he feeds you in no time a'tall. While the rest of the men on board here will be workin' for the New Basin Canal Association! Takin' in a whole American dollar the day!. That's six dollars the week!"

Patrick grabbed Rory by the arm. "Six dollars the week, Rory. Jesus, Mary and Joseph! I didn't think there was that much money in the whole world!"

But the priest interrupted, "Six dollars a week is a pittance, me lad, when you'll be dead o' the fever 'fore August is over. Come with me. Don't let the likes of his kind win ye over with promises of riches." And with that, Fr. O'Donnell spun around and bounded off down the gangway with his head held high, confident he had done the best he could with such an unscrupulous character as the captain. And as he put his foot on the good, solid ground, he turned back to the ship; folding his arms across his chest, he did fix his gaze upon those two young men above him. "Well?" he called out to them.

Patrick turned to Rory, "What shall we do, Rory?" he asked. "Six dollars the week!" But before his friend could answer him, he was palmed hard on the back of the head by one of the nuns. "Stupid oaf! Follow the Father there if you know what's good for you," she scolded. "Or be getting out of the way so me ladies may pass."

Rory Thomas O'Kelley yanked Patrick O'Bannion by the coat sleeve and pulled him down the plank with him all in a lope, all the way whooping and hollering out loud. They leapt off the plank together and landed for the first time in more than a month on the firm, warm ground. "Rory O'Kelley, I hope for me own sake you know what you are a doing," Patrick laughed. But Rory did not answer his newfound friend. Instead, he pulled up short and reached down to scoop up a fist full of the moist, delta dirt.

"Here, Paddy. Take it," he said as he held out his hand to his friend. Patrick took his friend's offering, but did look at him peculiarly.

"This? Ye want me to have this? Whatever for?"

"And don't ye see what it is I'm givin' ye, then?"

"Sure I do. A fist full o' earth."

"Nah!" Rory mocked his friend. "'Tis more than any handful o' dirt I've given ye there. What I've given ye there is what we've come all this way for. What I've given ye there is our destiny, Paddy. Our destiny!"

They followed along behind the Father, whose pace would seem to imply the end of the world was at hand, if not something more ominous. For a bit, they followed along in silence, but curiosity was soon to get the better of Patrick.

"Father," he asked, "will they really pay a lad six dollars the week just for the diggin' o' ditches o'er here in America? For true?"

"Some will," he replied. "But what would ye profit if ye earned six dollars a week digging ditches, and lost yer life in the bargain?"

Patrick did mull the Father's response over in his mind. "Ye mean to tell me, then, there's people over here who would work a man to his death?"

"In a manner of speakin', yes. They would and they do. But it's not the hard work I'm worrying about. Ye two are fine, strong lads, and anything that doesn't kill ye will only make ye all the better for it. No what it is that's a botherin' me isn't hard work; it's the digging of that accursed canal, in the first place. I tell ye, I'm morally opposed to it, lads. If I had me own way, they'd just drop their shovels where they are and walk away from it. Abandon it all together."

"Why, Fr. O'Donnell?" Rory asked.

"Because o' the cost. In human terms tis just too dear. Mind ye, this is no high and dry ditch they're digging through the blessed Irish soil here. This is a wide, wide waterway being dug through treacherous swamps and bogs. Mark my words the both of ye; ye go a diggin' in that canal and, likely as not, the malaria will get ye. And if it don't, the yellow fever probably will. And if that don't, the cholera's bound to kill ye off. And if yer're just plain lucky, and dodge all three of those musket balls, well then, ye still have the poisonous snakes and alligators to contend with."

"For sure, Father?" Patrick asked.

"Sure as I'm standin' here. Six dollars the week or no. That's why I keep me eye on the ships comin' in here from Ireland. Some like yer Captain Isbell, there, are devious men, indeed." Fr. O'Donnell halted to look the pair deep into their eyes. "Had it not been for me—callin' yer captain's hand on havin' yer names in the manifest—then I fear, likely as not, ye two wouldn't have been long for this world. Ye were lucky he's such a greedy rascal. He took and pocketed yer fares for himself, no doubt. That's why yer names don't appear in the manifest. He knew he could squeeze two more lads aboard without the ship's owners bein' any the wiser. And once he got you over here, he could collect from the association for bringing 'em two more strong, young bodies to use up."

Young Rory's mind commenced ticking like the movement inside a clock. "We thank ye for steppin' in to help us out there, Father. But tell us if ye will; is there work to be had, for the likes of us, around here?" Fr. O'Donnell broke out in a wide grin and took up leading the pair on along, once again.

"Aye, work there is, me lad. Work there is. On the other side of Canal Street in the American Sector where we're building a new cathedral," he said, pointing in the general direction. "Second only in size and beauty to St. Louis Cathedral." He pointed out St. Louis looming ahead of them, across the expanse of the Artillery Park. "St. Patrick's will be the new cathedral's name, and it's to be the gift of the

Irish to this city. Early Monday morning I will take ye there and introduce ye to the construction foreman. The pair o' ye shall indeed have yer work. Building on this monument to the Glory of God. And the Irish people. Never forget that." The priest chuckled a little. "Of course, we can't be payin' ye no six dollars a week. But the Bible says we must store up our riches in heaven, not here on earth. Wherever our riches are, there will be our hearts as well. Ye'll be doing well to remember that, ye will."

It was at that point that Susan shifted on the couch, her brow giving away that she was perplexed. "Can that be right? I mean, why would anyone want to dig ditches—especially in a swamp! —for a dollar a day." I thought to myself that it was a question only someone of means and advantage could ask, but I kept my thoughts to myself and answered her straight forward.

"Someone who'd just come to this country dirt poor. Someone even more destitute once he got here. Wouldn't have much choice. Unless he'd be so proud he'd starve to death first."

"Not only that, honey," T.K., the businessman added, "You'd have to factor in the present value of money. Remember, a dollar way back then was worth a lot more than it is today. If I had to guess, I'd say it was equal to twenty-five, maybe thirty-dollars today."

Susan just shrugged, unconvinced anyone could be so desperate for so little pay, so we continued with our reading.

Straight through the Artillery Park toward St. Louis Cathedral they went, hurrying all the way. Along either side of the cathedral ran narrow alleyways that were paved, not in gold as they might have imagined, but in the ballast stone the ships once hauled over with them from Europe—before human ballast became cheaper than rock. Fr. O'Donnell took the alley to the right of the Cathedral, between the church itself and the Presbytère Building, built on the site of the old Capuchin monks' residence. Down the way the trio scampered to enter the townhouse that is the rectory. Within, the boys were promptly escorted out through the courtyard to the service buildings at the back of the property, where they were given a bar of especially harsh soap, a scrub brush and a bucket of cold water.

"Wash yerselves now, lads. Make yerselves presentable for enterin' the church. I know ye'll be wantin' to make yer confessions before ye'll be expec tin' the good Fathers to feed ye now, won't ye?" It was in an obligatory sort of way that Fr. O'Donnell asked. "And empty your pockets there whilst you undress. Those clothes you're a wearin' will be in need of a good scrubbin' themselves. Have you decent clothes for church?" The pair cast eyes down to the floor and said nothing. "Well, can't ye answer me? What about ye, Rory. Do ye have decent clothes or no? Answer me."

Rory looked the Father straight in the eyes: "These clothes I have on," he held out his arms to show the garments Maggie had stolen for him, "are the finest clothes I've ever had in me life, Father."

"Well for cryin' out loud, then. Why were ye a wearin' yer best to cross the ocean in, lad?"

"Because they were the finest I'd ever had. I was proud to be seen in them."

"Then mark my words, Mr. Rory O'Kelley. Pride goeth before the fall. Ye'll remember that won't ye?"

"Of course, Father." Fr. O'Donnell had not meant to shame the boy, but he had. Men brought up in their kind of privation were easily shamed, though. Sometimes it just could not be avoided. More often than not, it was just their lot in life.

"Aw, well then. Don't be worrying yer heads over it. Go on and get yerselves washed up. I'll find ye something presentable to wear from the poor room.

It was careful attention they gave to scrubbing themselves from head to toe with the strong soap, shivering as they took turns pouring the cold rinse water over each other's head. And only when each was finally convinced he was clean enough to enter the church and the sacred confessional, did he take up the scrap of old bed sheet they had been given to dry off. Once Fr. O'Donnell returned, he was to find the two taking turns polishing each other's teeth with a corner of the sheet. "Ye'll be needin' some salt for the cleanin' o' yer teeth there, lads," he told them. "Feel free to take some from the table after ye eat. Salt is bountiful enough in these parts."

As respectfully as he could, he took each aside and examined his hair for the presence of the lice mites, and his mouth for rotted teeth he might need to haul. Only then did he present them with the hand-me-downs that were patched and faded, but which fit them well enough and were nice and clean. Once they were dressed, Fr. O'Donnell stepped back to admire his work. "Well, then. All cleaned up and handsome and ready to go to confession. I'd say ye two do the Irish in America proud." Then they were led away to the cathedral and their rendezvous with the confessional booth.

After confession, Patrick found himself sitting on the steps of the church, feeling better about himself whilst staring out across the Artillery Park waiting on his friend. It seemed to him that Rory O'Kelley had spent far too much time in the confessional and he had begun to worry about him, when finally his friend took a seat next to him on the steps where Fr. O'Donnell had instructed them to wait. "I thought ye were ne'er comin' out, Rory. Don't tell me ye were kneelin' in that confessional tellin' the Father that cock 'n bull story about your friend Maggie ye told me," Patrick taunted his friend.

"Ask me no questions, then, and I'll be tellin' ye no lies, will I?"

It was all the response Patrick was to get, but he was a wise enough boy, in his own right, and he did bide his time in silence. Eventually, he looked out across the Artillery Park and asked most casually of his friend, "What kind of penitence did ye get, Rory?"

"One hundred Hail Mary's and one hundred Our Fathers."

Patrick turned to Rory in disbelief. "For Heaven's sake, man! What went on betwixt ye and that woman ye've been keepin' from me!?"

It would be not until three in the afternoon that Rory and Patrick finally got to sit down in the rectory kitchen to a meal of hard rolls, buttermilk and a strange concoction of rice with bits of fish and shrimp in it. Fr. O'Donnell sat across from the two taking his meal with them, attended as they were by an older nun and her two novices. Once Rory had finished his meal, and his mind could turn to matters other than the growling of his stomach, he fished Maggy's letter from his shirt pocket and extended it to the nun, who happened to be refilling his glass with the thick, rich, tangy buttermilk.

"Pardon me, sister, but would ye be knowing where this address might be?" he asked. The nun snatched the letter without a word, read the front of it and tossed it to Fr. O'Donnell."

"What's this?" she asked as she read the envelope.

        Miss Mary-Kathryn Dunnigan
        Late of the H. Isaacson Household
        of Carondelet Street
        in New Orleans, America

"Letter me friend Maggie asked me to deliver to her friend, Father."

"Fancy address, that one. Wouldn't you say, Father?" the nun asked.

"That it is. That it is. And am I to take it, Rory O'Kelley, your friend's friend is in the employ of Mr. Isaacson, himself?"

"I dunno, Father."
"Well, that's whose house this letter is in care of, isn't it?" And once again it was that the good Father was forced to watch shame wash over the lad like the tide streaming over the shore.

"I'm just the son of a poor Irish farmer, Fr. O'Donnell. I can no more read than I can fly."

"What about you, Patrick? Don't tell me ye don't know how to read either!" Patrick merely hung his head. "Well lads. Then tell me if ye will. Be ye a pair of dullards? Feeble minded are ye?" he demanded of them.

It was Rory who looked up. "We're not dullards, Father. Just on account o' we cannot read. Feeble-minded we're not. You can just get that out o' yer head, for all the good it'll be doin' ye," he retorted.

The nun moved immediately to smack him on the back of his head. "Insolent imp!" she shouted, but Fr. O'Donnell lifted his hand to tell her to back off the boy. "But he's no more than a scamp fresh off the boat. And talking to you—a priest—like that." Again, the priest held his hand aloft, until the nun retreated to the corner to pout.

"Well, then, it seems to me I've got me work cut out fer me with the two o' ye. If yer not dullards and yer not feeble minded, then there's no reason ye can't be learnin' to read, now is there? Look at me the both of ye," he demanded. "Starting this Sunday, directly after Mass, the two of ye will meet me in the kitchen here for reading and writing lessons. Is that understood?"

"Yes, Father," was the soft reply from each.

"Fine. Just because ye're Irishmen doesn't mean ye don't need to learn how to read." The table was quiet for a while as Fr. O'Donnell studied the envelope. "This Mr. Hiam Isaacson is an important fellow in this community, Rory. That's the reason for my inquiry. I meant ye no embarrassment, ye must understand."

"Yes Father,"

"I take it ye'll be wanting to deliver this letter to this Miss Dunnigan in person, then?"
From her corner, the nun butted in, "I know of this Mary Dunnigan. A maid she is in the Isaacson house. Give me the letter and I'll see to it she gets it.

Rory tossed her a strong look. "If it's all the same to ye, sister, I'll be delivering the letter meself. I promised me friend Maggie I would, and I aim to keep me word. Or would you have me to do otherwise?" The nun refused to answer, a scowl being her only reply.

"Don't ye go getting' sullen, now, Rory. If ye go out to Royal Street in front of the cathedral and turn to yer right, ye can take the street all the way down to where it dies into Canal Street. It's a wide boulevard, this Canal Street. With stores, all up and down. Cross all the way over to the far side, and turn to yer right again. If ye walk up four, maybe five blocks ye'll come upon Carondelet Street. Match the letters with the letters on the envelope. It'll be a good many blocks on down Carondelet ye'll be a walkin'. The house ye'll be lookin' for will be a big mansion, now. Ye'll know it when ye see it, seein' as how it's far grander than any other one ye'll be a commin' upon. Mind yer manners and go around to the back door, ye know."

Rory nodded his head and Fr. O'Donnell handed him the letter. "Ye'll need to be runnin' on if you're goin'. It'll take ye a while to make the walk, and ye'll need to be back here before they lock the door at eight o'clock, if ye're plannin' on havin' a place to sleep tonight," the good priest warned him.

This then is the story of the journey that brought that boy with hair the color of the dark cherries in August knocking at the back door of this house. It is here that the story of what has come to pass under this roof begins. It was a story not easily told by the skinny Patrick O'Bannion. On five occasions did I pour him another splash of the master's fine whiskey, to get him over still another fit of tears, until at length he sat leaning against the wall, as totally spent as if he'd wrestled with the devil all the nightlong. Now that I've listened to his words, inside my head I wonder if maybe I've judged him too hard. His heart is all broken, this I can tell. It will mend in time, for sure, but the mending of a heartbroken always must be a long and painful course. Maybe it is, then, that Mme. Laveau is right. Maybe it is not the Irish kind the master let congregate around this house that has brought down the bad luck on it. Maybe it be the legions of those rotting at the bottom of that putrid canal—not the Irish spirit—that brings the bad luck. Maybe.

Still, that night in the carriageway I did worry about that dirty young mon before me. Drunk on the whiskey and in a pitiful state was he. His ti-bon-anj—his spiritual self—reached out and squeezed at my heart inside my chest. How long would it be, I wondered, before he would be gone, all used up and hauled away to rot away like some beast of burden? "You must mourn your loss, Patrick," I told him. "No one would deny you that. But your friend is gone now, and still you remain. What will you do with the time God's left you? Will you continue to risk your death of the fever, digging that awful ditch by day? Sitting underneath that big oak tree over yonder, crying like a baby by night? This is no way to exist. Those you mourn would not have you going on like this. What will you do with yourself?" I asked him in earnest. Slowly he lifted his head, like one so drunk on the whiskey, his eyes searching for my image to focus upon.

"I'll be makin' me way to that place they call Texas, that's what I'll do with meself," he finally told me. "Two, maybe three more months and I'll have saved enough money to find me way there. To get me self a little plot for the growin' of potatoes and sorts. And it's there I'll stay and try me best to make a go o' it. Still, one thing I've learned for sure: no one is quicker damned than an Irishman takin' his feet off Irish soil."

His words did burn the brain inside my head, still to this very minute. In another month, there could be yet another Irishman connected to this house, dead and decaying beneath the murky waters of that canal. How I regret the very day I ever heard the word 'canal.' How I curse the day the monsieur gathered his confederates together in the front parlor and told them of his idea for the creating of that channel. Sold them on the merits of a grand new water course running from Lake Pontchartrain to Canal Street, where goods would no longer have to make the long run up the winding river delta. Where goods from across the big lake and from Mississippi and Alabama could cut straight away across the lake, to the business district in no time at all. But regret is like the mud dug up from out of that canal: you can't build on it. All you can do is lie down and wallow in it.

"Is that why you quit your job building on St. Patrick's, then?" I demanded. "To risk your life, to earn the better wages the associates offer you? Is that it, mon? You abandoned your commitment to God to risk the life He gave you in the process? All to get you the price of passage to that Texas place. Untried like it is? What manner of mon are you? Look at me, then! Do you know who I am?" I enjoined him. An employee of Mon. Isaacson? Is that what you tink? I pointed back to the big house. "Inside there, he walks the halls, insane with his grief. So all look to me—known to the many as his natural born daughter, if acknowledged by only the few. It is I they look to, to guide his business interests. I tell this one 'do this', and he does it. I tell that one, 'do that', and he does it. And now I tell you, Patrick O'Bannion, go to that cursed canal tomorrow and upon my orders the big boss-mon will give you no work. But if you will come here, to stay in the loft and there take up your paints to paint me a fine picture, I will see to it you are paid even better wages than for ditch digging.

Slowly I saw his head look up to me in drunken surprise. "And did you tink I knew nothing about your painting? There's little what happens on this property I don't know about. Don't go looking so surprised. I've seen the drawings you did, hanging up there in Mary Dunnigan's old room. I saw the drawings you did there in the kitchen house at Christmas. Now, get yourself busy and paint me a fine picture—of anything your heart desires! More money will you be paid for that, than you will earn digging mud up from the swamp. And when the picture is finished, come to me for your wages. Then get yourself on to Texas if that's where your mind beckons. Go make you a home there before you end up just another Irish name lost in that canal. I stood up from my perch on the hay bale and extended my hand to the young man. He took it gently, too drunk to stand.

"I bid you a good night, Patrick O'Bannion," I told him. "But heed my words come the morrow. This house needs no more Irish death raining more bad luck down on it." And with that I walked away from the weedy one. The footman still stood his guard at the far end of the carriageway. "Take him up to the hay loft and let him sleep there for the night," I ordered, then handed him the decanter. "Leave the whiskey with him."

Saturday, 24 June 1837

I remember it just like it was yesterday—that knock at the back hall door. All night last night did it haunt my sleep. Kept waking me up, so that now I am so tired I must rely on the others to attend to my master. Yet I cannot—indeed I must not—forsake the writing in this daybook for the lack of sleep. The sooner this is finished, the sooner all this ill-fortune be lifted off this house.

Or so it is my hope.

It had been at the little table before the fireplace in the dining salon that I had been taking the evening meal with Mon. Isaacson. Oft times we would take our meals together that way, that we might discuss the affairs of the house. (And so monsieur would not so often be eating alone, I tink). It was near six of the evening. This I know because we had just sat down at the table and dinner is always served promptly at six of the evening. It was a most timid little knock. At first neither monsieur nor I was quite convinced what we had heard. No sooner had the steward, Sonnier, entered the room, bearing the first course, than there came a second knocking. An unmistakable knock at the door it was, yet still there was an obvious hesitancy in it. Sonnier looked toward the hall, then back to me for confirmation that he should investigate." See to it Mon. Isaacson is served," I told him, "And then you may see who it is knocking by the door." The first course Sonnier served and then he disappeared into the hall. We could hear the sound of voices coming from the back door, but we could not tell what it was that was being said. Soon, however, he returned to address the table, the silver card tray he bore being empty."

Mast Isaacson, dey's a young man at the doe, but he ain't got no card."

"What does he want?"

Wonts Miss Dunnigan, suh. Says he's got some kinda message fuh her?" I was furious with Sonnier and I did resolve to reprimand him at my first convenience for having not sent this unmannered caller away; that, and for bringing up the name of a servant-girl in front of monsieur whilst he dined.

"Go on about your affairs, Sonnier. I shall take care of this," I dismissed him. I left the dinner table and went straight forth to the door, and it was there that I first laid eyes upon Mr. Rory O'Kelley who stood a respectable step or two beyond the gallery door, his cap tucked up under his arm and an envelope held by each end as if it were so fragile it would shatter. I paid him little mind, I remember, I was so annoyed by the insolence of his knocking at someone's door during the dinner hour. What I did notice, however, were his big round eyes and hair the deepest of auburn-red. It was a most fair, yet most timid pose he struck, standing there in the doorway in the evening light. "Who are you and what do you want?" I demanded of him.

"Pardon me, ma'am. I've come a long, long way from Ireland a bearin' this letter for Misses Dunnigan. She does live here, does she not?" he answered.

"She does, but that should give you no right to disturb a household during their dinner hour. Leave the letter by me and I shall see to it that she gets it. At the proper time."

Back away from me the young mon did step. "Forgive me, ma'am. I wouldn't have disturbed your dinner for the world, had I known. But I promised me friend Maggie that I'd be deliverin' this letter to her friend personally. I mean you no offense." For the longest did I study this freckled young mon before me, shifting nervously about. I would have as soon sent him packing off and had my words with Miss Dunnigan about callers disturbing the peace of the household, but there was something irreproachable in his demeanor. This was nothing more than a working boy standing before me, I reasoned, common and unschooled in the intricacies of the mannered-class. I motioned toward the Negro kitchen.

"You should find her there in the kitchen house, taking her meal as well, I am sure. Go, find her, but don't come knocking at this door, disturbing the master again." And I watched him hurry off in search of Mary Dunnigan, before I did return to the table.

Little did I know then, that this was the beginning of the end; that this chance encounter would go down as a most unforgettable occurrence in our lives. Little did I know, then. And had I known, what could I have done? Run? Where to? To Mme. Laveau for some paquets Congo to protect us from the evil that was to befall us? No. I tink there are some tings in life God just gives us over to, in spite of whose magic we might invoke to get us past it. I tink this was just one of those tings.. I had no power to stop the master from bringing those Irish girls into this house, even had I foreseen the future. Bad there be in this world. Just like there be good. Now has the bad has gone and settled down over this house, but what can a mere woman do to stop it? A woman with colored blood pulsing in and out her heart, no less. It had been at that very same little table before the fireplace in the dining salon that monsieur first told me of his intention to bring two Irish womens to work in this house. The old Mother Superior at the Dominican convent had convinced him it was the ting to do. Times were bad for the Irish folk in their own homeland, and they needed the help of other people. It is out of the bounty of our monsieur's heart that I fear they may well have brought these bad times all the way over here, upon this fine home.

Reader, know this: Mon. Isaacson is a good listener. No high-muck-de-muck is he. He listens far, far better than he talks. My mother—may she rest in peace—told me he was such a good listener because he was a mon without vanity. As for myself, I tink this is true. But I also tink the monsieur doesn't talk so much out of being a very astute mon, as well; because he doesn't give away all his secrets trying to impress on people how smart he is. Always tings is moiling around in his mind, giving birth to more and more ideas. So he listened carefully to the old Mother Superior, and in the end decided to do what he could do to help out strangers less fortunate than he was. That's how those Irish womens came to live here.

I have run this house from the day it was built—even before it was built, when Mon. Isaacson and his architect were planning it. I studied the plans and envisioned the changes necessary to a smoothly operating household, befitting a mon of the monsieur's station in this life. For that reason, I was not pleased with the idea of foreign women being imported to work inside it. Even as a child, I had worked in the monsieur's house in Jamaica—at the side of my mother—from the time I was old enough to walk and talk. When the monsieur left Jamaica and immigrated to this great city, he left behind my mother and me, her thirteen-year-old child—the daughter he would never acknowledge. Eleven years later, my mother was dead and buried in the ground, and it was he who sent for me to come to New Orleans. "Amanda," he wrote to me, "You will oversee the running of my home. A fine, wonderful home, which shall be yours as well as mine." And thus it was I came to this city as a young, free femme de couleur. And thus it was that I took up my duty to our monsieur and have seen to the efficient running of this house for these past nine years—with never a problem from my colored help, and with no need of Irish help.

No good can ever come from white women working as domestics in this house, I thought to myself, that day Mon. Isaacson told me about the Irish womens. True it is, I resented his hiring these people without so much as the asking of my opinion. Resentment soon burns itself out, though. What bothered me more than resentment was the gnawing at my belly that came with anticipating my giving directions to those womens. Would they accept the orders of one not nearly so white as pearl? "Monsieur, I do hope you know what you do," I told him at the end of our talk. "Nothing good can ever come out of bringing white womens into the running of a house, I tink."

Now I wonder if it was the white of their Irish skin, why he let those two womens into his house: Mon. Hiam Isaacson is not a mon to hold with the owning of slaves. Not only does he not own them, anyone he knows who does, he will let them know they are mocking God. Eventually. Slavery is one ting the monsieur is not shy to speak his mind about. I guess it is because his people were the slaves once, too. For more years than I can remember, I have attended at his table for the Passover Seder and listened to his people recount their tales of slavery in Egypt; thank their God that they are free now; vow to be slaves no more. I tink maybe this is why the monsieur brought these Irish womens here, because of the white of their skin, because he didn't want anyone mistaking his Negro servants for slaves. Besides which, Irish servants be getting popular amongst the townsfolk of late. Good, hard workers they can make. Strong and accustomed to toil, I am told. And you don't have to pay the cash money for them.

A good healthy slave can cost you upwards of three thousand dollars-American in these days. Of course, some slave-mongers can make that back off the breeding of childrens from their slaves, but for house workers in town that just doesn't make any sense. Tings be way too close in a house sitting on a little plot of land in town, for rigmarole like that to be going on. It's different with the country folks. Slaves make good chattel for them. Slaves can turn a fine profit for their owners. Not so in the city, though. So, townsfolk have found Irish girls to be a good source of cheap house labor. Give them Sunday off to go to church and pay them a little each week and they be happy and you be happy. Or so some people would reason. But most of all you don't have to pay nothing for them. They get in your way, you just send them packing and you're out not a penny.

And so it was that there had come yet another knocking at the back hall door. A full year before the young mon with hair the color of dark cherries had come knocking, I would lay my eyes on Mary Dunnigan for the first time. There in that same doorway she stood, with her friend and companion Molly Connelly, who was to work in the house as well, both escorted by the stern Mother Superior. The old nun dabbed at the sweat tricking down from underneath her veil with a plain, unadorned kerchief, whilst the Irish womens stood tense, holding their little valises by shaky hands. "I bid you good morning, Misses Maneau. I've fetched over for you your two new domestics, Molly and Mary," she informed me, pointing to each girl as she pronounced their names. "Ladies, this is Misses Maneau, charge' d' villa." And will you believe it! Those two womens did do the strangest ting anyone has ever done before me. They did bow their heads to me like I was the Queen of Sheba! It was a foreshadowing of tings to come: for the rest of their time under this roof they would bow heads every time they passed me in the halls or one of the rooms, or even outdoors. No matter how strongly I did protest, they persisted.

"Thank you, Mother Superior," I said in the most formal tone I could muster from within my person. "Mon. Isaacson is in his library conducting business and not to be disturbed,

I'm afraid." And then I turned to the Irish, "Let me show you to your rooms and you may have the rest of the morning off to get your tings unpacked and settled in." Old Mother Superior departed from her charges with the admonition they were to work hard and cheerfully, and that any ill-report she would receive about them would only serve to bring down swift and certain punishment upon their shoulders.

No sooner had the old nun left than I escorted the womens up the grand stairs. "Unless you be cleaning, you're to use the outside stairs for all your comings and goings. With the exception of rain, of course. It does rain here with some frequency and the outside stairs can be impassable. At such times you're free to use this stairs. But only in such cases," I told them. At the second floor, I led them out onto the gallery and pointed out the kitchen building down below. "You will be taking your meals in the kitchen down there. Marie's the cook and she lives in the little room off to the side of the kitchen." Along the servants' wing we did walk, and I pointed out the door to Miss Miriam's room. "Miss Miriam's room is here. She's been our housekeeper for these many years now. Never needed any help until now. Henceforth, she will be in charge of the upstairs and you two will be in charge of downstairs." I pointed out the coach house, "Clyde is Mon. Isaacson's coachman and he lives upstairs there. The groom and footmen also live up there. Sonnier, the steward, lives directly below and Mordecai, monsieur's valet de chambre, sleeps in the ante room just off his bed chamber." Stopping midway between the two end doors of the servants' wing, I continued, "That is the staff you will be working with. You'll be given the opportunity to meet them over dinner this evening." I pointed to the far end door, "This will be your room, Miss Dunnigan, and this will be your room, Miss Connelley," I said, pointing to the other door. Timidly did they peek into their rooms, as if they suspected them to be dungeons of some fashion. Then Mary Dunnigan did poke her head into her friend's room.

"So new and modern, Molly. Can you believe it?" she whispered to her friend.

It was after they were given a little time to unpack and get their chambers in order that I showed them through the downstairs pointing out how I liked each of the rooms to be kept. Then, approaching the library I tapped at the closed door. "Enter," I heard the monsieur call out. I eased the door opened, and stepped just inside the room.

"Excusez, Mon. Isaacson, but the womens are here." He looked up from his desk with some confusion reading on his face,

"Women?'

"Oui, monsieur. The womens from Ireland."

"Oh! Yes. Those women. Please, show them in." I pulled the door fully opened and motioned for them to step inside next to me, which they did with all the shyness of little children. "Mon. Isaacson, may I present Misses Molly Connelley," I said, pointing her out to him as she curtsied and I made a mental note to let her know the monsieur would have none of that in his presence. A proper air of decorum would be more than adequate. "And this is Misses Mary Dunnigan," I said, noticing with some trepidation the color shading the monsieur's cheeks as he was introduced to that one. Why I should have been surprised at his reaction I cannot say. He was a mon, after all, with a mon's nature about him. And Mary Dunnigan, I noticed for the first time, was a strikingly attractive woman, with long hair as black as a moonless night, with an iridescence to it as navy blue as the deepest part of the ocean. She would be tall for a woman, I surmised, with the tiniest of waists. Cat eyes she had; almost green were they, and outlined in long lashes. Upon her lips she wore no daub, needed no tint; a perfect pink pastel had nature shaded those lips. But mostly I noticed her skin so smooth, the whitest, most flawless skin I believe I ever did see, like fine bone china, I thought to myself.

Not wishing to unnerve the girl, I turned my gaze back to the monsieur, who was preoccupied with a twisted tongue in his mouth. It was, to be sure, embarrassing that a mon of his level should be found stammering and stuttering over a girl young enough to be his daughter. I resolved to remedy this most unfortunate of situations and did speak up. "By your leave, monsieur, we will continue our tour of the house," I said, making sure to open my eyes wide at the proper instant, so as to convey to him that his silliness had not gone unnoticed.

"Yes. Yes. Please don't let me keep you from your..." With that I signaled the Irish women to exit the room and we did venture back down the hall, on outside to the kitchen.

Now, Sonnier the steward had always been a peculiar sort of mon. For true he had him a good heart; maybe too good at times. But there was some ting unsettling in his manner, for his was more the manner of a girl than that of a mon fully-grown. Maybe that was why he seemed to prefer the conversation of the women-staff over that of the men-staff. Or maybe the men-staff just didn't want anyting to do with him, being peculiar like he was. Whatever the reason, though, I was to notice that Sonnier and Mary Dunnigan did get along well together. I tink she had a fondness for Sonnier, in spite of his oddity; and I know Sonnier did possess a partiality for her, for it was from my own conversations with him that I was to learn much about the history of this Irish woman, this Mary Dunnigan.

The oldest of nine she was, and the daughter of a fisherman at that. But a happy family they must have been, for Mary was always to speak lovingly of every member of her family. On and on she would go with Sonnier, filling him with happy stories of her family life, not stories of the father beating the poor mother, or one of the brothers committing murder or the like as one is apt to hear from those born to the lower classes. Poor as church mice I tink they must have been, but tings were only to get worse for them. When Mary was but eleven, her father was lost at sea when the weather went bad out over his boat. Widowed at an age too young, her poor mother was forced to send out the oldest of her children. The two oldest boys went to sea before their primes, where they were both to perish like their papa before them. Mary and two of her sisters were sent forth into the service of manor houses, where at young ages they learned quickly how to work for their own upkeep. It was to the city of Belfast and to the manse of an English peer that Mary was apprenticed. There did she work for long hours, with little time off, when the lordship was in residence. And for wages not much better than none, although wages they were—and timely paid at that—and every pence she earned helped her poor mother feed and shelter the little ones left at home. No, long hours on her knees scrubbing at the floors bothered Mary Dunnigan not the least. Hard work she was accustomed to. Nor did the paltry pay bother her, for she had never known any ting much but privation. So, since such tings bothered her not, she was to remain in his lordship's service for five long years.

And then it began.

The first time it happened, she was walking down the darkened corridor to her chamber late of the night, after finishing with the scrubbing of the kitchen pots. The candle that lit her way flickered as she hurried down the hall, so it failed to illuminate the young lord lying in wait in the shadows. As she approached, he leapt from the dark, like a ravenous animal out to snare his prey, knocking her candle from out the holder. As planned, the candle went out, and in the darkness, where thoughts and deeds such as his belong, his hand did greedily paw at her breast, whilst his mouth sucked hungrily at hers. His face whiskers were wiry and they did burn their mark upon her face as she struggled. Finally, in her desperation she struck at her assailant with the candlestick she still held in her grasp. Instantly the coward did break his grip, slithering off down the darkened passageway with his palm held tightly over the wound above his eye.

A terrified Mary screamed at the top of her poor lungs, summoning the entire servants' quarters. All quickly assembled in the corridor where the womens whisked the stricken young woman away to her bedchambers, there to console her.

His lordship's butler did pace the hall for some time thereafter, lecturing the others that he would get to the bottom of the situation and expose the one responsible for so odious a misdeed. By morning he would have his answer. Around the morning table his lordship and her ladyship sat taking their breakfast with their children, the eldest of whom sported a bandage around his forehead. When asked by his father what had happened, he responded he had heard a cry in the dark and had hit his head on a door when he went to investigate. Never again would the butler look at the heir-apparent of such a fine old family with any ting but contempt, but there was little else he could do in Mary's defense. Underlings, he knew, were simply not at liberty to bring accusations against those noble of birth, absent severe repercussions. Especially accusations rooted in circumstance such as was the case. In the end, it would all boil down to the word of the son of a lord against that of a poor housemaid, and an Irish housemaid at that. No, there would be little that could be done, even against an affront as grievous as this, beyond seeing to it Mary was in the presence of others whenever the young lord was prowling about.

All willingly did their part, making sure she was accompanied to her chambers at night, lingering at the door until the lock had been turned from the inside. Keeping an ear out for her when she would be working in some part of the manor where the beast might be stalking. And the entire staff would have eagerly done more for her, but paramount among their responsibilities was the running of the house. It was impossible for Mary to have a bodyguard around her at all times. Moreover, the young lord was sly and did know his limitations. For months on end, he contented himself with eyeing inappropriate parts of her person as she would pass, a contemptuous smile always on his face. Or he would make a kissing movement with his lips, or even touch himself in her presence, when no one else was around to witness his actions. Once as he passed her on the backstairs, he touched the scar left by the candle stick with his fingertips and whispered, "Any day now, I'll be claiming me bounty."

And he did. Finally, he did come to claim his prize, stalking down the servants' hall in the dark. A key to Mary's room had he procured from the butler's cabinet. Silently as an apparition he unlocked the door and let himself into her room, to stand over her, there with the moonlight washing through the window, watching her chest rise and fall with each breath. Nothing did she mean to him; his own desires were his only concern. Gently, then, did he lean over her, then slapped one hand over her mouth to muffle her screams. In the other hand, he bore his jewel-studded dagger, which he stuck up against the side of her throat. "Make a sound and I'll cut your head off your very shoulders, you Catholic mongrel," he whispered in her ear. Paralyzed with fear, she lay still as a corpse, her eyes traveling down her own body as the young lord drew the dagger down to cut loose her bed gown. The tip of the cold blade he used to lift the gown up and away from her body, the very sight of which overtook him with his own base lust. He laid the blade to his side and slid atop Mary, mouthing her breast, thrusting a hand down between her legs locked tightly together. She struggled that he might not enter her with his hand, but he was just too strong for her and did manage to touch in that certain place only she has right to surrender. It was more than she could take.

She wiggled her head about and managed to get her mouth over the leading edge of the young lord's hand, then chomped down. Hard! So taken by surprise was the fiend, that he yelped aloud like the animal he was, but Mary did not let go her bite. She only bit down harder as he struggled to jerk his hand free from the grip of her teeth. She could feel the warmth of his blood on her lips when, finally, he pulled his hand free. One short scream was all she managed to get out, before the monster did double up his fist and pummel her face. Once. Twice. Three times, until she lay bloody and unconscious upon her bed. Up he leapt and bolted through the door, knocking down Rory's friend Maggie, who had come to investigate the commotion that had awakened her. Off into the shadows he disappeared, not realizing until he got back to his apartments that, in all the confusion, he had left his jewel-studded dagger behind.

None of the staff was to sleep that night. Those not attending to Mary gathered in the kitchen to map out a strategy for dealing with the unfortunate incident. It would be only after much arguing and bickering among themselves that they would send for the local monsignor, who arrived just as the morning meal was being served to the lordship and his family. There in the morning room it was that the lord first noticed his son's bandaged hand. "What have you done to your hand there?"

"A scrape, nothing more, father," came the reply.

"Well for goodness sake, be careful," the older admonished the younger. "You're always going around injuring yourself these days. And what is going on in that kitchen. It sounds like the House of Commons out there!"

It was a peculiar atmosphere that pervaded the estate that morning, both his lordship and her ladyship sensed. The butler seemed particularly abrupt with his duties, more interested in hurrying back to the kitchen, where some sort of caucus was taking place. Within the kitchen, everyone was most animated. "Yes, but can ye be sure it was the young lord who's done this to the lass?" the Monsignor asked. The butler pulled open a drawer in the long, oak worktable, around which all had congregated and took out a fine linen napkin. Carefully he unfolded the napkin and held aloft the jewel-studded dagger for the priest to see. "

"Tis the proof ye'll be needin'. This dagger is known to be the personal possession of the young lordship. And everyone gathered around this table will tell ye twas left behind in poor Mary's room last night. That's where we found it all right."

"Used it to cut off the poor girl's nightgown, that's what 'e did!" Molly Connelley exclaimed.

The butler waved a hand at her. "Molly, there'll be none 'o that talk in front 'o the monsignor here." For his part, the priest attended to the dagger for some time, before laying it back on the napkin. He took a deep breath and looked to the others in the room.

"Well, it's an untenable situation we have here, that's for sure. Mary Dunnigan can no more remain under this roof than any one of us can swim the channel…" He was interrupted by cries that the unfortunate girl needed the work to help out her widowed mother. "And that may be," the monsignor continued. "But the fact remains, this is not the only house where work is to be had. I think it may be time for me to do a bit 'o bargaining with his lordship in there," he said as he lifted his chin toward the morning room door. He collected the dagger and looked to the butler to escort him to the family's table. Up from his cup of steaming tea the lord did look with some surprise, as the butler quietly entered the room escorting a man of lesser cloth. "Beggin' your pardon, sir. The monsignor here will be havin' a word " he announced.

"Unacceptable!" her ladyship exclaimed, obviously incensed that an uninvited guest—and a Catholic one at that! —had invaded her breakfast room.
"

"Your ladyship, m'lord," the monsignor acknowledged as he bowed. "The meaning of this is that one o' your female servants was accosted and savagely beaten in her room last night."

"Which servant?" the lord inquired, as his elder son bolted to his feet and made to leave the room.

"Not so fast there, me young lord," the priest called out. "Is it not this that you'll be a lookin' for?" he said as he laid the dagger beside the lordship's plate. The young one fairly collapsed into his chair as his father took up his son's dagger and studied it.

"I don't understand. How is it you came into possession of my son's property?

"So? This is the dagger of your eldest son, there, m'lord?"

"It would appear so," came the reply.

"Well, sir, it was that very dagger that was found left behind in the chamber of poor Miss Dunnigan after the attack last night. If you'd be carin' to undo the bandages there on your son's hand, I think you'll be findin' the young lady's teeth marks there as well." The lord slowly took up the dagger by the handle, then plunged it into the table as he rose from his chair. Up out of his own chair his son did jump upon reading the anger welling up in his father's eyes.

"She... She invited me to her room," the younger lord claimed. "She's a sport, father! Everyone knows that. Only she..." The lordship made to round the table after his son, but his wife was to intervene.

"Sit down, my lord," she demanded. "Do it! Sit down this instant. And you," she turned to her son, "Go to your room until your father and I come for you." Quietly, the he turned and departed the room, as his mother turned her attention to the monsignor. "Well, now sir! It would seem we have quite an unpleasant situation on our hands, does it not?"

"We do indeed, your ladyship."

"And what would you propose we do about this? Consult the authorities? My son says this woman invited him to her chambers. I doubt you would want that to become public knowledge, would you? And we," she looked to her husband, "We certainly would not want our son's fine name dragged through the mud by some common house servant. Now what should we do, then?" Surely the monsignor must have been a mon wise in the ways of life and did know when he was being finessed.

"By your leave, m'lady. I'm open to your suggestions."

Her ladyship rose with grace from the table and made way to the dagger still stuck in the table beside her husband. "It is my understanding these Irish wenches are leaving Ireland for America by the boat loads. Is that not true?"

"There are opportunities in America not available over here, ma'am," the monsignor responded, reading the direction she was leading him. She took the dagger by the handle and with some difficulty extracted it from the table.

"Miss Dunnigan's services are no longer required by this household. Please see that she is packed and off this property today," she said most coldly. Then, taking the dagger by the blade she presented it to the priest. "My son's blade should fetch more than enough to buy her silence. See to it she has passage booked on the next ship to America. See to it she's on it or she will suffer the consequences."

The monsignor smiled and politely accepted proffer. As you wish, m'lady. As you wish." Then without further ado, he turned and made his way out of the room, the butler following in after.

Five days later all the staff, save Maggie, had left for other positions, so disfavored was the lord and his family within the upper classes of the community that no references were expected of anyone coming forth from that house. Five days later the monsignor saw Mary Dunnigan off for America, aboard a passenger ship bound for New Orleans. Molly Connelley and the other women in their group shed tears as they watched the ship slowly pull away from the Irish shore, but not Mary Dunnigan. Her assailant's dagger had fetched a price adequate to provide for her mother, younger brother and sisters for the foreseeable future, the price of her passage having been paid by Mon. Isaacson. Maybe that was why she shed no tears. Maybe. Or maybe it was because her eyes were still too swollen shut to make out Ireland fading away in the distance.

This then is the story told me by Sonnier our steward. It is the story about how I did come to find this Mary Dunnigan—who brought such a flush to my master's face—standing at the very same back hall door where I would find Rory O'Kelley standing, almost a year to the day later. It is a story I wish had never been told. It is a story I wish had never taken place. But then, some tings God just gives us over to, despite our own wants. This I believe.

Gloria Patri.

A few minutes before, the hall clock struck six and shortly thereafter Aunt Alice appeared in the doorway to order us to the kitchen as soon as we reached a stopping place. With that day's entry finished, we dutifully filed out of the library to make our way through the dining room and out into the kitchen. There we found the table set before the window overlooking the back garden and pool.

"I sent Galvez out for Popeyes. Y'all kids are going to be reading until late evening if you plan on finishing the book. Didn't want any of y'all going home telling folks I left you to read on an empty stomach," she told us. "Wouldn't be hospitable of a southerner to do so."

As we dined on spicy fried chicken, dirty rice and Barques root beer served in the glass bottle, Susan paused to ask, "Where is the kitchen house Amanda wrote about?"

"Long gone," came Aunt Alice's response. "My granny had the kitchen moved into the little room that used to be the butler's pantry way back in the twenties. Wasn't until my husband and I took over that we moved the kitchen in here. This room used to be an old servant's bedroom. By then the old kitchen building was just a shell so we it pulled down and paved the patio with the bricks when we put in the pool."

"Well, your garden is lovely. In fact, your whole house is beautiful. It must have been wonderful growing up here."

"No, not always. For a long, long time it was about to fall down around us. Mother wouldn't let us do anything to it. Kept saying it wasn't necessary. That she'd die if we changed things. Hell, we didn't want to change anything, we just wanted the roof to stop leaking. To walk down the hall without falling through the floor. No, it wasn't until she died that my husband let me put it back together. Even then, he wanted to just unload it and move someplace else. The neighborhood went into decline after the war and he didn't see putting a lot of money into the place. I held my ground, though, and this is the result."

Alice gazed around at her kitchen. "In fact, when you take over, Pamela, you'll want to update this kitchen. I was thinking just the other day that you could get rid of the butler's pantry—no one uses those things anymore—and blow out that back wall between here and the other old servant's room and open this up into one big kitchen/family room. Wouldn't that be nice?"

Pamela was caught off guard. "I... I suppose. Yeah. But you've still got a lot of years ahead of you, Aunt Alice. That's a long way down the road to be worrying about today."

"Oh, I don't know. Wednesday bridge met at Lila Hebert's new apartment in the Carrol last week and it was nice! Just the right size. Everything on one floor. Y'all don't need to be paying a mortgage on that house you're in when you've got this one. Sell that Pine Street place. Invest your equity. Move in here. I could get a place in the Carrol and my people could still keep their rooms here and just walk the block over to take care of me. Just makes sense, doesn't it?"

I could not help smiling at the look of horror that overtook my wife's face. It was a high-wire act we walked with Aunt Alice and her house. These places were built for a different time when you had someone like Amanda Maneau to oversee a large staff keeping it up. Mansions like my aunt's were not just extraordinarily expensive to maintain, they could take a toll on your sanity just managing them from day-to-day. Although we would never let her know it, our plan was to sell it to someone with more money than common sense, or perhaps turn it into a museum, once she was gone and it was dumped in our laps. This was one of those moments that called upon me to rely on my legal training: "Now Aunt Alice, you were born in this house and you're not leaving it until they carry you off to the funeral home. Right now, though, there's an alligator bound journal in the library that's beckoning us. Let's go read some more."

And with dinner finished, we got up from the table and made our way back to the library. Another bullet dodged.

Monday, 26 June 1837

Now that look back over it, I tink Mary Dunnigan was happy, that year she spent in this house, before that boy came knocking at the back door. True, she was overcome with the homesickness when she first came here, but that was to be expected. And she didn't let it interfere with her work. I, myself, remember being homesick for Jamaica when first I came to this place. But the homesickness is some ting what eats at you and eats at you, till you get used to it and don't notice it any more. Then it goes away, like it did for me and like it did for pretty Mary Dunnigan. No, I tink she was indeed happy, that first year she spent in this house. I know this place was happy up till then. But that knock on the rear hall door changed tings, made every ting all different, somehow.

She was a good, hard worker, this Mary Dunnigan. I must give her that. Never had I occasion to follow in behind her, pointing out this and that she had missed. She went into a room to clean, and she would clean it like it was her very own. Never once did she break any ting. Never once was I to point out some speck of dust she had missed, or the likes. She took it on herself to do what she was paid to do, and she did it cheerfully—always humming to herself—just like the old mother superior had told her to do. This much I must give her. And she was always pleasant to me. Never once was she to question me about an order. Always it was "yes ma'am and right away ma'am." I'd tell her to take one of the big carpets outdoors and beat it and what do you tink? Next ting I know, I'd see her hauling it down the back stairs by herself, humming under her breath all the way. "Mary

Dunnigan," I'd call out to her, "Why you don't get one of the stable boys to help you with that?" And always she would just smile to me and say they had enough work of their own without having to help her with hers to boot. So, pleasant she was to me, I have to give her that much, too. All my anxiety about orders had been for naught. Still, in another way I tink I was right, that no good was to come from having her in the house.

It was the effect her presence had on Mon. Isaacson that caused me all my distress. Whenever she was around, his face would light up like he had not a care in this world. This from a mon of business, of all tings! She could change the monsieur, this I tell you—take him from a mon with obligations weighing heavy on his shoulders, to some stumbling, bumbling school boy, drooling all over himself at the mere sight of some pretty face. This I did not like. This I did not like at all. It was just like she took and cast some spell over him; over that poor O'Kelley boy, too. They were mens, and mens be at their weakest when it comes to the females, and those two mens did prove to be most sorry matches for her fair magic. Not that I am to say she was servi loa or the like. Les invisibles, I tink, just clung to her spirit—to her nam. Always be it those whose magic is inert who's the strongest.

When Mary Dunnigan first came by us—while she was still overcome with the homesickness—she would spend much of her free time wandering the gardens, enjoying the plants. And as she did wander these gardens, it was that I first noticed the effect she had on the monsieur, for on more than just a few occasions did I catch him standing at a window spying on her, a big smile plastered all over his face like a poultice. Later, I was to witness the transactions between the two, when I would see him enter a room where she would be working. Mind you, Mary Dunnigan was a girl trained in the ways of a house of this one's stature. Well did she know that when the lord of the house was to enter a room where she was, she was to silently gather her cleaning tings and leave at once. This was protocol for a house such as this; a protocol Mon. Isaacson always required. Always, until this Irish maid with rosy cheeks came into this house, that is. It was then I saw tings start to change. Always, the monsieur would be telling that one and only girl never to mind him, but to keep on with the work she was making. And then as she went about her work, he would sneak peeks at her, engage her in idle chitchat. Never had I seen the master prattle on with a servant, not even my very own mother, not even with myself, I say!

And then there was that occasion in the library—in Mon. Isaacson's very own library, his inner sanctum in the entire house! A mon of books is the monsieur, a mon of great study and contemplation. From the Torah he does read and argue daily, to the works of the modern European philosophers, his books and his library be the very essence of his life. And such was a core he could not easily bring himself to share with others: on very rare occasions had I witnessed him to lend one of his books, but always with the point belabored that if the book was not timely returned, in the condition it was lent, such would be equivalent to a breach in friendship. Anyone lucky enough to have Hiam Isaacson lend them a book would know, only too well, that the privilege extended was not one to be taken lightly. And yet, I on my own did witness this very same master tell Mary Dunnigan she could feel free to borrow any book she might want to read from his collection. Imagine that! A servant girl—one who was only just learning how to read herself—being given the run over the monsieur's precious library. Bowled over I was, I tell you. Bowled full over! But mostly I tink it was what happened that day in the music room that started it all on a downhill slide, that drove the wedge deep between my monsieur and me.

My love of grand opera I can easily profess. And while I may be a woman of some means—whose gowns and jewels would put to shame most of the mistresses who occupy dress circle in the magnificent Théâtre d'Orléans, the income from whose properties and bonds could buy and sell many of those same ones, yet still am I nothing more than a femme de coleur in their pale eyes. My jewels and gowns, by law, I cannot wear in public, lest I offend the dignity of some white man unable to provide for his wife a standard equivalent to mine. My money is not pure enough to purchase a seat for one of their operas. The touch of my less-than-holy-white hands has tarnished the gold, I suppose. By monsieur's good offices, however, have I been able to attend almost every opera performed in this city in the last nine years. Always do I follow in his company, the proper three steps behind, in lieu of the de reguir footman. I would seat myself outside the door to his box, which he would leave ajar so I could better hear the performances. Only on those occasions when he was to occupy the box alone, was I permitted to sit inconspicuously in the darkened corner, but only after the lamps have been lowered, and always well before they had been raised again. Such is not an ideal vantage point from which to observe the goings-on of the stage, but it is far preferable to a hardback chair in the hall. Most see past Mon. Isaacson's scheming I do reckon. Most, I tink, know full well it is on pretense that I am brought along to be of possible service to him rather than a proper footman, but they raise no exception to this, provided we are diligent in presenting my presence in a subservient demeanor. The whole mess is an humiliation, but one my love of opera has given me the strength to endure.

Now, often of the morning after a performance, Mary Dunnigan would engage me to give her a complete accounting of the set and costumes and so forth. Frequently would I be surprised to learn she had read the libretto on some work and was quite knowledgeable about the story. Often too, the monsieur would engage me to play at the pianoforte selected pieces from the opera we just attended. Thus, it was such occasion of a Sunday afternoon that I sat down before the his Bosendorfer imperial grand (imported from Europe only the year before), there to play passages for him from Mozart's magnificent Don Giovanni. Outside, on the rear gallery, Mary Dunnigan did sit herself to listen to the music through the opened window; which, of course, was acceptable, was properly servile in demeanor. It is just that no sooner had she sat, than my master did spy her and rose to interrupt me. To my astonishment, he did invite the servant-girl to sit with us in the music room whilst I played! Imagine, then, my consternation when I realized I was fully expected to entertain in the presence of a common house maid! Imagine, then, my further astonishment when my monsieur, upon learning Mary Dunnigan had never attended the performance of an opera, the very next day would tell me of his intention to take her to the next performance. The surprise in my eyes must have been evident, for the monsieur did blush and mumble what a shame it would be for someone so interested in music to never have the opportunity to experience grand opera.

"I tink there must be many persons in this town, monsieur, who loves the music but will never be setting foot inside the Théâtre d'Orléans," I responded. "And if I may be direct, sir, what would you be expecting such a girl to wear to the opera? That pitiful frock she wears to church Sundays?" It was then and there that Mon. Isaacson did squint his eyes at me for the first time in my life.

"If she has no gown to wear, then call for the seamstress and have something made for her," he said to me, his voice all full of authority.

I tell you, his words did knock the wind from out of my very lungs. I could scarcely reply, so struck was I. Never in my life have I challenged the monsieur; never in my life have I imagined I would have the need to challenge the monsieur. But some ting was changing in him and he was becoming different before my very eyes, like he was taking leave of his senses. Less thoughtful, more flippant was he. "Did I hear you right?" I implored of him. "That you would have me send for the seamstress to fashion a gown for...a servant? Master surely—" But I was not to finish.

Anger welled up in his eyes and he did lash out at me, "I don't seem to remember asking your permission on any of this, mademoiselle. You will do as I say or— "

"I will not do as you say, sir!" I cut him off, the anger I felt welling up inside me by then. "I fear you do forget yourself. The very idea! That I should be sending for the seamstress so you can ferry a pretty, young cleaning woman off to the opera with you. What will people be tinking when they see the two of you, I wonder? And who will I be sending the seamstress for next? There are others in this house who have never been to the opera. What about them? Next ting I know, and you'll be giving Marie the cook my seat outside your box door!"

There! I had said it. Never in my life had I raised my voice to my monsieur. Never in my life had I reason to raise my voice to him. Yet now I had; now I stood before him, his face red like fire and trembling with a burning rage. "You would do well not to challenge me on this. This or anything else." he said to me through gritted teeth, never raising his voice. "May I remind you that it was I who gave you your freedom? And it is I who can take that freedom back from you?"

To the bone was I cut by his remark and it made my blood run cold within me. He was right and I knew it: it was narrow ground that one mixed in the races like me occupied. All my property and bonds notwithstanding, I was without legal position in this nation. Should the monsieur choose, all he need do would be to summon some slave-monger to steal me away and stand me on the block somewhere else. There my claim to be free would fall on deaf ears; it would be the word of one who had no right to speak, against the word of one for whom those rights were written. Freedmen had been sold back into slavery before; it could be done again. This I understood and well. I moderated my tenor. "So you may. So you may, monsieur. I shall see to it the seamstress is called forthwith," I responded, holding my anger in check, for my own sake.

"Good."

"And will you be telling Miss Dunnigan of you plans, yourself?" I asked. The mon did stand and eye me for some time before responding. "Perhaps it would be improper for me to extend such an invitation. You do it," he said, then spun and left the room.

I felt the tears brimming up in my eyes and tried hard to hold them in check, as I stood there staring at the door though which he had left. Dumbstruck I was. In the briefest of time, had my whole world been changed. Later, he would have a change of mind, and it would be that both Mary Dunnigan and Molly Connelley would have new gowns, and tickets in the balcony instead of chairs in his prestigious box. But from that day of confrontation forward, tings were never again to be quite the same between the two of us.

The night of the opera, I accompanied Mon. Isaacson to his box and took my seat outside the door, as usual. From there, I could see him take his seat near the railing and survey the balcony, a smile overtaking his face when he did spy that little Irish peasant-girl, sitting up there in the balcony like she was any ting but a common housemaid. No good could come from all this, I knew. But what was I to do about it?

Like it or not, this all had made the monsieur happy; and happy he had been.

At least until that Irish boy came knocking at the rear Hall door.

Yes, I remember it. I do. I remember it like it was yesterday, when that boy came knocking and I sent him off to the kitchen, in search of Mary Dunnigan. Had only I sent him away; taken a kitchen knife and plunged it into his heart! Had only I done most any ting but send that boy off to find her, then I might have spared this household all the ill-fortune that now holds it tight in its grip. But, alas, I did not.

It would be Sonnier who told me about the staff all huddled around the long table in the kitchen, finishing up their suppers, when they noticed the stranger in their midst, standing in the door, eyeing them up and down. "I'll be a beggin' your pardon, but I'm lookin' for Misses Mary Katherine Dunnigan. Previously o' County Antrim in Ireland," the young O'Kelley spoke up and everyone's head turned to the girl who slowly she did rise up from the table.

"I'm Mary Katherine Dunnigan. Who is it that asks about me?" she inquired in return. And it was the instant Rory laid eyes on fair Mary Dunnigan that he fell under her spell, just like our monsieur had. Sonnier told me as much; he said he sat there and watched the spell take effect right before his own eyes. He said the boy's face did flush, a tremble over took him, and he thought the mon would choke up his very Adam's apple. Barely could he speak to the girl.

"Beggin' your pardon, miss. I don't mean to be disturbin' yer dinner there," he said with wavering voice. "I'll just be a waitin' outside..."

"I've finished with me dinner. Who might you be, and what is it you'll be wantin' of me?" Mary interrupted

"I'm Rory O'Kelley of County Fermanagh in Ireland, and I am a... An acquaintance of yer friend Maggie. What works in his lordship's manor near Belfast."

A fit of giggling overtook Molly Connelley, Sonnier told me. He said he thought the girl was going to burst of laughter. "Aye. It's well and long me and Mary been knowin' Maggie. And I'll bet you're indeed a fine acquaintance of hers, now. Knowin' the reputation that one has," she teased the young man. And poor Rory O'Kelley looked for all the world like he wished he'd never been born, as all joined in to cajole him.

"I know not what yer a talkin' about, lass," he defended. "All's I know is Maggie give me this letter to deliver into Miss Dunnigan hands, personal." He held out the envelope to her. "And here it is, if ye'll kindly be a takin' it."

Mary took the envelope from him. "Never you mind Molly there. She means you no shame, Rory O'Kelley. She's no manners to her. And I thank you for bringin' me this letter."

And with that, she tore open the letter as Sonnier fetched the boy a chair. "G'on and sit you'self down. Let me fetch you a nice glass o' buttermilk," he offered, but Rory declined, as he took the seat offered him.

He watched with interest as Mary greedily read the letter, a smile flaring up on her face, only to disappear with a furrow of her brow. Finally, she laid the letter aside and looked up to Rory. "Eleven days you stayed on with Maggie, did you there, laddie? And whilst his lordship was in London, no less," Mary said, tossing the boy a knowing wink of her eye that caused the flush to return to his cheeks. "She highly recommends you," she continued, and again the kitchen broke into good-natured taunting.

Even more defensive did Rory O'Kelley grow. "I didn't come here to be givin' the likes o' ye a good laugh," he said as he stood up. "Ye have yer letter, there. Now, I'll just be biddin' ye a good day." But before he could reach the door, Mary intervened.

"Mr. O'Kelley, where's your sense o' humor now. Haven't I told you we're not out to get your goat. It's just a playin' with you we're a doin'. You must take no offense."

"Fine. Then it's no offense I'll take, if ye say so. But I don't aim to stand here and be the butt o' yer jokes. Good day," he said, and again made for the door, only to be stopped by Mary once more. "

"No. Please wait." She looked to the letter, "Our friend Maggie asks that I help you find work. I'll check with Misses Maneau, but I don't think there's any jobs to be had around the house here."

"And I thank you mighty kindly for takin' an interest. That I do. But if it's a job for me what Maggie was a writin' about, then never ye mind. It's only one day I've been in America and already I have me a job."

Instantly all around the table but Mary and Molly erupted in laughter. Tooley, the stableman, punched Clyde the coachman on his arm. "See whut I done tole ya, Clyde!" he bellowed. "'Nother Irishman for diggin' the masser's ditch."

Then Clyde added, "I tell y'all, I rather Massa Isaacson turn me back to a slave than put me to diggin' in that ditch." And so the commotion continued unabated for a while, as Rory did bide his time until all was quiet again before speaking back up.

"Tis not a diggin' ditches I'll be a doin' there, me friends," he said, as he looked each carefully in the eye. "Tis buildin' on St. Patrick's Church that'll be me occupation, thank you." And with that, he did turn and leave, as silently as he had first arrived, leaving Mary Dunnigan looking somewhat distressed that the boy had taken such offense at all their teasing.

Thursday, 29 June 1837

Molly Connelley left today. Said she could no longer stay under this roof. Said too many were the memories weighing too heavy on her soul for her to stay on any longer. Another position has she secured in a fine home in the Garden District. I tink she will be happy there, in time, but I fear she has gone off and left all the bad luck behind.

There is so much to be done right now and so little time to do it. For the most part, the monsieur is quiet. He rests upstairs in his chambers, sleeping off the effects of old Dr. Penney's pills and elixirs. Sedatives, the old physician calls his potions, but they seem to work and this is what is important. Mordecai and Miriam take turns sitting up with him, lest he awake in one of his fogs and do himself harm. Dr. Penney worries about this, so they take turns sitting up with him. For the most part, he sleeps as peacefully as the infant that old Marie, the cook, watches over out in the kitchen house. But once the effect of the doctor's medicine wears off, he wakes and begins anew his promenading up and down like a caged animal.

So much of my own time I find taken up with the administration of the monsieur's business interests. I break to check in on him whenever I can find the time, but I must confess that it tears me apart to see a mon of such elevated station reduced to such a pitiful state, all broken down and left a drugged and slumbering heap upon his bed. It is a long way he has fallen; even a longer way, I fear, than it took to pull himself up in the world.

Though few would imagine it, given his deportment, Mon. Isaacson was not born a rich man. It was into a family sans privilege that he came, the youngest of eleven children to be born to descendants of Spanish Jews. The year was 1781, the city was Liverpool and another mouth to feed was the last ting his papa did need. He sat back and bided his time, though, allowing his wife to dote over her youngest, sending him to Hebrew school until he was eleven years old. Then did his papa step in and take over. Off to work he sent the boy, to a textile plant where he worked from seven of the morning until eight of the evening, with only forty minutes for lunch at the noon hour. It was hard work and dangerous; many were the little ones he knew and worked with that were maimed and killed in that factory. But always the young monsieur did heed his mother's lament, paying careful attention to his work. And always did he did bring, straight home to his papa, his full week's pay of 7 shillings.

Whatever it took to help the family, the young monsieur would do, and suffer quietly for it. But in his seventeenth year, his papa died and Mon. Isaacson did set his sights beyond the blackened factories of Liverpool. To London he fled, where he soon found himself a job running messages between brokerage houses. Day in and day out, dozens of messages would he deliver. Soon it came to be that the monsieur would take to reading those messages he carried, gleaning any advantage he could from their contents. He took to playing games in his mind: using the information he found in the messages, he did pretend to invest in schemes, following the results to see how he would have come out. The results only served to encourage him on, to the extent that when he read, one dreary, English day, of an early and terrible hurricane that had devastated the islands of Cuba, Hispaniola, and Jamaica, he did act. The message he carried told of great loss of life and property, but stated the effects on the sugar cane crop could not be ascertained at the time.

Monsieur was, indeed, an astute young man. During the day he would run errands and during the evening he would forage through London's libraries, devouring whatever tasty morsels of information that may have whetted his appetite. When waiting for messages to run, he would while away the time reading the newspapers, trade journals and position papers that always littered the brokerage houses. This is how he came to be so well-versed on the sugar cane industry. Well did he know the cane grew in tall, wood-like stalks that were particularly susceptible to high winds, which could cause them to snap in two, or pull up by their shallow roots. There that day, with the message in one hand and his pay envelope in the other, he did reason that a hurricane strong enough to cause great death and loss of property, most likely would cause devastation to the cane crop. As he hurried along to deliver his message, he argued with himself in his own mind, until finally after he had made delivery, he went straight away to the trading floor and invested his whole week's pay in fall sugar futures. If there was one thing the monsieur understood innately, it was that the market would be slow to react to certain information, but once that information trickled on down through the echelons of investors, the reaction could be swift and decisive. If he were going to make the move and put his own hard-earned money at risk, now was the time to act, whilst he had the upper hand.

The storm did devastate the cane crop and sugar prices were to go sky-high. It was handsomely monsieur was to profit; handsomely, that is, but not excessively so. For one ting, his poor salary was not ample to get him far enough into the sugar market that his profit would have turned other heads. Far, far too astute was he to call attention to himself like that, even if he'd had more money to invest. Nothing good would come from his being caught making big profits off investments that could be traced back to the priority information he dispatched each day. And being a mon not given to boasting about himself, he did manage to lay low. Slowly, steadily he did build up his bank accounts, to the extent that within the next four years, Mon. Isaacson did go from being a boy of inconsequential prospect to a gentleman ready to enter commerce.

At age twenty-one years, his means were fully adequate to allow him to seek his fortune in the new world. To Jamaica he sailed, to found a business built upon the brokerage of sugar cane and spices. Frequent trips to New Orleans would he make, making more and more contacts, lining up purchases of sugar and even buying up lands when the opportunity presented itself. Soon, his would be a thriving business, with employees old enough to be his father answering to him, day in and day out. Soon he would own a stately, blue house in one of the finer neighborhoods of Kingston. And soon it would be that he would spy my very own mother, standing on the block in the New Orleans Slave Exchange, waiting to be sold at public outcry to the highest bid. Before the gavel could be dropped on her, however, monsieur did barge in the room and outbid all for her title.

"So now we know," Susan interrupted. "Hiam Isaacson *did* come to this country a rich man. Right?"

"We were speculating outside earlier if he immigrated to this country in such high-style or not," T.K. explained. "I was contrasting this house with how humbly my mother's family lived when they first got off the boat at Ellis."

"Well, he may have been born penniless but by the time he got to New Orleans he seems to have been pretty well fixed," I added before continuing.

To his fine new home he took my mother, where in so doing he gave her freedom: slavery had by then been outlawed in Britain and her colonies. There, my mother was given charge of the home—that same home where he would often share his bed with her. In return, she gave him her love, and in time a baby girl. And I, the product of their love? I readily confess I was a reared in a most fortunate style: a liberal education instructed by private tutors; mentoring in the social graces; music lessons. Jewels and dresses of the latest Parisian fashions were lavished on me, the apple of my father's eye, even if I was never to be recognized as such. Such was the destiny of we love children born mixed in the races and outside the bounds of Holy Matrimony. By no means could I be considered a mere servant in his house, yet by no means could I be acknowledged as his true daughter.

It would be eight years they would be together, but their days were to be numbered. With Mr. Eli Whitney's invention of his gin, cotton was to become king, and the monsieur's cotton accounts in New Orleans soon proved to be far more lucrative than the sum of his cane and spice accounts combined. His move to New Orleans was inevitable; all could see it coming. And when the time for him to leave came, he provided well for my mother, allowing her to remain in his Jamaican house the rest of her days; providing her with a generous allowance, deposited into her bank account each month by the Kingston brokerage house. Frequent trips— once, sometimes twice a year—would he make, back home to Jamaica, where he would check up on his business affairs; and where he would spend the rest of his time with my mother and me. Those wonderful days when our monsieur would return to us, that is how I make myself remember him, nowadays. Tender and loving; shrewd and powerful. Nothing like the shattered shell of a mon that sleeps away his days, no different from that pitiful infant out in the Negro kitchen.

To be sure, it is so much of our time the monsieur does these days consume, that I fear the house has been neglected. Already it is the ending of June and the weather has grown hot and heavy. Yet the house still waits to be made ready for summer. The heavy, wool carpets from Persia must be taken up and stored; the grass mats put down in their place. The winter drapes must be taken down; mosquito netting needs to be hung in the windows and the cool white cotton curtains put up. The chandeliers must be wrapped up in the netting, lest the big flies pit the crystals with their excrement. And everywhere, chairs and settees lack their crisp white slipcovers. But what shall we do? Monsieur and that little infant require so much of our time.

This very morning did I venture out to the coach house, there to call the stable boys to take up the parlor rugs, when I remembered that skinny Patrick O'Bannion up in the loft. I asked one of the boys about him and was told he spends most of his time up there, painting on the picture he will let no one see until finished. He ventures out only occasionally, usually to empty his chamber vessel, or fill his water jug, or fetch a morsel of food from the kitchen. Little has he to say to anyone. Hearing this, I ordered the boys to clean their boots and go to the house and take up monsieur's rugs for me. And then I did stand in the courtyard and call up to Patrick in the loft. In time, he was to appear at the door, shirtless, smeared with oil paints and wringing wet with the sweat that would not evaporate in the damp air. "Tant ready," he called down to me. "It takes time. I'll tell ye when it is I'm finished."

"It's not the picture I'm inquiring after. It's you," I replied to him. "It's hot up in that loft, is it not? Get yourself down here and enjoy a glass of citrus water." I could tell he was about to decline the invitation when he thought better of it.

"If you say so," was all he could muster.

I ordered cook to fix up a pitcher of sweet lemon water and bring it out to us, then took a seat in the shade of the banana trees and waited for the skinny boy. When, finally, he appeared, and sat himself nearby, I saw the shirt he had slipped on was stained yellow and coated with white patches of body salt from all the sweating he had done up in that baking loft. "Is the loft adequate for your painting, up there?" I asked him.

"Fine. North light it gets, and that's the best. Leaves no shadows on the canvas to go foolin' me."

"But what about the heat? It's hot up there, I can tell from looking at you. Does the heat interfere with your paints?"

"Tis a good cross ventilation ye get up there. The breezes help keep the paints from takin' too long to dry."

The cook appeared bearing a tray with the pitcher of sweet yet tart water and two glasses. Upon her back, the little slumbering infant was bound up in a scarf and I did notice young Patrick eye him closely. Nervously. Then quickly did he look away, and I hastened the cook on with a wave of the hand. "Here, this should cool you down some," I said as I poured him a glass. "You know, no one expects you to be hidden away up there in that loft of yours. You can come and go as you wish.

Patrick accepted the refreshment, then waited until I had my glass filled before tasting it. "I've a job to do," he said, smacking his lips with the taste of the water. "I owe ye an honest day's paintin', just like I owed the mister an honest day's diggin' when I worked on his canal."

"That you do. I've no qualm with that. But it's miserable hot up in that loft. All I was intending to imply was that you take your time and do a good job whilst you're at it."

"Oh, I'll be a doin' a good job. Don ye worry yerself none on that account. Tis a labor o' love I'm workin' on up there."

"Good," was all I could find to reply.

The two of us sat in silence for a while, he studying the flowers and the birds in the courtyard; me studying the house, so neglected on the inside. I studied the window to monsieur's chambers and deduced that all was quiet within. Then I did turn my eyes on the door to Mary Dunnigan's room, there on the second floor of the servant's quarters. A padlock had I caused to be installed on that door, with instructions that no one was to enter that room under any circumstances. "Tell me, Young Patrick," I said, still looking up at the door, "How was it your friend Rory and Mary Dunnigan came to be acquainted? I know he brought with him from Ireland a letter for her. But it was my understanding their meeting over the delivery of that letter was brief and uneventful."

He took a gulp of the water and swallowed it down hard. "That it was. And rude on yer people's part. Fairly mocked the lad, they did! Cheeky lot. I know because I came to this house with him, that day. Stood just outside that gate, I did," he pointed to the rear courtyard gate. "This much I'll tell you, Rory O'Kelley was provoked when he left these premises. Said to me he'd not so much as empty his bladder on one of those people, if he was to come upon them afire in the street. Still, that very Sunday-after, while we were standin' in the side aisle at church, waitin' on the Holy Sacrament, who would you think he should see in the line to receive the Host but that Mary Dunnigan herself. She glanced over to him, and wouldn't you know it? He broke out in a silly grin and all. Right then and there, it was, I could tell he was smitten. Patrick rubbed his neck with the cool water glass and stared up to Mary's door.

"After church, he made us to hang back so he could meet up with her. She and that high-and-mighty Molly friend o' hers. I tell you, I've known women like that one before. Think just because they work in these big fancy houses they own 'em. Wouldn't give the likes of me a sip o' water if I was starvin' o' the thirst." Sheer disdain resonated in the young man's voice and he was right, I knew, about Molly Connelley. She was a good, hard worker who never was to give me much worry, but she could have her high-handed ways with the others. As much as I missed having her here, with so much to get done, I was glad she was gone. If only she'd taken the bad luck with her.

Noticing that Rory's glass was empty, I refilled it as I agreed with him, "So I've heard from the others. Miss Molly has never been out of line with me, but she can get a little grand in her own estimation with the others. Especially those with color." Patrick thanked me for the second glass and drank it down like a mon nearly parched. "That was it, then? They met at church and that was it?" I inquired.

The skinny boy did ponder me for a bit before he answered. "Tis a mighty powerful curiosity ye have in these dead ones now, isn't it Missus Maneau? And why might this be, I wonder?"

I did give the boy the eye. "Do you tink you are the only one who has been unsettled by these tragic events of late? I hope you don't, because then I fear you'd be disappointed when you find out different. My reason for making these questions has to do with my need to make some sense out of what's taken place of late. That's all. Or would you be denying me that?"

He dropped his eyes to the glass he held in his big but delicate hands and said to me, "No. That I won't deny ye." Then he looked me back in the eye. "But if it's any sense ye can be makin' outta' all this, I'd be appreciatin' yer explainin' it all to me."

"If I can. If I can make sense out of it, I will," I promised him.

It was for a moment he seemed to pull thoughts out of the air, before he continued. "I'd been around him night and day for the seven, maybe eight weeks by then. I'd gotten to know the lad pretty well durin' that time. That, and tis not like I ne'er saw a young man in love. I could just tell that Sunday that Rory O'Kelley was taken with Mary Dunnigan." He turned his gaze on the water shimmering in the well pond as he continued, "Like I say, we waited around after services and he caught up with her. Bold he was, but shy at the same time. Ye know what I mean?" He looked around to me, like it was important to him that I understand what he was telling me.

"I tink so," I said. "His desire to talk with her some more made him bold, but he was shy about what to say. Is that what you mean?"

" Aye. Tis."

"Well, I expect most men's be like that. That's why I tink women of French heritage makes tings easier for their menfolk. Always giving them their little signs with the fans and all. Helps the menfolk along."

"Well, Mary Dunnigan wasn't one o' those fancy women carryin' no fancy fan. That she wasn't. So poor old Rory had to just bite the bullet and step right up to her. He asked her how she was a doin', I remember, and that awful Molly woman made some remark about it not bein' none o' his business. But Mary turned to her and gave her a look that caused her to drop back and let them go on in peace. I myself, had manners enough not to go elbowin' me way in between them two, but not that Molly woman. So she dropped back and walked along side of me the whole time. Without ne'er sayin' so much as a word to me. We just sort o' followed them. They didn't have much to say, there at first. Walked on like they both had a cat get their tongues, for a whole block or two. You know, sometimes I think it's not an easy thing—men and women findin' common ground to talk on."

"Sometimes it's not. Sometimes. But once a mon and a woman learns they have more in common than they give themselves the credit for, then it's not so hard. Then they find it's good to have someone to make talk with."

"Spoken like a true lady, mademoiselle," he teased me, and for the first time I was to see a smile on that skinny boy's face. A fine, handsome smile he could be proud of, I thought to myself.

"Did they ever get around to talking. Or was this just another one of those awkward strolls you menfolk be so famous for?" I teased back.

"No, they talked. It was her, I seem to remember, who asked him what brought him to America. That was it. What had brought him to America, she wanted to know. And he told her his father had died, and she said she had lost her father too, and it just sort of went on from there." The smile returned as he stared off into space, reminiscing aloud to me. "I remember Rory sayin' to Mary that he heard somewhere that the man she worked for was a Jew. Rory said he'd never seen a Jew before. Mary reminded him right quick he was not back in Ireland, that there were all kinds o' people what made up New Orleans. She told him in the year or so she'd been here, she'd even seen a Chinaman. Ole Rory asked if she'd ever seen an Indian, but Mary said no, an Indian was the one being she reckoned she'd never seen in America."

Once again, the boy wandered off, lost in his own thoughts. Eventually, I moved to stand and retire back to housework, tinking he had no more to say to me, when he spoke back up. "They just walked along slow-like, talkin' to each other, all the way back to this house. When we got back here, Rory asked if she had to go inside and she said no, that she had the rest of the day off, so the four of us went and sat underneath the tree over yonder. The one growin' out into the street. Me and that Molly-woman listenin' to those two gettin' to know one another." It was then Patrick O'Bannion's eyes watered up again, threatening to flow down his cheeks like so much water so close to home.

I sat in silence to let the boy's pain run its course, realizing his must be such a tender heart for a grown mon. Beyond the back gate, the old oak tree those four had spent so much of their time under, stood spreading its branches all the way across the street. How often had I seen those four young ones gathered under the shelter of that tree, talking and carrying on like young peoples always do. How often had I found the monsieur standing at his chamber window staring down at those four gathered there under that oak. How little thought had I given it at the time, to now find it burned so deeply into my memory. How vividly do I remember that night I was to accompany Mon. Isaacson home from the Théâtre d'Orléans. Clyde had guided the landau into the carriageway, and as we had stepped down, laughter was to be heard emanating from the direction of the darkened tree.

"What's that?" The monsieur asked of the footman, "Who's that out there in the dark?"

"Dat? Dat ain't nothin, Massah Isaacson. That's jest them crazy Irish women o'er there carryin' on with a couple of Irish boys they done met somewheres."

"Boys? What boys?" he wanted to know. How quickly did he then turn to me. "I can't have my help loitering around in the dark like that. What will the neighbors think? Send those boys on their way and order your housekeepers inside." Then off he stormed, leaving me wondering if his concern was so much with the neighbors, or the presence of boys in Mary Dunnigan's company.

Nevertheless, Clyde did accompany me across the street, bearing a lantern for the light in the moonless night. At the tree, all four stood at attention, concern registered on their faces, like school children about to be upbraided by a stern sister. "Molly. Mary," I addressed the ladies, noticing for the first time one of the boys was none other than the one who had knocked at the rear hall door at such an unfortunate hour. "Mon. Isaacson wishes that you come in now. It is not seemly before the neighbors for you to be loitering about out here in the darkness."

"Yes, Misses Maneau," they said quietly and promptly followed in behind me, without so much as a word of farewell to the two young men in their company.

Throughout the rest of the summer, I was to notice, more and more, that young Rory O'Kelley showing up at the rear gate, where he would often just stand on the outside conversing with Mary Dunnigan through the iron bars. It would be in the late afternoon of the weekdays when he would usually show up, after he was finished with his work on St. Patrick's and Mary's duties allowed a few minutes of free time. I found my eyes fixed upon that gate, as I remembered the strange dance I had witnessed between the two there. Like it was the door to a jail, keeping him out and her in, they would stand for a spell, each clutching at the bars as they talked. From time-to-time, he would allow his hand to slide down the bar and over hers. Momentarily. Then she would discreetly extract her hand from his caress, before his affection became obvious to all watching from the house.

At other times, I was to witness the ritual of their differences; first the one would grab at the bars and lean inward toward the other, while driving home a point, with the other one always taking a step back, refusing to acknowledge that point. And then the stances would be reversed, when the other would grab at the bars and lean inward to the first one and attempt to force a contrary point. It was indeed a strange ritual, one that often ended with Rory O'Kelley storming off down the street in a huff, and Mary Dunnigan fleeing to her room in tears. The course of love, I have observed, does not always flow smoothly, but that is matter for another entry, another day. It grows late and my candle burns low, so I will conclude this day's entry by mentioning young Patrick's tears ceased to overflow the dams that were his lower lids. Soon his eyes had dried sufficiently for him to excuse himself without further shame on his part.

"If ye'll be grantin' me leave, mistress, I've me work to attend to."

"Moi oui," I responded. Then I did sit and watch him disappear into the coach house. Such a sad young mon, I remember tinking he was. Yet what is done is done and can't nobody make it any different than it is. His whole life has Patrick O'Bannion in front of him; it's time he got over his grieving and on with his living.

But then, is it not time we all put this tribulation behind us?

Friday, 30 June 1837

All has been busy, but peaceful, around the house these past two days. Monsieur seems to rest quieter nowadays, requiring less and less of old Dr. Penny's elixir. Out in the coach house, young Patrick O'Bannion still keeps to himself, consumed with the picture he is painting. And I? I am still taxed with the volume of business matters to which I must attend in monsieur's absence, but I have made some progress in getting the house in order for the sweltering months. Sunday-last, after church, I did happen upon Molly Connelley, and inquired if, on her day off, she or perhaps someone she knew, would be available to help me with some of the household concerns. To my astonishment, she most agreeably did offer her own services, and was able to procure the help of two other girls. Most of the hot and sticky day we worked, and worked hard, managing to get the summer drapes hung in all the windows, all the chairs slipcovered, and most of the chandeliers netted up. So relieved was I at our progress, that when I doled out wages to send the ladies on their way, I did ask Molly to wait behind and take tea with me in the front parlor.

Molly offered to fetch the tea from the kitchen house, but I did insist that she take her rest and allow herself to be a guest in the house for a change. When I returned with the tray, however, I must confess I was struck by finding her slouched in one of Mon. Isaacson's elegant Louis XV side chairs. I can only assume the child just didn't know better, given her unfortunate class. "Molly, my dear," I said to her as I proceeded to pour the tea, "You must sit forward in the chair. A lady never allows her back to touch the back of the seat. See? Notice how I sit."

Straightaway, she took my cue, not begrudgingly as I would have thought, but with what I sensed to be a want to better herself. I handed her a cup of tea, which she took with adequate skill, spilling not the slightest drop, as I confided in her, "Lately, I have been going over all that transpired of recent in this house. I've taken to talking about Mary and that Rory O'Kelley with young Patrick O'Bannion—" I was unable to finish my sentence, as Molly instantly interrupted me.

"You'll just be a wasting your time talkin' anything with that one," she said. "A horrible excuse for a man he is." I poured my tea in quiet, allowing Molly's breach to dissipate, lest she be led to tink such behavior was acceptable. A sip of the tea I took, then continued, as if my train of conversation had never been halted.

"You know, I was never privy to what was going on between those two. Oh, I'd seen them talking at the back gate from time-to-time. But I'd never thought much of it. Now, I find myself pondering more and more about that back gate. About how one day they looked like a young couple all infatuated with each other; and then the next time, they'd look like they were ready to do battle."

"That they were. Ready to go to battle that is. Those two was always arguing over what the other one never said."

"What the other one never said?" I considered aloud Molly's odd statement. "I don't believe I understand."

"Twas like they was always a readin' somethin' into what the other one had to say. Always interpretin' utterances the wrong way from what they was meant. I blame it all on that O'Kelley boy. I'll be a tellin' you this much: Mary Dunnigan was never one to be all that worried about what someone else thought o' her, till that lad came along."

"Oh, I don't know. I found her to take great pride in her work," I mused. "That leads me to conclude she was a little concerned over what others thought of her. I wonder, though. Don't you tink love, itself, can make us feel all...insecure. It's an awful scary business, you know, giving your heart to someone else. To go and lose that love, that would be a awful happening, wouldn't it? No wonder, then, that we're all so wobbly, so much of the time we be in love. Maybe that was why they were always misinterpreting each other's words. Out of feeling so vulnerable."

"I suppose. Still and all, I blame that Rory O'Kelley. I'm glad he's dead in the ground. He got what was comin' to him, if you were ask me."

I was astonished. I knew not what to make of this brash young woman sitting before me. How could anyone speak so unkindly of the dead? "Molly Connelley," I said as adamantly as I could, leaning forward to emphasize my words, "You will do well not to be speaking unfavorably of the deceased. It's not in your interest to rile the spirits of the departed. Nothing good can ever come from such as that." I straightened my back upright, then, and moderated my tone. "You must learn to forgive, like our Savior has taught us. Is that not right?"

"It's and eye-for-an-eye, and a tooth-for-a-tooth, what the Bible tells us to take," she shot back at me.

"Indeed, it does. In the Old Testament, it says just that. But what that means, Molly, is the punishment must be proportionate to the crime. Now the fact of the matter is, Rory O'Kelley never killed a living soul. So, it's unreasonable you should say he got what he deserved. And even if he'd killed the Bishop himself, in the New Testament our Savior teaches us that we must not take eye-for-eye. We are to forgive; we're to show love even to our enemies," I said as I sat my cup aside. Then I did entreat of the girl, "But all that aside, I cannot help but wonder why you do hate that mon so much."

"Ha!" she barked out loud. "I'll tell you why I hate him so. Because if it hadn't been for him and his pretty face and sweet-talkin' ways, me friend Mary Dunnigan would be alive today. If it hadn't been for him poor Sonnier would b,e alive today! If it hadn't been for him, Mr. Isaacson wouldn't be confined to his chambers up there, plumb absent of the mind. And you ask why I hate him so? It's burnin' in hell I wish on him!" she cried out, her words reverberating throughout the house.

I had allowed Molly to become too perturbed, that I could see. I said nothing further, merely took her teacup from her and refreshed it in silence, allowing her time to regain her composure. Yet I thought to myself, my God how high passions do run against that pair of ill-starred lovers. I realized how fortunate I was to have been so removed from the situation.

At once it seemed an eerie quiet overtook the room, the only sound to be heard being the ticking of the tall clock out in the hall. I returned Molly's teacup to her and thought to myself for a moment, before saying. "I do believe you are too young to let all this eat you up like it is." And then I had to stare at the floor to collect my thoughts before I could go on. Finally, I looked up to her and asked, "Is it possible, mon petite, that you yourself were in love with Rory O'Kelley? Could this be why your feelings run so hard against him?" I had fully expected an explosion of denial from the girl, but all I was to be given was a gentle shake of her head.

"No. I could tell by the way he looked at me that he cared not the least about me. Tis a fool who falls in love with someone who's got no use for the sight of you."

"Was that it, then? Rory O'Kelley was standoffish and you took offense?"

"Wasn't that he was mean by me. More like he didn't even know I existed most o' the time. A blind beggar could see twas Mary who'd stolen his heart. Tis a fool, as well, who falls in love with a man who's heart belongs to someone else. No, I was never in love with him. I just had me feelin's hurt that he didn't give a hoot for me."

As I churn it over in my mind, I confess I must have known that it was a question my better angels told me was none of my business; a question that I'd be better off leaving unasked. But it was a question, I also knew, that begged for an answer. I could not keep silent on it. "So he had eyes for someone else, not for you," I heard myself say. "Still, let me ask you this: do you not suppose that if they threw themselves on the mercy of the confessional and repented of their sins, gladly performed their penitence—do you not tink they both would have received assurance of forgiveness?" I asked her. "And if no less than God Himself can forgive Rory O'Kelley, then why can't you?"

My words must have cut into Molly, for she sat for the longest, saying not a syllable, only the sound of her stirring her tea competing with the ticking of the clock. I endured the silence lost in my own thoughts, realizing the question I'd put to Molly was equally applicable to me. If God Himself could forgive these poor Irish, why could I not put my own disfavor behind me, I wondered. Was my own prejudice against these ones any less odious than that of the powder-white Caucasians who expect me to step aside into the mud as they pass me on the street? Slowly, somewhere in the fertile furrows of my brain, a notion took root and I came to wonder if maybe all the bad luck hovering over this house had passed from Mary Dunnigan by no design of her own. And if that were so, would it be any more reasonable for me to blame her for our present misfortune, than it was for Molly to blame poor Rory O'Kelley for all the death that's visited here lately? There, in the back of my mind, I argued with myself, about whether my anger was misplaced, was unreasonable or not. Could it be that because so much unhappiness does so pervade these halls now, that I need someone to blame, some direction in which to vent my anger in order to make some sense out of it all? My rumination, however, was to be interrupted when Molly Connelley finally did look back up at me.

"I came to this land an orphan, ma'am. Twas no family I left behind in Ireland, like the others. All I had was me friend Mary Dunnigan. Twas like a sister I loved that girl. I had no jealousy against her for fallin' in love. I fell in love too, don't you see. Twas Patrick O'Bannion who had my eye. But if Rory O'Kelley had never come to this place a carryin' that foolish letter o' his, I'd still have me friend Mary. And maybe even a chance with Patrick."

"Maybe. Maybe you'd still have your friend alive. But that be second-guessing the will of God, would it not? There's usually two sides to every story."

"Wasn't all his fault," she replied. "That much I'll accept. But most o' the bumps in their road were from his own makin', I reckon."

"In what manner?"

"Well, take for instance the time we was all down to the riverfront. You know, by the Artillery Park. Ever one was happy and havin' such a good time. Then that Rory did spy such a dandy in his kilt, his pipes slung o'er his shoulder and all. Wouldn't you suppose he could make do with just a 'hello'? But nooo, not that one, he couldn't. Right up to the man he marched and started carryin' on such a conversation about Ireland, leavin' poor Mary and the rest o' us feelin' all left out. Always that man had such a mind about Ireland. Could talk for days on end about dear old Ireland." Molly Connelley looked me straight in the eyes and raised her voice, "If you ask me, if Ireland was such a fine place, he should have just turned right around and gone right back home, he should! But not him. Noooo! Not Rory O'Kelley. He just took up with the man, talkin' and talkin' o' Ireland. Leavin' us all waitin' round on 'em, like he'd bleed blue if you cut 'em. Like he was the king himself."

"Why did you all have to wait around on him? If he went off with another, why couldn't the rest of you just go off on your own, as well?"

And, don't you know, Mary Connelley did put her finger on the crux of the matter when she thought out loud: "Oh, I don't know. He always had such sway on people, that Rory O'Kelley did. People just naturally took to him, I reckon."

Reflecting on it now, I must admit that I have observed people like that myself. Certain people there are who, for whatever reason, just seem to pull the affections of others right out of them. Though one would not know it by looking at him now, it had always been my impression that Mon. Isaacson was just such a individual. People, it seemed, just naturally gyrated toward him. All, that is, except that bunch harboring unfounded dislike of the Jews. I wondered if it was like that with Rory O'Kelley, being fresh off the boat from Ireland. As much as those of commerce do relish all the plentiful, cheap Irish labor, among the lower, unschooled masses, I've discerned an ever-growing prejudice toward the ever-growing Irish numbers. I soon found myself studying the leaves in my teacup, as I thought about that young Irishman I never really knew too well. I pondered aloud, "Having never been around him, myself, I wonder? What was his demeanor? Was he a loud and pushy sort? Quiet and shy?"

"No. I wouldn't say that about him; he wasn't loud or shy, just sort of in-between. At times, though, he could be downright distant. Had a mind like a steel trap, that one. When he had his mind fixed on somethin', likely as not he wouldn't even know you was in the room. Drove poor Mary crazy that way, he did."

"I see," I said. And I did. It is my observation that these people who exude such magnetism are seldom brash or overbearing. To the contrary, they are, almost without exception, reserved but self-confident beings, not given to bragging and strutting. Often, like Mary and Rory both, they possess a measure of that very trait Molly ascribed to Rory. And certainly that is a trait I have observed many times in the monsieur. That, I imagine, is a general attribute of the human male, however. Too often is his focus on some matter or some task so intense that others—especially the women—feel excluded. That, it seemed to me, was the state of tings Molly was describing. Preoccupied or not, however, these ones we others find so captivating, so beguiling, often seem to take an unusual stake in the lives of others. Or so it seems to me." Molly's mumbling soon interrupted my thoughts, however.

"Course, the other thing that drove Mary crazy was his drinkin'."

"He would partake of libations, then?" I asked with some surprise.

"Not really. Not all that much that I ever noticed. I've no big problem with a man takin' him a wee nip from time-to-time, mind you. But not Mary. Not Mary Katherine Dunnigan. She just couldn't abide drinkin' in any form. Especially by the man she was in love with. That night down by the Artillery Park? I tell you, the dandy in his kilt took out a flask and offered it up to Rory. He took it; he was a man, after all. And as well, it would have been down right impolite to refuse the bloke, I reckon. Still, this much I'll be tellin' you: Rory O'Kelley caught hell for takin' that swallow o' whiskey. Mary flew into a rage. Demanded poor Patrick escort the two of us back home, she did. And then Rory chimed in, and it was such an argument those two got themselves into. Mary stormed off vowing to never set eyes on him again, and Rory just shouted back to her he hoped he never sat eyes on her again, neither. It was a spectacle they made o' themselves."

And then, there in the front parlor where we had worked so hard that very afternoon, Molly did turn inward on herself for a spell, sitting and staring at her teacup as she did. I indulged her silence, respecting her right to keep to herself, to attend to her own thoughts. And so it was for some while that she sat quiet as a pebble, as unmindful of the world around her as that little infant strapped on old Marie's back. Yet when she did come back to the world, her words came babbling forth like waters from a spring that the earth can no longer hold deep down inside. I allowed her a free reign, to sit and muse on the courtship of that Irish couple and she spoke at length about their wooing. Sitting there with her teacup in her hand, she told me of the many times Mary would invite her, whilst Rory would invite Patrick, to accompany them down Josephine street, to the riverfront—lest Molly and Patrick be left alone to themselves, with nothing to do of a fine afternoon. There they would lie in wait for one of the elegant paddle wheelers to come steaming down the river and dream of the day they could take a trip aboard one of those modern vessels. Or the men would throw a fish line into the waters, but always the swift current would just bring the cork back around to the bank, and never were they to catch any ting. But mostly, Molly and Patrick, themselves, would marvel at how long the young lovers could sit and talk with each other, about even the most mundane matters. To Molly, it seemed the two enjoyed the words and sounds of the other's voice, to the same extent as I do so love the words and sounds of operatic music.

There would be more—much more—that Molly was to share with me that afternoon. There were stories of the pair strolling down Canal Street, after Sunday Mass, admiring all the pretty notions in the store windows, tings they could only dream they would be able to afford someday. There was even the story of the time Rory caused Mary to pack them a picnic lunch, whereupon he met her at the back gate and escorted her across the back street to the big oak tree. There, he did convince the girl to climb with him, up in that tree, where they spent the rest of the day sharing their picnic lunch and admiring the view from such a lofty perch, like they were a couple of children content to watch the world go by beneath them. I tell you, Molly's recounting of Mary climbing up in a tree in her dress did cause my heart to palpitate and I thank God that none of the neighbors came wandering by, looking up amongst the branches! And yet, at the same time, there was something in the story I found heartwarming and wonderfully whimsical.

And then there were the accounts of the dances at the Irish social hall and afternoons spent beside Bayou St. John, but mostly there were reports of the times those four shared together beneath the shelter of that big oak tree across the back street. There was even the recounting of the time of a Sunday afternoon the pair spent strolling down Canal Street, whilst poor Patrick did attend to his reading and writing lessons with Fr. O'Donnell. At the window of the seamstress Melencon's boutique, Mary did pause to attend to the notice in the window:

JUST ARRIVED
NEW SHIPMENT OF FINE FRENCH SILK
SEE US TODAY ABOUT YOUR GOWNS
FOR THE CULTURAL SEASON

And as she gazed on, admiring the fancy frocks in the window, Rory's mood did turn peculiar. "Ah, Mary me love. What're ye a doin' waistin' yer time on the likes o' me? Ye deserve to walk right in shops like this and have those fancy women workin' in there waitin' on ye hand over fist. Ye should be on the arm of a fine, rich gentleman what can open up doors like this to ye. I've neither the money nor prospect o' gettin' any to do that for ye. You must know that."

Mary Dunnigan turned to look on Rory with amusement. "You talk like you just fell out of a tree on your head. I've an elegant gown made up at this very store hanging behind the door in me room. Most uncomfortable thing I've ever put on in me entire life, that's what it is. I've worn it but once, so I don't see what I'd be a needin' with another one, now. Do you?"

"From here? Ye have a fancy gown from this fine shop? Saints be praised, Mary! It must've cost ye a fortune."

"Twas a favor from Mr. Isaacson, it was. He had dresses made up for me and Molly, the both of us. When we first went into his service. Presented 'em with a ticket to the opera, sayin' it was a 'welcome to America' tradition."

"Did he, now? Ha! Didn't no one present me and Paddy with no fine present when we first stepped off the boat. Still, it was a grand gesture that yer employer made ye. And ye deserve a whole room full o' dresses like these. One for every day o' the week. Shoot, one for ever day o' the year, that's what ye deserve."

"You carry on too much, Rory O'Kelley. You just be getting' all your high-minded ideas about me out of your head. It's not that kind o' woman that I am. Even if I had the money to spend on a bunch of these expensive dresses, I'd far rather use that money helpin' the sick and poor than wastin' it like that. I'd have thought you'd know that about me."

Looking back now on this little account Molly gave on Mary and Rory, I can hear her saying that. For all the grief she may have brought down on this good house, she did have a good side to her. That much I'll allow. There was one occasion that comes to mind when I overheard a controversy she and Molly had when Clyde and I did offer them a ride home from Mass. Sitting up in front beside Clyde, I suppose they did not realize the wind carried their words straight back to my own ears. Molly, I remember, was chastising poor Mary about putting a silver piece in the poor box. "You needn't be always actin' like you was no fancy ladyship, Mary. You don't need to go puttin' money in the poor box every time you go inside the church. Makes the rest o' us look bad when we don't. You ain't exactly rich you know. In fact, rather than be puttin' money in the poor box, you outta be getting' some out! That's what you ought."

It was on her perch up front that Mary turned squarely to face Molly and then let her have it, much to the amusement of Clyde and me. "Molly Connelly, I'll have you to know that I may not be rich, but I ain't exactly poor neither. Mr. Isaacson pays me good enough as it is. Besides, back home Fr. O'Maley once told me that it says in scriptures that we ought ne'er to turn our backs on strangers, because some folks have actually taken care o' angels that a way! Without never bein' the wiser about it."

Mary's was a retort for which Molly had no ready answer. And so it was that on and on Molly did talk about Mary and Rory's times, that afternoon in the front parlor. But always her conversation, like that fishing line the boys kept throwing into the Mississippi, would come back around—

back around, again and again, to that night by the Artillery Park. Eventually it was to dawn on me that this was a story that kept bubbling up inside Molly, struggling to find a way out. I sat quietly, therefore, and listened carefully once it finally poured out of her. And the more I listened, the more I did realize that the story Molly was telling was nothing less than the foretelling of the days of our discontent. This, then, is the story she shared with me. It is the story of what transpired between Mary and Rory, that night they went down by the Artillery Park. And yet, in another sense, it is much more than that, for it is the story of two Irish lovers, trapped in a nation still searching for its soul, and cursed by an unfortunate fate.

By the time they had gone off with Molly and Patrick to the Artillery Park that night, Mary and Rory had known each other for six months, maybe a little longer. Long enough had they known each other, that they had learned all the little secrets and mysteries of the other that so intrigue a mon and a woman when first stepping out together. Long enough had they known each other, that they no longer had to put on the airs and masks a mon and a woman uses to lure the other. By then, they knew each other well; by then they had abandoned the strain of always being on their best behavior, in favor of acting their natural selves. By then had they come face-to-face with that awful truth that confounds us all when we take to the course of love, for each had uncovered in the other that little cache of imperfection we all hold deep down inside us. And so it would seem—that evening down by the Artillery Park—that it was poor Patrick who was caught in the middle of that lover's squabble. Mary was adamant she would not stand idly by whilst Rory drank himself drunk, all the while talking sentimental gibberish about dear old Ireland. "Rory O'Kelley, you know I don't approve of you drinkin' that old whiskey," she told him, in no uncertain terms. Rory paused with the bottle held aloft, ready to take another nip.

"And who the hell asked ye, lassie?" he demanded of her, like she had just gone crazy. Mary stood there, her face turning red and trembling all over, eyeing the lad like she could wring his head off, as he choked down another swallow of the evil spirits.

"I'll not stand idly by whilst you make a drunken' fool o' yourself, I wont! Come, Molly! We're a goin' home." And with that Mary grabbed her friend by the elbow and pulled her on along. Ah, but poor Patrick O'Bannion; what was the lad to do? He watched the ladies stomping off down the street, knowing he could not let them go sans escort. It was dark already. He looked back to his friend Rory, fearing if he tallied off after the girls, he would incur the wrath of his best friend in the entire world. Torn he was, not knowing what he was to do. Fortunately, Rory sensed his friend's predicament.

"Go on after 'em, then," he told Patrick. "They can't be moseying down the street alone after dark, anyhow."

So did Patrick rush after the ladies, to see them safely home. All the way along, Mary grew more and more sullen, while Molly grew more and more insulting toward Rory. "It's not like he don't know you don't hold with drinkin'," she said at one point. "It's more like he just don't care. I tell you,

Mary, I don't know what you see in that one, I don't. You'd be better off droppin' him like the handful of filthy dirt he is, if you ask me." But that evening, Mary was in no frame of mind for any of Molly's rambling on.

"Well I didn't ask you, Molly," she shot back. "And I'll appreciate you mindin' your own business from here on out."

Molly was, of course, devastated. Keeping her thoughts to herself, tinking beforehand, before she spoke, these were traits she could not master for the life of her. It was her tongue that was always getting her in trouble with others, but she was helpless to control it. The sad irony was, Molly Connelley was most adept at bringing out the rancor in others, but she was far too insecure to take such displeasure in stride. Thus it was that she had been, indeed, riled by her friend's reproach that night. Yet, along the three trudged on, in complete silence, all the way back home.

At the back gate, Molly bolted right on in, without so much as a parting thank you to Patrick. Up the back stairs she bounded, rushing into her room and slamming the door behind her in a temper-fit. Mon. Isaacson, that very evening, was corresponding at the writing table in his quarters, where the windows to the rear gallery stood open wide in the warm night air. There, the loud bang of the slammed door did alarm him and he rose from his desk to present himself onto the gallery to see what was the commotion. Down below in the dark, he could make out the shadowy images of a mon and a woman at the back gate. Now, by the time they had reached the house, it seems Mary's anger had eased, though not completely subsided.

She had paused at the gate to thank Patrick for seeing them home. "For the life o' me, Patrick," she told him, "I can't understand why drinkin' that old whiskey is more important to Rory than me."

"Ah, Mary now," Patrick tried to assure her, "Don't ye go a believin' such as that. I know full-well Rory thinks the world o' ye, girl. Told me as much, he has. I'll be havin' a talk with the lad. Seein' to it he apologizes to ye and all."

Upon the rear gallery, the monsieur took one of his fine Cuban cigars from his jacket pocket and struck a phosphorous-match to it. The flare of the flame caught Mary's eye, and she realized her employer was most likely watching the pair of them, down there below. "Don't you go a sayin' nothin' to him now, Patrick," she implored. "It'll just make things all the worse. I have to go. Mr. Isaacson's out on the balcony up there and it wouldn't seem right for us to be hangin' around the gate down here in the darkness."

"Good night then, Mary. Go get yerself some sleep. Things will look much brighter in the morn."

"God Bless you, Patrick O'Bannion," Mary whispered as she pushed the gate closed and turned toward the house. In turn, as Patrick rotated and started back down the dark street, some ting did hit him on his shoulder, bouncing off into the street dust as it did. He turned and surveyed the dark but could see no one. Nothing. Suddenly, another object—a small pebble—hit him on the ear. "Ouch! Who's there?" he called out.

Back from the dark came a shush. Then a whisper, barely audible, "Patrick. Over here. By the tree, laddie." It was the sound of Rory's voice. Even in a whisper, Patrick could recognize the sound of his friend's voice. Quietly, he made his way over toward the tree, ultimately making out the image of his friend lingering in the dark. Patrick started to ask him what he thought he was doing, but was prevented from doing so. "Shhhh," Rory warned him. "Up there. She's talkin' to someone on the balcony. See?"

"And who might this someone be, talkin' to someone on the balcony?" Patrick inquired.

"Mary. That's who. She didn't go straight to her room. Someone's up there smokin' in the dark and he stopped her when she went up the stairs."

Now that I recall it, I remember that I, too, had heard the bang Molly had made, slamming her door like she did. I had stepped out into the upstairs hall and had taken up station by the opened rear door leading onto the gallery. There, I saw the shadow of Mary climbing up the outside stairs, and I heard the monsieur call out, "Who's there in the dark?"

"Just me, Sir. Mary Dunnigan,"
"Miss Dunnigan? Are you all right there? I thought I heard a noise out here."

"I'm afraid you did, sir. One o' the doors in the servant's wing slammed shut. That was all."
"I see. And was that you down there by the gate, in the dark?"

"That it was, sir. Twas me. I was just a thankin' a friend o' a friend what was kind enough to see me and Molly home this evenin'."

"You were out this evening?"

"Aye. We were. Down by the Artillery Park. In front o' St. Louis Cathedral, we were."

"In the Veiux Carre? Whatever were you doing down there, of all places?"

"Nothin' really. Just congregatin' with some of the other young people."

"Well, you be careful down there, do you hear? The Creoles don't always take kindly to anyone not French being around their part of town."

"Surely, Sir. I don't think I shall be a goin' back down there anytime soon."

"Very well. Good night, then."

"Good night, Mr. Isaacson."

I heard the monsieur as he disappeared back into his room, while Mary made her way down the gallery to enter her own room, not noticing in the dark that Molly had reopened her door to catch some of the much-needed night breeze. I, myself, had returned to my room to make ready for bed, completely unaware that what was about to transpire that night would alter the course of this fine home's history.

In the darkness down below, by the old oak across the back street, Rory turned to his friend. "Did ye see that, then, Patrick? That old man was spying on me Mary. Grillin' her over about where she'd been, I expect."

"Tis a moonless night, Rory. Dark as a cave it is out here. I don't know how ye could tell who it was up on that there balcony. Much less whether they was havin' words with Mary or no."

"From the light of his cigar. That's how I could tell twas a man up there. And you could hear 'em talkin' in the dark, though I couldn't make out none o' their words."

"Yeah? Well, it's getting' late and Mary's gone on in now. Let's us be a makin' way on home now."

"Go on, Paddy. Don't bother about me none. I'm just goin' to wait around a bit longer."
"Wait around? Out here in the dark? Whatever for?"
"Just go on Paddy. I told ye I'd be along directly."

"I know not what ye're up to, Rory O'Kelley, and I don't think I want to know. It's to home I'll be a goin' now." Patrick turned and wandered off down the street, disappearing into the dark night, whilst Rory sat himself on the ground, beneath the old oak. There he watched the yellow candle glow in Mary's window until it went out. Then he waited a little longer, until the light in Clyde's room above the coach house went out as well. Slowly he rose, his heart beating in his chest like it was struggling to break free. His breathing grew deep and labored, as he stole across the street, softly as a cat, and slipped inside the back gate. He made his way to the garden area, between the rear of the servant's quarters and the brick fence, directly below the window in Mary's room. There, in the dark of night, he fumbled, digging in the soil until he had found himself a handful of shell fragments. Tick! He tossed a shell up against the upper sash in Mary's room. Nothing. Tick! Tick! Two more shells did he strike against the glass, until presently he could barely make out Mary's image, as she stuck her head out of the opened window.

"Who's down there?" she called out in a whisper.

"Mary, me love," Rory whispered back. "tis me, Rory."

"Rory O'Kelley! You get yourself away from this property before Mr. Isaacson calls the constable on you."

And with that, Mary disappeared back into her room.

Tick! Tick! Silence. Only the barking of a dog off in the distance. Tick! Tick! And more silence. Rory looked all around him. The house was darkened. The coach house was darkened. All was quiet. Peaceful. Slumbering. "Mary!" he called back up to the room, in as loud a whisper as he could muster. "Mary Dunnigan, I love ye so much and want ye to know I'm sorry." Still nothing but the dog barking in the distance. "Mary please! Come to the window," he begged in a hoarse whisper. Then he did hit upon an idea. "Mary

Dunnigan, come to yer window right now. Don't make me wake the whole house callin' out after ye, woman."

His idea worked. In an instant Mary was back at the window. "Don't you dare," she whispered down to Rory. "You're drunk! Go on home where you belong and leave me alone."

"Ah, can't ye see, Mary; tis not whiskey that makes me drunk. tis me love for you that keeps me this way." Mary disappeared back into her darkened room, only to quickly reappear. In her hand, she held the water pitcher from her dressing stand and blindly in the dark she did dump out the water, managing to splash poor Rory across the face and chest with it.

"And what did you do that for?" Rory moaned but Mary had disappeared back into her room, leaving the mon standing there in the herb garden, his hands on his hips, his head bowed as water dripped off his face. For the longest did he stand, considering his next move. Should he give up and go on home? No. In his mind, he knew well he could not do that. Softly, quietly he left the garden, stepping carefully along until he had made his way to the gallery stairs. There he looked all about, and once he was confident no one was stirring about, he sat himself upon the bottom step and removed his boots with great care, stowing them aside, under the stairs. In his bare feet he did tiptoe up the staircase, softly, quietly down the gallery, past Molly's open door, toward his Mary's own closed door.

In her room, that night, Molly had been unable to fall asleep. Still agitated was she at her friend having been so curt with her. She had sat up in her bed, staring out the doorway while playing around in her mind all the clever answers she should have given Mary in rebuttal. Then suddenly! Her blood did run cold. There outside her very door a figure passed in the dark, a shadowy, ghostly silhouette wandering along the balcony. She froze in panic. Her eyes opened wide to take in as much of the spectacle as she could; her hearing became as keen as an animal's. Who could this be, prowling the property at night? A murdered? A slave out for revenge? A ghost? Yes! Surely it was a ghost she had seen, for she could hear it subtly scratching at poor Mary's door. Scratching like a cat!

And then she heard it.

Softly, ever so softly she heard the voice whispering, "Mary. Mary open the door."

Much to her own surprise, Molly felt herself drawn out of her bed, slowly making her way toward her opened door. What she would have done, she knew not; she knew only that Mary Dunnigan was in danger and she meant to be of aid to her. Before she could get to the door, however, she heard Mary's door quietly open, the hinges squeaking slowly, gently in the night. In an instant, her blood ran from cold as ice to boiling hot, as she heard Mary whispering in the dark. "Rory O'Kelley! You get yourself off this balcony and off this property before I call Mr. Isaacson on you. You drunken fool."

Rory stepped in close to Mary; too close for her comfort. "I am not drunk, and I'll be a thankin' ye to stop sayin' I am."

"Then what do you think you're a doin' here? Takin' such a chance."

He stepped back so as not to appear threatening as he replied, "I'm here to tell ye I'm sorry about tonight. And to tell ye I love ye, Mary Katherine Dunnigan."

"O' Pshaw!" Mary let him have it. "You don't love me. You don't love anyone. Except maybe yourself."

Mary's words stung like a scorpion bite. Rory stood studying her outline in the dark. He was hurt, and he responded the only way that a mon who is hurt could respond—with anger. "And how would ye be a knowin' what I feel inside me," he hissed at her. "When have ye ever been inside me mind? Privy to all me thoughts? Never! If you had ye'd know all I ever think about anymore is you. And when've ye ever looked back at the world through me eyes? Never, that's when. If ye had, ye'd know there's nothin' in this whole universe I want to see but you. When have ye ever been in me heart?" he asked, tapping his chest, as he did. "Knowin' all the feelin's I have inside me? Never. If ye had, ye'd know I can't feel nothin' no more, cept me love for you. Taint nobody what can be a knowin' the feelin' another person's got inside 'em, but God Himself. Or do you think yer're God?"

Rory spun around on his heels. He grabbed the railing with both hands, his shoulders slumping as he gazed out into the darkness, trying to find composure somewhere out there in the night before he lost the last vestiges of his monhood and burst out bawling like a baby. For her part, Mary watched the rising of his shoulders as his breathing struggled to keep up with the pace of his pounding heart. In time, Molly was to see Mary's outline in the dark, stepping forward and taking Rory by the hand.

"I know you love me, Rory. It's just that..." She was not to finish her sentence, though.

Rory wheeled around and slipped his arm around her waist, pulling her to him. Tight against himself did he hold her, even as she fought to break free. She arched herself backwards, away from his lips that searched for hers, but he found her neck, instead, and planted urgent kisses up and down the length of it. So tightly did he hold her that he could feel her heart beating against his, her breasts crushed against his chest. So tightly did he hold her that she could feel the hardness of that part of him that made him a mon, all pressed up against her. Only once before, in his lordship's manor house, had she felt a mon so firm against her. That she had found revolting; this she found intoxicating, even though she continued to struggle against him.

"Rory, you let me go right now," Mary demanded. "Do you hear me?"

He stopped kissing her neck, but held his cheek tight up against hers, his whiskers scratching her tender skin. He struggled to speak, his breathing even more heavy and labored, like he had just run a mile. "Not...until ye...listen to what...I have to say...to ye...Mary. Do ye...hear me?" He was equally adamant in his tenor.

Molly poked her head around the corner of her doorpost, just as Mary ceased her struggling against Rory's embrace, and allowed herself to be cradled in his arms. "What is it, then?" she asked of him.

Rory eased his hold on Mary. With his hand, he stroked her hair as he spoke. "First of all, please let's not fight no more. I can't take the fightin', Mary. It takes too much outta me." He looked as deeply into her eyes as he could in the coal black night, but she said not a word to him. "Second, I am not drunk. What I have to say to you, right here and now, comes straight from me heart. Do you understand that?" Mary nodded her head. "Fine. Then from the bottom o' me heart, Mary Dunnigan, I profess me love for you. I loved ye from that first time I set eyes on you. I knew then and there that there could be no other for me. I love you, Mary and I want to be yer husband, if ye'll be a havin' me?"

Molly Connelley could not believe her ears. She wanted to shout out loud for Mary not to listen to the silver-tongued devil, but she knew she had to hold her peace. On she scrutinized the dimly lit pair. Mary did not at first respond to Rory's profession of undying love. From Molly's perspective, it appeared that she took her time studying the mon's face before finally easing herself into his waiting arms. "I love you too, Rory. I would have never thought I could love anyone as much as I love you."

Rory reached in hand inside his britches pocket and took out plain silver band. "This here's about all I have of value in this world. This and me daddy's pocket watch. This here's me own dear mother's wedding band." He fumbled in the dark to slip the ring on Mary's finger. "If ye'll consent to be me wife, then wear this ring as a sign of our betrothal to each other."

Still Molly spied, even as the pair merged into one in the darkness, in a fervent, arduous kiss. Then, they melded in the darkness into Mary's room. Behind them, Molly was to hear the door gently close.

Then silence, nothing more; just the barking of a dog off in the distance.

Saturday, 1 July 1837

I sometimes ask my God if all that has happened would have happened, had Mon. Isaacson not eaten such a big helping of Marie's spicy rice that one particular evening. I declare, how the mon did love that dish, but always it would give him the worst of indigestion. So much saffron and filet and three kinds of pepper—symbolizing the three sides of Marie's soul—made sleep impossible for him. Yet craved it he did. He would beg poor old Marie, "Bel ami, why you don't make me up a little of your spicy rice for my supper tonight?"

"Mon, what you talk about?" She would spar with him. "You know you done got too old to be eatin' no spicy food like that."

Of course, she would give in to his begging, his groveling. In the end, old Marie would always give in and cook him up a little of the rice dish, as a surprise for his supper. The three kinds of pepper she would pitch into the pot: red, standing for the passion of her soul, which gave her passion for her cooking; white, standing for the purity of her soul, which helped her stay true to the ways her mamma had taught her to cook; and finally, the black, which stood for the color of her skin, the nature of her soul, which gave her the talent she had for cooking. That was what she prepared, the night Molly listened to Mary's door closing in the dark. In the dining salon that very evening, I watched master take a second helping and I just knew he would be up, walking the floor before the sun could rise on him. And that's just what happened, too. His stomach was bothering him so badly he could not lie prone on the bed, and so he had risen in the faint hours of the morn, to pace the upstairs hall in his distress. Now, I sometimes walk the very same hall, asking my God if all this would have taken place had our monsieur not had a second helping of that spicy rice.

Naturally, He does not answer me—my God, that is. I talk to Him, but he does not talk back to me. Not in words, at least, which is good, because if God did talk out loud to me, I should tink some ting was wrong with me. We all talk to God, of course, but still I tink it must be a little arrogant of us to expect him to talk back to us in our own native tongue. And so, I continue to pace the hall, now and then, inquiring of God if all this would have taken place, but for Marie's spicy rice.

You see, what poor Molly did not know—could not know—when she heard the door to Mary's room being closed behind those two lovers that night, was that six hours later the monsieur would be standing in the upstairs hall, gazing out the back door. There he would stand, belching and swearing never to touch that rice dish again, when what to his astonishment do you tink he should see, standing there in that darkened hall like he did? Outside on the balcony, there in the faintest hint of the light that would come with the new day, he did witness the door to Mary's room open up and Rory O'Kelley slip out onto the balcony. Monsieur watched as, like a thief in the night, the boy paused long enough to slip into his shirt, as he presented Mary with a most fervent kiss, before hurrying on down the outside stairs.

Silently, Mary closed the door behind her, and the monsieur did step up to the hall door to watch in wonder as, down below Rory retrieved his boots from under the stairs and dashed out the back gate, out into the street beyond. There he stopped long enough to struggle to pull them over his bare feet. Then, before heading off like old gooseberry himself was after him, the biggest of smiles crossed his face and he waved up wide to Mary, standing in the window at which he had tossed pieces of sea shell earlier that same night.

Surely my master must have been stunned at the spectacle he witnessed. As stunned, no doubt, as he would have been had he been struck by David's rock. What must have gone through his mind? What agony must he have been suffering during this time? It had become painfully obvious to most of the staff—not just to me—that the monsieur had lost his heart to some pretty little Irish girl of no consequence whatsoever. Now, to have this happen to him! Under his very own roof! As I had said to Molly, it's a pretty awful ting to lose your heart to someone else, only to have it trampled underfoot. Had only I known. Had only I known, perhaps I could have been of some comfort to him; as it happened, it would be several days before he was to say so much as a word to me about the matter. Then, three or so days after witnessing Rory O'Kelley leaving Mary Dunnigan's room at that most inappropriate hour, he did summon me to the dining salon during his breakfast time.

There I did find him seated at the small table before the fireplace, the same table over which we had so often shared the evening meal, before Mary Dunnigan drove such a wedge between us. He motioned for me to take a seat at the table with him, and dismissed Sonnier with the admonition we were not to be disturbed. "My Dear," he began as he poured a cup of coffee for me. (Not since our argument over Mary Dunnigan's going to the opera had he referred to me as his "dear.") "I am afraid I was witness to a most unfortunate event that happened at this house a few nights ago. While pacing the floor with my indigestion, at about four and a half past the morning hour, I saw a young man leaving Miss Dunnigan's room."

What Mon. Isaacson said! His very words did astound me. They left me dumbfounded for a bit until I found words to utter: "Unbelievable! That someone you have taken in and given your good aid and assistance should repay you by disgracing your home like this!" I did so want to add that I had forewarned the monsieur that no good would come from having those Irish women in his house, but such as that is tantamount to poking fun. It is best, I understood, to do one's gloating in private. "By your leave, monsieur, I shall turn her out immediately."

"No," he responded, quietly. So quietly, in fact, that I became acutely aware that Mon. Isaacson was taking this whole situation quite calmly. I knew that somewhere in the back of his mind he had him an idea, a plan. A mon like the monsieur does not reach such an elevated plane without learning how to remedy the little unpleasant parts of life. "You will let me handle this in my own way," he insisted. "What I require from you is this: find out for me what you can about this young man. Get me his name. Where he lives.

Where he labors. That sort of stuff. But be discreet! I'll handle the rest."

A chill did suddenly run up my spine. "Master, you wouldn't be tinking of challenging this mon to a duel, would you?"
Up he looked at me with surprise. "A duel? Certainly not! Dueling has been outlawed in the United States. I thought you would have known that." And I did know that dueling was illegal in this country. I also knew that duels seemed to be fought every week in New Orleans. The more duels that were fought, the more the authorities seemed to turn their backs on it. But if the monsieur said he had no intention of dueling with the boy, then I knew he had another plan up his sleeve. My master is a mon of his word, and I knew he would not knowingly lie to me. So I took my cue and rose from his table.

"As you wish, monsieur. Will there be any ting else?" It was with a shake of his head that he dismissed me, as he returned his attention to his newspaper. I knew, of course, the ideal source for acquiring the information on Miss Dunnigan's suitor. Later that afternoon, when I did come upon Sonnier in his cabinet, polishing silver, I made myself busy examining the crystal vases on display on the shelves.

"What you lookin' fo' in here, missy?" he asked me.

"Oh, I thought I might cut some flowers from the garden for the library," I lied. "I'm just looking for vase, that's all." Sonnier returned to his polishing, a tedious task made even more tedious by the degree of detail he applied to it. He even went so far as to use a broom straw to clean the indentations in the filigree. As he labored over a soup spoon, I perused the vases and used the occasion to casually inquire, "Sonnier, tell me some ting. Who might be this young mon Miss Dunnigan's been seen about with lately?" He immediately looked up to me with a grin extending from ear to ear: there was nothing Sonnier enjoyed quite so much as the sharing of a snippet of gossip.

"O' Lawd, mam'oselle," he crowed, "that be her beau. Dem two's done gone and gots demselves head over heels in love wid each other."

So it would appear, I thought to myself, but I responded most casually, instead: "Is that so? And what might be the name of Miss Dunnigan's new beau?"

"Rory. Rory O'Kelley," he told me. "He come from over to Ireland, jist like Miss Mary do."

"I see. And is he employed?"

"Is he!" Sonnier emphasized. "He works cuttin' stones on that new cathedral. You know, the Irish one down by the Lafayette Square. St. Patrick's! That's it. St. Patrick's. He's apprenticed down there to make a stone cutter," he explained as he broke into a high-pitched chuckle. "Lawd have mercy how dat boy do like he's job. Dis nearly drives Miss Mary crazy, always carryin' on about what he does. Yass'em, dey gots into a quite a li'l squabble here the other day. Next day she was still all in a huff, tellin' me dat's all dat boy ever do, is talk about dat church. How dey did such-n-such yestiddy. An' dey's goin' to do such-n-such tomorry.

Yeah, tole me she was plumb tired of hearin' 'bout his job. Said he talks mo' about that job o' his dan he do 'bout her."

"Is that right? And what did you have to say about that?"

Suddenly, Sonnier found his soup spoon fascinating again. "Aw, you knows me, mam'oselle. I don't go puttin' my two cent-worth in where it don't belong," he claimed, although I knew better.

"You gave her no advice at all?" I goaded him on. "You didn't say any ting to make her feel the better?"

"Weeel, I mightta tole her she needs to get dat boy in line. Ain't right, you ax me, fo' no man like him to go ignorin' a fine young woman like Miss Mary o'er no job. Church work or no. Man's place is to put the woman above 'em, pure an' simple. But as it turns out, dat wasn't what wuz a botherin' Miss Mary in the first place. Seems after dey got into dat big squabble, an' she tells him she's tired o' hearin' 'bout work, work, work! He gets real quiet like. Swole up like a stomped-on toad frog. Finally, when Miss Mary axs him to quit his poutin', he tells her dat church is goin' to be a monument to his life. Kin you believe that. A monument to his life! He say it's part o' his destiny—dat means what God put 'em here on earth to do. Plumb tore up Miss Mary, what he said. Cut her like a a fresh sharped knife."

I lost interest in the vases, suddenly, and watched Sonnier, so fastidiously polishing the monsieur's silver. "I suppose that's a noble enough sentiment, though, don't you tink?" I finally posed. "Every mon should take pride in his life's work.

Look at yourself, Sonnier. How earnest you undertake cleaning the master's silver. If that doesn't evidence pride in your work, I don't what does."

"Still, you don't have to sit round listenin' to me carryin' on about polishin' the silver all the day long. Like right now. I kin polish this here silver, an' give you some of my attention at the same time. Don't you see?

"Oui," I said. And I did. I understood what Sonnier was saying.

"But now you takes the menfolks. Seems like when it comes to dey work, dey just can't let it go. Dey just aways carryin' on over it like it was the most important thing in the world. You ax me, dat jist ain't fair to the womenfolk."

"I suppose. Sometimes. Still, if I were to marry, I'd want my husband to be proud of his life's work. I'd rather he has a calling than just a job. No matter what it was. No, I tink I could put up with a little of his chattering about his occupation."

"Yeah, I reckon you right on dat. You ax me, Miss Mary and her beau still be jist a couple 'o kids. Dey gots dem a passel o' learnin' 'bout each other to do yet. Give an' take. Dey gots to learn to give an' take." And Sonnier turned to polishing a new spoon, giving it his utmost attention for a bit, until his train of thought roared back out of the tunnels of his mind. "Speakin' o' love, Miss "Manda," he said to me, "Why in the world ain't you never gots yo'self settled down yet? You a fine, free, educated woman an' all. I been seein' that rich

Etienne DuBoisblanc commin' round here vistin'. An' don't go tellin' me he's commin' round here to talk no business with Mast Isaacson, neither. Cuz I knows better."

Sonnier had a way of taking people by surprise; it was a trait he practiced with some facility—with most people, but not necessarily with me. "And when would I have time to devote to running a second household?" I asked of him. "Most every waking hour I have is devoted to our monsieur and this house. When would I have the time to make a mon a proper consort?"

Sonnier threw his head back and howled. "Yass'em. You got me dere, mam'oselle," he laughed. "You got me dere." I let his laughter die down and randomly snatched a vase from the shelf.

"Tell me," I asked, as I paused at the door, "Do you know where this O'Kelley boy lives?"

And thus it is with great trepidation, with stomach bound in knots, that I reduce to writing the preceding events. My every instinct tells me that what follows would be better off lost somewhere in the annals of the ages. I have consulted with Mme. Laveau about the absolutely necessity of setting forth on this page what I have learned of recent, yet she has assured me such is critical to the eviction of the ill-fortune that now visits this house. Accordingly, it is with much foreboding that I here continue with my writing, for you see that same evening after my visit with Sonnier in the butler's cabinet, I did pause to knock at the door to the monsieur's library. His dinner finished, he had, as usual, retreated to his private domain to read, or perhaps work on some incomplete business affair. He did bid me enter, which I did, finding him at his desk piled high with papers. Approaching him, I handed him a sealed envelope.

"What is this?" he asked, appearing somewhat puzzled.

"The young mon's name is O'Kelley. He labors at the site of the new St. Patrick's Church," I explained. "I tink you will find all the information you need in there."

He offhandedly tossed the envelope aside and returned to the papers he was studying. "Thank you, Amanda. I'm sure this is all I shall need. Please remember you are to discuss this with no one, now."

"As you wish, monsieur," I said and took my leave from the room.

Now before I continue further, allow me to state this: Mon. Hiram Isaacson is a good and kind mon. He is not a perfect mon, for perfection is not to be found in the human kind. But he is a mon with a heart of wisdom, not prone to making mistakes. So much good has he done for his community; witness his taking in of poor Mary and Molly, upon old Mother Superior's request. Witness the two school buildings paid for by his generosity. Indeed, he is a mon whose generosity and compassion are not relegated solely to his own race, or religion, or heritage. To the contrary, Mon. Isaacson has always been a mon most eager to lend his support to any cause beneficial to his community-at-large. Such was certainly the case with his most generous of benevolences to the St. Patrick's building fund. To be sure, the monsieur is not Catholic; nor does he find the Catholic faith to be generally compelling. What he does recognize is that, in this day and time, there is a wide gulf that divides this city between French and American, and it is, therefore, high time New Orleans had a second Catholic parish, remote from the French dominated St. Louis Cathedral. It would be in the better interest of New Orleans, he reasoned; and for that reason, and that reason alone, has he given generously of his money to effect the building of the new church. Such is simply the nature of Hiam Isaacson.

"That sounds to me like your family, Mr. Isaacson," Aunt Alice declared, peering over the tops of her bifocals.

"Really? In what way?" T.K. wanted to know.

"You read the article in the *Picayune* about you donating that painting to the art museum?"

"No. I'm afraid I haven't. Why?"

"Well... Because. Old man Hiam was a generous old coot, but he didn't want his name plastered all over town. Don't get me wrong, I think that's admirable. And the paper said your family was pretty much like that. Maybe more so."

"Did they now?"

"Is it true y'all use lawyers to keep your name off Forbes richest list?"

"The newspaper said that?"

"Said something to the extent the Isaacson family was paranoid about keeping their wealth private. Said the foundation y'all underwrite doesn't even carry the Isaacson name. That none of the properties y'all own have the family name anywhere on them. Is that right?"

Now my auntie is one of those people you can't help loving, but that doesn't mean her bluntness isn't a nuisance. I tried telling her it was none of our business, but T.K. didn't seem to mind.

"To paraphrase Amanda Maneau, Mrs. Monroe: nothing good can ever come of flaunting your good fortune in others' faces. So, no, we don't put the Isaacson name on public display. And as far as Forbes is concerned, just let me say this about that: Hiam Isaacson left our family a substantial legacy and I like to think we've been good stewards down through the generations. That's why we've always run our interests as a corporation—to keep the occasional rogue cousin from squandering everything and making a spectacle of our good name. But what you must understand is that there are sixteen of us owning an interest in the family estate. *Sixteen* of us, not one of whom would come even close to belonging to the billionaires' club. That's why you don't see the Isaacson name on any Forbes list. Even if we wanted it there, which we don't."

T.K.'s explanation seemed to satisfy Aunt Alice, who returned to her needlework as T.K. returned to our reading.

Unfortunately, even one as selfless as our monsieur can lose his way when tinking with his heart in place of his head; when led by his emotions, rather than his conscience. This, I fear, is the case with what occurred after I did deliver to him my sealed envelope, that evening in the library. I might have dismissed the rumors I heard from Patrick O'Bannion and Molly Connelley as childish surmises, nothing more. I might have dismissed the whisperings of old Mr. Wells at the bank and young Mr. Webster, who directs the Canal Merchants Association, as pure pettiness. But I cannot so easily dismiss the confidence of my beloved Etienne. Allow me to digress before I go on, that my words may not become unintelligible ramblings.

Etienne DuBoisblanc is my love, my dearest friend in all this world. And he is my confidant. It was to him that I turned, as my suspicions against the monsieur grew and grew. You see, my Eitenne is a mon of learning, himself. He is a French national, of aristocratic lineage, who has been sent to Louisiana by his older brother, the marquis, to manage the family's extensive plantation, just down river of the city. I was first introduced to Etienne when he called upon the monsieur at the house, in the fall two years ago. Thereafter would he send little notes inquiring as to whether he could call upon me when next he would be in town. Eventually, I would come to realize that during his little visits he had managed to steal my heart, bit-by-bit, without my even knowing it. Perhaps, then, it was only natural I did turn to him during my hour of concern over the monsieur's behavior. On my behalf, Etienne did institute an investigation, which only served to confirm what had already been intimated to me.

What I am about to write, therefore, is in no sense hearsay; it is nothing less than the truth. For, you see, what was confirmed by Etienne was that monsieur did take my information to the head of the St. Patrick's building committee, whereupon he did demand—upon threat of his refusal to make future money advances—that the young apprentice Rory O'Kelley be turned out of his job. Young O'Kelley was to be taken from the church work-site and delivered out to the canal laborers' camp, where the gang-boss would see to it that he was given new work. That very day, the lock on Rory's boarding house room was broken and his few meager possessions gathered up and thrown into the back of a wagon. At the church work-site, two constables did pull him from his labor, whereupon they beat him unconscious with their sticks. They threw him in the back of the rig and drove away toward the north, to dump him in the squalor that was the workers' camp, a collection of worn-out army tents, throw up in the swampy mud beside the canal that was being dug.

This then, was what my Etienne did find out for me: that upon witnessing young O'Kelley leaving Mary's room that evening, my master schemed against him. His was an act of anger, not of reason; an act of blind revenge, not of perceived compassion. But mostly, it was an act for which all of us who dwell within these walls still suffer, even unto this very day. And I do so fear it is the heart and core of our undoing.

Monday, 3 July 1837

Ofttimes, over the course of the past two days, have I sought to take up my pen and continue my writing, only to find I had not the strength to face what must be written. Were it not I who had to face this awful truth, who had to tell this tale of betrayal! Alas, I know—I understand—there is no one but I who can do it. Mme. Laveau must have seen that when she charged me with the task. And so much and the welfare of so many depends upon it, that I now force myself to go on. What I cannot help but feel inside, however, is that I am like one balanced atop a high, high mountain. And if this exercise should bring about my downfall, I do so hope and pray there will remain behind a little part of the me that was before.

But I wander too much in my writing; I must trudge onward. By the evening next, the house had been gripped by a sense of turmoil brewing just under the surface, much like occurs when the storm clouds gather in the south in August, signaling what could be the approach of one of the dreaded hurricane storms. Within the great house, all was placid; too placid, to be sure. Monsieur, I did notice, was in a particularly light mood, to the extent he complimented me on my appearance and invited me to take dinner with him when I encountered him on the grand stairs that afternoon. Otherwise, the house was as still and quiet as a tomb long-since sealed. Through the dinner meal I sat confused, listening to master's gibberish about how bright the future did look, and didn't I suppose we should plan a splendid ball, once the weather went cooler.

It was after the dinner that I confronted Sonnier in his cabinet. "Is there some ting I do not know about, mon ami?" I beseeched him. "It's like all the life's been sucked out of this place all of a sudden-like." The expression on his face told me there was, indeed, trouble at hand.

"Aw, mam'oselle, I swear. You ought to go on out to the kitchen an' see if you can't be of some hep to poor Miss Mary. She be in a powerful bad state right now." Was that it, I wondered? Was the entire staff gathered around Mary in the kitchen house? Was that why the place seemed so deathly still and quiet?

"Whatever is the matter with Miss Dunnigan?"

"Lawd have mercy! One dem Irishmens dat works down by the new church done come runnin' up to here this evenin', tellin' her two constables showed up down by the church an' beat up on her beau! Dey done drug him off somewheres an' ain't nobody knows where he be at. Ruther he be dead or alive."

"Constables, you say? Well he must have been in trouble with the law. He must be in jail. They're always getting drunk and getting into some sort of trouble—those Irish are. You know that for yourself, Sonnier."

"Oh no ma'am. Dat's de first place dey done looked. Dem polices don't have no record of 'em. Go on out to the kitchen, mam'osell. See you can't be some comfort to Miss Mary. I'z 'faid somethin' bad's done happen' to dat boy."

I could see Sonnier's concern was most genuine; sometimes it could be touching how sensitive he could be for a mon. It was as much for him, as for that bothersome Irish housemaid that I went directly to the kitchen, where I found the staff gathered around the grieving Mary. Seeing the anguish on her face (her eyes all swollen and red as she sat with her head cradled in her hands, her elbows propped up on the table) I understood the source of Sonnier's concern. I did not particularly care for this daughter of Irish soil, who had elbowed her way into my home against my wishes, and who, in turn, had proceeded to turn my master's head, but she was a human being and she was in agony. That much I could see. I could not help myself, I felt for her. I went to her and put my hand upon her shoulder to comfort her. Around the room I did gaze at my staff, pleased they were of the stock that could rally around one another in times of crisis. And as I did gaze around the room, my eyes fell upon Patrick O'Bannion, sitting alone in the dark corner by the back window, a worried scowl furrowed upon his brow. I recognized him as one of the young men underneath the tree, that night Mon. Isaacson had sent me to order the girls into the house.

I motioned for Marie to move aside, that I might take my place next to Mary. "Miss Dunnigan, tell me: what is it that bothers you? Some ting has happened to your beau?" But Mary never looked up from the blank stare she cast in front of her. She spoke as if to an unseen specter, floating somewhere off in the distance.

"You tell her, Patrick. I can no bear it." As I looked up from Mary, my gaze caught Molly Connelley and she rolled her eyes at me. What a peculiar girl, I remember saying to myself. Everyone else was most given with Mary's distress, yet this one seemed dulled to the whole, unfortunate situation.

"'Twas at work, Missus," I heard the young mon in the corner say. I gladly looked away from the distant Molly, to young Patrick, as he went on. "Two men showed up. Big men they were, with badges on their chests. They called for Rory to come down off the scaffolding and when he did, one took off his belt and began to beat him hard with the buckle-end. Blood would spurt from poor Rory with every strike, I tell ye. But Rory, he was just like the rest o' us, he was too surprised to know what to do. He just stood there with the goon a hittin' on him. Finally, he made to try and defend himself, and that's when the other one took out his stick and hit him twice upside his head. And that was it. I don't know whether Rory was dead or no. He just went limp."

Mary erupted into sobs and Patrick momentarily halted his recounting of the day's events. I stroked her hair until she quieted down, then nodded for the boy to continue. "Anyway, them two goons just picked him up, like what he was a corpse, and pitched him in the back o' a wagon. Told us all that we'd seen nothin', that's what they did. In a real threatenin' way, too. That was it. They just drove off and that was it."

Mary sat up straight and blew her nose loudly, then wiped her eyes. She took in a deep breath. "What I don't understand is why anyone would want to harm me Rory. He wouldn't hurt a flea, that one wouldn't." No one seemed to have an answer; the room stood still. My mind, though, was any ting but still and I did not relish the anxiety brewing within it.

"You say these men had badges, but the police know nothing about it?" Patrick nodded his head and said softly, "Nothing."

"And there is no one you can tink of who would want to harm your beau?" I asked of Mary. She merely shook her head. I looked to Patrick but he in turn shook his head as well. Once again the room grew quiet, as I pondered the disturbing thoughts that kept cropping up in my mind. Like weeds choking out the pretty flowers, these thoughts began to flourish and I soon found myself wondering if Mon. Isaacson could be so infatuated with pretty Mary Dunnigan that he could have a hand in all this—that he would resort to wicked play against her suitor.

Such was most certainly an idea abhorrent to every fiber of my being, but an idea, nonetheless, that must be proved or disproved, no matter what the outcome. Much to my own surprise, then, I found myself taking charge of the situation. "Well, I perceive we can't have all this hanging over our heads if we are going to get our work done around here," I found myself saying. "None of you say a word more about this to anyone. Do you hear? And you," I squeezed Mary's hand, "Try to go on about your work as best you can. You must trust me. I have the sources to get to the bottom of this, and I shall. It's going to take time, though. So you must be strong. Strong and patient. Can you do that for me?" She tried to put on a brave face as she nodded her head, but I did notice her bottom lip quiver. "Good," I told her as I rose from the table. "Clyde," I said to the coachman, "In fifteen minutes I shall have a letter for you to deliver down river. Come to me in the upstairs hall then." And with that I turned and left the kitchen. Hurrying on to the privacy of my chambers where I took pen in hand and wrote to my Etienne, beseeching him to come to me without delay. I feared some matter was bad wrong at the house, I related to him, but cautioned that he must call discreetly, telling Mon. Isaacson nothing of my summons.

When Clyde did find me in the upstairs hall, it was decided that at the first light of morning, we would send off the smaller of the footmen upon my personal riding steed. Down river to the DuBoisblanc Plantation we would bid him go, there to discreetly deliver my letter into the hands of Mon. Etienne. By nightfall the footman did cause a commotion at the plantation, arriving alone and unannounced as he did, shouting aloud "Urgent message for Mon. DuBoisblanc!"

Commotion or not, he did timely deliver my message and by the third day I was most relieved when Sonnier did present Etienne's card on the silver tray, the right-hand corner turned upwards as a sign he was calling on me, lest the monsieur should be about. I found him waiting upon me in the front parlor, and as I entered the room, he did rise and bow low to me—to me, a woman he fully knew to have dark blood coursing through her veins. I distinctly remember tinking how I do admire the chivalrous French. How I do prefer the French to the English; the English over the Americans.

Behind closed doors did we sit on the settee, there before the cold fireplace. Etienne held my hand as I related to him all that had transpired of late. Patiently did he listen to me, his eyes roaming across the terrain of my face, as I related to him the facts, as I understood them. Once I had finished, he rose and paced the room with hands clasped behind his back, as he thought to himself, then turned to me and expressed his concern. "Of course I shall assist you," he assured me. "Together we shall get to the bottom of all this. But I must warn you: if Mon. Isaacson has been involved in anything so plebeian as murder, such could well rain down ruin upon us all. We may not be able to tell your domestique the truth about her beau. Do you understand?"

He was right. I knew he was right. My concern, though, was that my master had possibly taken leave of his senses and involved himself in some doing so ignoble as the spilling of innocent blood. That Mary Dunnigan might never know what happened to that young mon caught leaving her room early that morning was of little consequence to me. Had the worst happened to him, the fault would be hers and hers alone, for being so foolish in her behavior. Lovers have arranged trysts since time Noachian, with no one the wiser for it. Theirs was behavior most indiscreet and by reason, therefore, no fault of mine. While I did feel for Mary's anguish, I also did fully recognize it was of her own making. "I shall, of course, have to meet with your servant girl. And the young man who was witness to the violence," Etienne advised me.

"Of course. I shall send someone for the boy right away." Which I did. I instructed Clyde to send one of the stable boys to the work-site, with notice for young O'Bannion to come to this house forthwith, once his workday had ended.

Later that day, the four of us gathered behind closed doors, out in the Negro kitchen, where Mary and Patrick did relate to Etienne all they knew of the affair. Intently did he listen to their stories before finally rising to dismiss them. "I must say," he started out, "I can't imagine police—if the two beasts were in fact police—would be so reckless as to carry out a murder in broad daylight, before dozens of witnesses. However, the fact remains Mon. O'Kelley has been abducted, and I intend to find out what has happened to him." Etienne bowed low before Mary Dunnigan, "Mademoiselle, you have my word as a Son of France and as a gentleman, I shall endeavor to inform you of the condition and whereabouts of your amour. Take courage."

That same evening, Etienne and I took the evening meal with the monsieur in the dining salon, where it was evident his spirits were still high. Etienne professed to be in the city on business, and monsieur did insist he stay the night as his guest. We were to meet again over breakfast in the morning, after which I saw him to the door. There he took my hands in his and offered them a gentle kiss. "Don't worry yourself, mon ange," he assured me. "I shall sort all this out for you."

I remember closing the door behind him as he departed and wondering how long it would take for him to muddle through this sordid affair. Well did I know he had little time to spend away from the plantation, for while the land turned a handsome profit each year, Etienne's brother l'marquis siphoned off all the profits and then some, to maintain his high modus vivendi back in France. By virtue of Mon. Isaacson's bank loans was the plantation maintained from year-to-year, the task of keeping the land ahead of his foreclosure becoming more and more difficult. Thus did I concern myself that my beloved Etienne would devote too much of his time to my cause. Such was not to be the case, however, for that very evening before sunset he did return to me.

Fortunately, the monsieur was at the synagogue sitting Shiva for the dead daughter of a business associate. We adjourned to the parlor, where Etienne did reveal to me all he had learned in so little time. Much to my relief, he advised me that Mary Dunnigan's beloved had not been murdered, as feared. Because the abduction had taken place on Church property, Etienne had sought the wisdom of the Bishop, who in turn referred him to Fr. O'Donnell. From Fr. O'Donnell, he had learned most of the story: yes, it was rumored that Mon. Isaacson had ordered that the boy be turned away from his job. Indeed, the ruffians who had abducted him were not constables at all, but to the contrary, were employed as guards and enforcers of monsieur's Canal Bank. Fr. O'Donnell, of course, was not privy to why young O'Kelley had incurred the wrath of one so powerful as Mon. Isaacson, but he was aware of his having been taken to the canal diggers' camp. A seminarian had the Father dispatched to make sure the boy was in good health, and he did assure Etienne that, upon his seminarian's impeccable character, he was satisfied Rory O'Kelley was well enough. A little worse for the beating perhaps, but he was, to be sure, alive and well when last seen, covered in mud and struggling to dig with his eyes swollen.

"You can't know how you have eased my heart," I told my beloved. "Monsieur has been so enamored with that Mary Dunnigan that I did fear he had gone and done some deed most rash. How it eases my mind to know the young O'Kelley is safe." But Etienne suddenly rose and went to the window, where he passed a spell gazing out across the way, as if some ting bothered him. "What is it, then?" I asked of him. "Surely there be some point you're not telling me?"

He turned to me, his hands clasped behind his back in classical French fashion. "For now, Mon. O'Kelley is well enough. For how long, I'm afraid I cannot say." He returned to the settee, where he took his seat beside me. "Amanda, this new canal Mon. Isaacson is so instrumental in having dug... I am afraid I have learned facts about it that, as a gentleman, I find most noxious. The conditions under which these Irish immigrants are made to labor are so atrocious that the pitiful souls are dying like flies. Literally, each day the Church is so overwhelmed with the number of deaths they cannot even provide all the dead with the Last Rites, much less that of Christian burial. Already have hundreds—perhaps thousands—died."

I was struck by the words. "Etienne!" I exclaimed. "Whoever has told this is no respecter of truth, I fear."

"But don't you know? Fr. O'Donnell related all this to me. A priest, no less! I am told these Irish are made to work in the swamps from first light of day until sunset. With only a brief respite for nourishment. Cholera, dysentery and malaria—they all run rampant throughout the camp, and already the Yellow Fever season is upon us. I am told that as the workers fall, they are cast aside and covered over with the putrid mud dug up from the channel. Or sometimes, other workers dig holes in the floor of the canal. There they bury the bodies, weighing them down to keep the evidence from washing back up."

I was not sure what to say, so appalled was I at what my Etienne had related. My mind immediately went to Mary Dunnigan. She had anguished so over her beau. Now I had the good news for her that he was alive and well. Was I to build her up, only to then dash her hopes, by telling her he was yet in grave danger? Oh what turbid waters my monsieur's scheming has left behind, I did so lament that evening. If I should tell the poor girl of her darling's danger, her anguish will only serve to further muddle the operations of this household. Yet, had I the right to withhold news of such import as this from her? On the other hand, would it not teach our master a good lesson, should the sorrow of the one who has his eye upset the smooth operations of his home? No. No, he is too far gone with that girl; he would only place the blame on my shoulders, I reasoned. I turned, then, to Etienne and begged of him, "Under no circumstances should we divulge any of this deathly business about the canal to Miss Dunnigan. We've problems enough in this house, without further compounding them. As you said yesterday, we might not be able to tell that young woman all we know. Let us not, then. Let us keep this disturbing part of the news from her. At least the part about all the death and misery. At least for the time being."

Gentleman that he was, Etienne naturally acquiesced to my request. It was to prove to be a request, however, I wish I had never uttered, for in the final analysis, all it had served to do was to delay the inevitable, and make the consequences even more horrible than I could have imagined.

Foolishly, blindly then, did Etienne and I proceed to the kitchen house where we found Mary Dunnigan gathered around the supper table with most of the other staff, staring at her untouched supper plate. Upon our entrance, she looked up to us with all the anticipation in her eyes of a puppy-dog not knowing if he's to be praised or punished. Immediately did I smile to ease her fears. "Good news," I said. "He is alive and well. Mon. DuBoisblanc will elaborate for you."

So much hope washed across the child's face, I could almost see the color of hope-in-tomorrow return to her cheeks. Etienne elaborated about her Rory having been dismissed from his vocation at the church building. Like a lightning strike, a puzzled look flashed across her face. "But why?" she begged. "Workin' on that kirk's me Rory's reason for livin'." Etienne looked to me for guidance, so I took over.

"We don't know, child," I lied for her sake. "Some sort of a falling out with someone of authority, I suppose. The point is he no longer has position at the church site."
"No?" she asked, seemingly even more puzzled. "And what will be a happenin' with him? He's got no money. How will he survive?" Again, Etienne looked to me for direction and I nodded him on.

"But he does have work," he told her. "Not to worry yourself on that account. That's where he is now. This very day he labors on the new canal." Instantly, the room grew restless, as everyone seemed to look around at the others, questioning whether their ears had deceived them or not. Instantly, too, did I grow most uncomfortable, as Mary did narrow her eyes at Etienne, then look to me.

"Mother of God, Miss Maneau, why? Whoever it is that's sent him there's played a cruel trick on a lad not familiar with this town nor its ways, I tell you!"

"I don't understand," I lied yet again, attempting to feign confusion. And then did the woman's beautiful eyes, as green as summer, quickly grow as cold and turbulent as the Gulf in the dead of winter. She stared deep into my own eyes, as the others in the room did fidget and stir. Most uncomfortably did I stand before her, before finally she spoke up, saying, "Would you take me to be a fool as well, now, me lady? Don't you suppose I've heard the rumors and the sermons goin' around about how awful the Irish diggin' that gruesome canal are a bein' treated? Don't you think I've ears to hear the talk 'bout how many of 'em it is that dies every day? And you stand there tellin' me Rory's been given the boot from his church job, and now he's diggin on that ditch! For Heaven's sake, woman!" she exploded, "If this be good news, God save me from hearin' any of the bad!" Up she leapt from the table, fleeing out the kitchen door, out across the courtyard and up the outside stairs. Down the gallery she hurried, disappearing into her room, even as all gathered around the table watched with troubled souls.

Was I the only one who knew nothing of the wicked repute in which that canal was held? This I wondered to myself, as I stood there in the middle of that silent room, observing Mary fleeing to her chambers. I looked about the room, only to find all faces, by then, turned upon me. I motioned to Marie to go to the girl and as she rose to leave, so did Etienne and I turn to take our leave. At the door, however, old Marie paused, looking to me and asking, "Ain't there nothin' you kin do, mam'oselle? Most likely is not, that boy'll be dead in no time, if'n he stays too long in them swamps. Fool knows that." But old Marie could read the answer on my face. That I could see. It was as if she bore upon her shoulders a cross of granite, the way she took in a deep breath, then dragged on out the door, making her way across the courtyard to poor Mary's room. And I? I could do nothing more than hang my own head, as Etienne escorted me back to Mon. Isaacson's grand home. Every privilege I may possess, I retain at his pleasure; and yet the looks on my staff's faces had proclaimed to me that, in their eyes, my more elevated position rendered me the defender of justice.

If only they understood what a weak warrior I would make in such a battle.

Tuesday, 4 July 1837

Although he insists on keeping to himself in his room, allowing the company of none but Mordecai, for the most part does it lighten my heart that Mon. Isaacson is up and about these days. Dr. Penney is still most concerned with his despondency, however, and cautions me he is far from well. Still, progress has been made, thanks be. And substantial progress it has been, giving hope to my heart that one day mon protecteur may yet be his old self again. My hope in this is such that it does encourage me in the continuation of this daybook. Can it be that Mme. Laveau's magic has begun to work, even before my writing is concluded?

This very morning had I stolen away early, to the quiet of the monsieur's library, where I had sat reading my last entry and collecting my thoughts on the next one, when there came a knocking at the back hall door. When I did investigate, I was to discover a young priest calling, one I had never properly met, but who introduced himself to me as Fr. O'Donnell. He had come calling to inquire about the infant old Marie tends to out in the Negro kitchen, where it sleeps most of the day strapped to her back as she goes about her chores. I had shown him into the music parlor with every intention of receiving him in the hospitality befitting Mon. Isaacson's home, only to soon learn the young priest was more interested in calling me to task for not having presented the nursling for rite of Holy Baptism.

I must confess, I did experience some pang of guilt at my dereliction of duty as a practicing Catholic in not protecting the demise of the child's soul by seeing to its prompt Baptism.

In the back of my mind, though, I suppose it just never occurred to me that there would be urgency in the blessing of a bastard and an orphan. Fr. O'Donnell had other opinions, though, and it was quickly decided the child would be presented at St. Louis Cathedral at eleven of the morning tomorrow, there to be blessed with the Sacrament of Holy Baptism. Having won that battle so handily, however, the young priest then did commence to press me on the issue of turning the little one over to the Catholic orphanage. I did my best to explain to him that Mon. Isaacson, as master of the house, would have to make such a decision, and that he was indisposed to the extent he could make no such judgment at this time. I suspect young Fr. O'Donnell did harbor fear that the monsieur, as a Jew, might entertain ideas of the babe being brought up Jewish, rather than Catholic. I did my best to allay any such concerns, but ultimately the priest was forced to retreat with only half his holy war won. There would remain that one last battle to be fought another time. Once he was gone, however, I returned to the library, where I sat at the monsieur's desk for some while, trying to regain my direction of thought. Only now do I feel sufficiently composed to continue with my writing, and I thus do so.

The morning after Mary had rushed in tears from the kitchen house and locked herself in her room, Etienne left with the first light of day. It was a long and strenuous journey he had ahead of him. I had allowed myself to get caught up in imagining the worst, in allowing my fears to run ungoverned. The sting of guilt invaded my serenity, that morning, at the very thought of my having brought him hence on business, ultimately so unimportant, and I did deride myself for so inconveniencing him. I petitioned St. Christopher that Etienne's return to the plantation would pass quickly and uneventfully, and so it did.

That morning we had taken our breakfast alone in the kitchen house, attended only by old Marie who, as was her custom, rose before the roosters to begin her preparations for the daily meals. And a fine breakfast it was that she had prepared for Etienne: eggs, some fried potatoes with onions, biscuits and gravy. Marie had even whispered in my ear for permission to go next door and fetch a nice ham steak for Mon. DuBoisblanc. "This one time," I told her. Mon. Isaacson would have him a temper fit if he knew pork had been brought into his kitchen.

Taking advantage of Marie's absence, Etienne confided in me some of his thoughts about previous day's affairs. "I've been thinking about this business preying on your staffs' attention. I think it's too dangerous for this Irishman to be digging ditches in the swamp. But I also think it's not good for him to be staying in New Orleans. He's found Mon. Isaacson's bad side, I fear. I think it would be better for all concerned, were this young man to dig in the canal just long enough to save himself up a little money. Wouldn't take much. Maybe just enough to take him up river to Donaldsonville. Maybe Baton Rouge. If he's young and strong, he should be able to find work there on the wharves. There'd be a future for him and his Mary Dunnigan there, I should think. And you would have all this mess out of your house, no?" My Etienne did have a way with finding a resolution to the most perplexing of problems. His was a most excellent solution, I did perceive, and I vowed to take up the matter with Miss Dunnigan at my earliest convenience.

"Indeed, I do so wish that woman had never set foot inside this house. But she has, and I tink you must be right." I told Etienne. "Let that boy earn them a little money first, then get that Mary Dunnigan on along with him and out of this house. And the monsieur's sight."

Marie then returned, beaming from ear to ear as she placed the fine, thick ham steak in front of Etienne. "What is this?" he exclaimed. "Ham served in Mon. Isaacson's kitchen?"

"Hush up!" Old Marie teased him. "I not do dis for nobody but you, Massah Etienne." My Etienne ate heartily that morning, and gladly accepted the satchel of food Marie had prepared for his trip. I walked him to the coach house where the groom had his fine roan stallion saddled and ready to ride. There he bid me farewell with a kiss, then mounted his horse and rode away from me. I watched him disappear down the street, once again invoking St. Christopher to watch over him along the way, then turned back to the house wherein my responsibility resided. And a heavy responsibility is was to prove to be. More so than I could ever have imagined that morning.

I had slept fitfully the night before and I was tired the rest of that day. Once our monsieur was out of the house and off to his office, I retreated to the front salon where I took up my needlework and instructed Sonnier to send for Mary Dunnigan. I sat on the same settee I had only the day before shared with the one I love, gradually growing aware of the disorder I felt inside my being. Always, it was like this when

Etienne would come to call; while he was with me, my delight would be as warm and bright and lofty as the sun itself, only to grow as black and cold as the dark side of the moon once he had gone. Often did I question whether the joy of having him at hand was worth the distress at seeing him go. In a few days, I knew, the torment I felt within would subside and I would ease back into one of the humdrum interludes of life, which are nothing more than intervals wasted while awaiting the dust and ash foretold. And so, I sat with the emptiness inside me growing with every step farther down River Road my Etienne's fine mount did take him. Oblivious to the world I was, even to Mary Dunnigan's appearance into the room.

"Beg pardon, ma'am," she said meekly, as if delicately clearing her throat. I reacted with a start and immediately she commenced her apologies. "Forgive, ma'am. I meant you no scare. For the life o' me I didn't." I caught my breath and motioned for the child to take a seat, trying my very best to offer her a smile, so as to ease her concern over startling me.

"Please take a seat, Miss Dunnigan. I didn't see you come in." I held up my needlework for her inspection. "It's to be a basket of grapes. For Mon. DuBoisblanc. His family has vineyards in France and I thought..." I did not finish my sentence. I could see Mary was most preoccupied with her own concerns, her interest in my handiwork being perfunctory at best. Rory O'Kelley weighed heavily on her mind, I could see from the dark circles under her eyes, from her pallid coloring, from her stooped shoulders. Here, before me, I thought to myself, sat one who slept no better than I had last night. "Did you rest at all last night?" I asked her. She simply shook her head in the negative, almost child-like.

I returned my eyes to my needlework as I continued, "Mon. DuBoisblanc did speak with me this morning about your predicament," I said. "And I do believe he has come up with a most interesting solution to the quandary. What he proposed was this: that your beau continue for just a little while with his ditch digging—just long enough to save up enough money for the two of you to get yourselves on up the river. To Baton Rouge perhaps." I lifted my eyes from my needlework to gauge her reaction, only to find her appearing more confused than ever..

"Baton Rouge?"

"Oui. It's a fine city, Baton Rouge. Many opportunities should present themselves to a young couple like you, in such a place. This Mon. DuBoisblanc has assured me of this."

"Leave New Orleans?" she asked with some incredulity registering in her tenor. "Is this Baton Rouge far away?"

"Not at all. Nothing more than a short ride up the river, I believe. The journey would be safe enough these days. No savages on the loose, you know."

"Savages?"

"Oui, savages. Indians. Louisiana's Indians are kept in check. Not wild like they be in the west. You can make the trip with no problem, I 'm certain. If I didn't tink so I wouldn't recommend this to you. Nor would Mon. DuBoisblanc."

But the confusion remained on Mary's face. Perhaps this was an inopportune time to broach the subject, I thought. Her's had been a fitful night, that she had told me herself. And I was certain she was still in a state over her beau's plight. "I don't understand, ma'am," I heard her say, barely audible. "Why can't we just stay here and work in New Orleans?"

I laid my needlework aside and turned to face the girl squarely. "Now Miss Dunnigan, that would not be advisable. Would it? For one ting, what other work is available for a mon like your beau? One with no reference to his name. Only a black mark. We've already told you he's been turned out of the building trade. Digging on that terrible canal is the best he can do right now. At least in this city—". I was not to finish before Mary interrupted me.

"But he wouldn't need to be earnin' all that much. I have me work here and—" It was my time to interrupt her.

"Hold it. I do hope you're not assuming you'll just settle in here once you get married . In your room out back. That's not what you're tinking, are you? Just move in here and raise your family?" She dropped her head and her shoulders sagged again. "I don't want to sound mean to you, Mary, but house service has always been a maiden's work. And you do plan to marry the boy, don't you? Because if you don't, I see no reason why you should be so concerned with his present-day welfare." Then came her tears, but I persisted, trying hard to make my point. "And I hope I don't need to remind you that beau of yours has already had a falling out with the wrong people in this town. It's for your own good that the two of you move on along. If you're planning to be married that is. Otherwise..." I shrugged my shoulders for emphasis.

"O' I don't know!" she cried out. "I don't know! Rory promised me we would be married, but everything's changed now." She looked up at me with her face all contorted in misery, tears streaming down her cheeks. "I need to see 'em. That's what I need. I need to see Rory. To talk to 'em. See what he thinks."

My patience I found to be rapidly wearing thin. "Well you can't be going out to the worker's camp, now, can you? Put that out of your mind if that's what you be wanting. That camp would be no fit place for a young lady. House maid or not. You do realize that, don't you?" I asked with some exasperation in my voice. But Mary Dunnigan was to have no answer for me. Up she flew from her chair, knocking it over backwards, and out the door she fled in tears, back to the sanctuary of her room.

What was a body to do? I tossed my needlework aside and allowed myself to lean back in the settee. My stomach was in such a lump that I did place my hand upon it for comfort. This Mary Dunnigan was a kind girl. That much I would allow. And she was in fact a good hard worker, not given to complaint. That much I would give her, too. But the baggage she had brought with her into this house was simply not worth the bother. For my own peace of mind, for Mon. Isaacson's better interests—indeed, for all concerned—I wanted her out of this good home. There that very morning, as I sat with my stomach in a knot, I did resolve that by my will Mary Dunnigan would depart from this house with all dispatch.

Wednesday, 5 July 1837

This morning did we arrive in front of the Cathedral in Mon. Isaacson's luxurious landau, even as the bells struck eleven. Old Marie, the baby and I rode in the back of the carriage. Molly Connelly rode between Clyde and Patrick O'Bannion, freshly scrubbed and fitted out in clean trousers and shirt. Within we were to find Fr. O'Donnell, arrayed in his vestments and waiting patiently by the baptismal font. Upon our approach did he reach out and take the little one from old Marie. For some time his eyes darted back and forth over the infant, much like he was contemplating a fine painting for the first time, unawares of the smile of affection occupying his face. It would be with a kiss to the baby's forehead that he would commence the ceremony.

"Who might the Godparents of this child be?" the good Father asked, most formally. Molly did respond that Patrick and she would accept the charge.

"And what is the name given this child?"

Patrick responded, "Thomas O'Kelley. After his papa and grandpapa."

Father opened with prayer, and then a shiver did run up my spine as he continued softly, holding the little baby aloft. "Thomas O'Kelley, I knew yer parents. Not well, but I loved 'em nonetheless. Their lives were short and full o' sorrow. But I suspect their brief time together and all the love they had for one another, more than made up for all the suffering they endured. And one has only to look upon you, me little one, to know their lives were surely worth the livin', in spite o' everything." Patrick and Molly, I did notice, quickly averted their eyes, and even old Marie had to reach inside her veil to dab her kerchief at her eye, as the young Priest went on, his voice rising with authority, whilst fairly echoing down the aisles of the venerable sanctuary. "Therefore, wee Thomas O'Kelley, I Baptize ye in The Name o' The Father; and o' The Son; and o' the Holy Ghost."

In one fluid motion, T.K. Isaacson dropped the journal on the coffee table and slumped back in his chair, looking much like he had just been blindsided. He stared straight ahead for a moment or two, touching his fingers to his brow; his eyes opened wide in disbelief. Eventually, he turned his gaze to me.

"My God," he whispered, "I hope this isn't going where I think it's going."

I knew what he was thinking, even before he said anything. In one short paragraph, Amanda Maneau had finally begun to piece together the puzzle; I saw what T.K. saw, but still I questioned him: "So where do you suppose it's going?"

He shook his head as if to clear away the cobwebs. "Don't you see. 'Thomas O'Kelley,'" he said, emphasizing the 'O' in O'Kelley. "Whose mother just happened to be Mary Katherine—with a K—Dunnigan." He paused with words hung on his lips, seemingly afraid to give voice to them.

"You think Mary Dunnigan may be your real great-great-great grandmother. Thomas O'Kelley your great-great-great grandfather. Right?"

But he offered no response to my observation. He continued to sit preoccupied. For the longest he sat, lost somewhere inside himself, and once he finally looked up it was toward the ceiling he gazed until eventually he handed the journal to me to continue the reading.

And as Fr. O'Donnell invoked the blessing of the Holy Trinity upon the child, thrice did he dip his fingers in the blest waters and touch them to the baby's head, then looked to the rest of us saying, "Now, let us pray." And pray we did. We prayed for little Thomas, that his days might be full and productive in God's will. We prayed for the souls of his departed mother and father, and when that was done, we prayed for guidance for those in charge of deciding the child's future. Then, and only then, did Fr. O'Donnell dismiss us to return home to the toothsome lunch Old Marie had prepared of stewed hen, collard greens, field peas and squash fresh out of the garden.

Early on, we had been fortunate enough to find a reliable wet-nurse whose milk the infant did tolerate, and she was waiting for us in the kitchen house upon our return. Little Thomas had begun to fuss and the nurse immediately took him outside, in the shade of the banana trees next to the kitchen window, to change his diaper and let him nurse. Through the opened window above the bench where they sat, we could hear the soft sounds of the wet-nurse's humming to the infant, "Bye-yo-baby-bye. Bye-yo-baby-bye." Molly, Patrick and I took places at the table, as Marie went about heating and serving up our lunch. All during the ride to and from Church, all through the service, the two youngsters had spoken not a word to one another. Now I noticed they exchanged quick, uneasy glances, until finally Molly was to speak up.

"Twas a fittin' Baptism, don't you think, Patrick?" Patrick looked up at Molly and nodded deeply.

"Twas for a fact." Then he looked to me. "I thank you, ma'am, for lettin' me be a part o' it. For Rory's sake."

Molly quickly added, "And me for Mary's sake."

"It was just proper you were both there," I told them. "We've had nothing but tragedy around this house for too long now. I do pray this morning lifted your spirits—seeing that little one baptized—like it did mine." And everyone's spirits did seem to rise, for the short while at least. The chatter around the table had more liveliness to it than I had remembered in a long, long while. That is, until the conversation inevitably turned to reminiscing about the missing parents. I could tell he could not help it, but it was only a matter of time until young Patrick's thoughts were to return to his friend, Rory. Looking back on it now, I confess it was cruel that my spirits, so lifted at the child's baptism, should plummet so far, so fast. Yet as he and Molly did recount what had been related to them, I soon found myself even more horrified, as I learned what had happened to Rory O'Kelley that first day he spent in that God-forsaken camp, digging on Mon. Isaacson's God-forsaken canal.

That first night there, Rory told Patrick he slept dreaming he was holding Mary in his arms. He could feel the contours of her back, her breasts against his chest, her legs wrapped around his, the smell of her hair so near his face. So real was his dream that he was unaware of the suffocating heat inside the canvas tent; and that made it all the more cruel when the cold water insulted his nerves, just as the room began to flip over. It was with a hard thud that he hit the packed-dirt floor, even as his cot landed atop of him. He awoke in a fog, confused—cognizant only of the pounding inside his head and the sound of laughter all around him. He struggled to focus his vision through his badly swollen eyes as he heard the booming sound of a mon's voice.

"Get yer arse up and outta that bed, mick! Whadda ye think this place is, some fine an' fancy hotel!"

Before he could gain presence of mind enough to understand where he was, he felt two massive hands grab him by his collar and belt and lift him up. To and fro, a time or two, did he feel himself swung, before being hurled like a rag doll through the flaps of the tent door. To much laughter did Rory land hard in the foul-smelling mud outside the tent. He struggled to sit upright and wipe the mud from his swollen eyes when yet another splash of water struck him full on the face. At least it washed enough of the mud from his eyes that he could look around somewhat. "Where am I?" he heard himself asking, as another round of laughter erupted.

"I'll tell ye whur you're at," he heard the booming voice resound again, as the bear claw of a hand grabbed him by his collar and lifted him to his feet. "Yer at the New Basin Canal, that's where yer at. And if yer plannin' to eat and get paid around here, I advise ye to get off yer sorry arse and get to work. Otherwise ye might figger on stealin' off through the swamps and seein' if ye couldn't hook up with some dirty Indians what would take you in. If ye make it through them swamps, that is. But I wouldn't go entertain' no ideas of goin' back into town if I were you." Again the laughter rang out. "Not if I planned to stay alive for any length o' time. Yer about as popular as a epidemic o' the smallpox in New Orleans, from what alls I gather."

Suddenly, a shovel flew through the air like an arrow and stuck in the mud right before Rory's feet. He jumped backwards to avoid being hit by the handle and almost fell down in the mud again. "That's a shovel, mick! Ye know how to use it?" he heard a new voice say.

Rory took the shovel by its handle and jerked it out of the mud, his daze quickly being replaced by anger. "'Course I know how to use a shovel. What would you have me to do with it?" he said, only to be serenaded with another chorus of laughter.

"I'll tell ye what to do with it," the booming voice rang out. Again, he took Rory by the collar, dragging him to the edge of the wide ditch. There before them, someone lay prostrate on the ground, a piece of canvas laid haphazardly over his head. "See him? Twas a good night we had last night. He was the only one to croak. Yer the rook around here right now. That means til someone newer than you comes along, ye get to bury all the dead, first thing of the morning. Now get to it!"

Rory struggled to make out the image of the burly figure storming away from him. He was about to ask where to bury the body when he heard a voice next to him, a young voice by its sound, perhaps not much older than he was. "I'll show how to do it, lad. Me name's James. What's yours?"

Rory moved his head around wildly, trying to find an angle in which to see through his swollen eyelids. "Rory. I'm Rory O'Kelley."

"Well, now, Rory O'Kelley. I don't know who it is you crossed there in town, but for the life o' me, I 'd be avoidin' him at all costs, if I was you."

"And for the life o' me, James, I don't know who it was neither. I wish I did. Ye could rest assured I'd be avoidin' 'em like he was a leper."

"Ah! Come on then. Let's us get poor old Gerald here buried. I'll help you with this one, seein' as how you've taken this responsibility from off me shoulders for me. Most times they just cover the dead ones o'er in the levees. Or bury 'em in the road. Trouble is, this ain't rocky Irish soil we're a standin' on these days. Ain't nothin' but soft dirt 'round these parts. You go diggin' much deeper 'n a few feet and you hit water. Twill float a dead body up to the surface in no time atall. Gives grown men a good scarin'. That's why the boss sent into town for them there ballast slabs over there." James motion to a stack of slate tablets stacked nearby.

"Ballast slabs? What's that?"

Ships a comin' o'er here empty would use them rock slabs to keep 'em from tippin' o'er in a storm. When they'd go back twas the cargo that acted as the ballast, so they'd be a leavin' all this good stone behind. Mostly folks in town use it to pave their walkways—banquettes they call 'em. Boss, though, decided we'd commence a buryin' down in the canal bed and rely on the ballast to keep the dead from getting' up outta their graves.

James reached down and jerked the canvas off the dead man's face and for once Rory was able to focus his eyesight. There before him lay a man no older than himself. Emaciated was he, his eyes open wide and fixed in a blank stare. His lower jaw hung down low and inside his mouth Rory could see his swollen tongue played host to the flies. "Puuu weee! Let's get 'em covered o'er quick-like. Died o' the dysentery, this one did. Shit 'em self plumb to death. Be careful where you put your hand on 'em or you'll be getting' it all o'er yourself for sure." James bent down and took the young man by his dead hands while motioning for Rory to take his feet. "Old Lawrence got his shoes," he said as Rory lifted the corpse by the ankles. "Good thing too they fit; old Lawrence'd just about worn plumb through his own shoes. Okay, now. On three... One, two..."

"What! You aim to just toss 'em o'er the side?" Rory asked in disbelief.

"I reckon he'll not be a feelin' nothin', O'Kelley. Now, on three. Ready? One. Two. Three!" And with that, poor dead Gerald's body was flung over the side of the ditch, landing with a dull thud headfirst on the muddy floor of the canal bed, five feet below. James and Rory eased themselves down a makeshift ladder and walked over to the corpse; the landing had broken its neck, making it more grotesque than before. Bewilderment quickly settled over Rory like the suffocating heat inside that tent. He grew sick to his stomach and tears welled up in his eyes.

"Go on and have yourself a good cry, there, Lad," James consoled him. "Just don't let none o' the others catch you at it. You'll be a getting' used to all this in no time. Meanwhile, if you're gonna cry, try doin' it while you shovel out poor Gerald here a grave." He handed Rory the shovel, which he took as he wiped his eyes with his other hand.

"I'll not be a cryin', thank you mighty kindly. How deep should I dig this grave?"

" Ah, deep enough to get 'em covered over. No need to go diggin' to China. It'll just fill up with water as fast as you shovel it out. We'll be a dumpin him in it and then be puttin' one o' them slabs o'er 'em to keep 'em from floatin' back up and scarin' folks."

Rory dug diligently at the grave, but indeed, the more mud he shoveled from the hole, the more water would slowly percolate up into the void. When he thought he had the hole deep enough, he drug the body over to it and rolled it over into the murky pit, then summoned James to help him with the heavy slab of slate. Together, they grunted and they groaned and they bogged down in the muddy canal floor as they struggled to get the stone to the poor soul's grave site.

There, James did show Rory how to stand the slab on end at the foot of the grave and push it over onto the body. The water had filled the hole enough to float the body and so when the stone fell over it, it was the pitiful corpse that took the brunt of the impact. It was, as Rory was to relate to Patrick, a sound that he could never get out of his mind. "Just shovel a bit o' mud o'er that slab there, O'Kelley. That way, nobody'll be the wiser 'bout poor Gerald bein' buried down there," James told him, as he turned to walk away.

"Wait!" Rory demanded. "Ain't we gonna say a Hail Mary or nothin' o'er the poor lad?" James, though, just shook his head and laughed in spite of himself.

"For cryin' out loud, O'Kelley! Ain't you figured it out by now, laddie? Even the Blessed Virgin Herself ain't got time for no prayers o'er another piss-poor Irishman." And with that James turned and walked away, chuckling and shaking his head in amusement at the new kid's innocence.

And now I tell you this, though it leaves my very soul in turmoil: no sooner had Molly and Patrick finished telling this tale of such repugnance than I happened to notice out the corner of my eye none other than Mon. Isaacson standing by the window, there in the shade of the banana trees. For the first time in weeks had he left his chambers to wander in the fresh air of the courtyard. There had he spied the wet nurse and infant and had taken little Thomas up into his own arms, only to be captivated, then tormented, by Molly and Patrick's horrid recollections, so audible through that open window. There he stood, staring though the window, uttering not a syllable, moving not a muscle. Like a ghost he stood and stood, before being distracted by the baby's fussing. He looked down to the infant, handed him off to the wet nurse, then silently, like the ghost he was, he trudged off across the courtyard, toward the main house. A more pitiful sight I had never seen than the one our monsieur made that afternoon, walking along with his head hung low, a broken man for all the world to see.

Thursday, 6 July 1837

As I sit here this morning, revisiting that day after little Thomas' Baptism, I can still see Mon. Isaacson making his way across the courtyard, wandering aimlessly back to the main house. I remember tinking he moved like a thoroughbred whose spirit had been broken, like so many of the old slaves I have seen who have just given up on life. Gone was the spring in his step; in its place were stooped shoulders and a head of hair turning silver overnight. I declare that in all my life I've never seen a more pitiful sight than that, and it caused my heart to grieve for him, in spite of all the hard feelings I'd been harboring against him of late. I, apparently, had been the only one to see the master there in the window, eavesdropping on Patrick and Molly's recollections of times now past. On had they continued with their recounting, unsuspecting, I imagine, that old Marie and I were even in the room with them, their recollections being more in the nature of a purging of their own sorrow. So it was in silence I sat minding their word, and in so doing more did I learn about Rory O'Kelley's first day in the canal diggers' camp.

No sooner had they gotten that pitiful mon's corpse covered over, than Rory was whisked away to what would become his usual chore. Slowly had the canal inched its way toward the narrow isthmus a few yards shy of the lake, down through the swamps, like a great crocodile gobbling up the poor workers as it meandered along, unfazed by its actions. Once the ditch reaches its destination, those few yards between the beginning of the canal and the lake will be dug away, and lake waters will then rush in, filling it up like some mon-made river—a river to the end of the world, for so many.

That first day on the job, however, Rory was to find the digging going slow. By then had the canal reached the Metairie Ridge, a ribbon-like crest that runs around behind the city. There, did the canal have to be dug deeper than its six-foot mean depth, to account for the rising up of the ground. And where the rest of the way had proven to be easy digging through the slimy mud, cutting a trench through the ridge was proving to be no easy task. That morning after the burial, Rory was shown to the forward edge of the canal. The big boss-mon had paced off a few steps and drove stakes into the ground to demarcate the distance the workers were expected to dig that day. As the morning started out, the work proved to be easy enough for the boy. At the front line of ditch, the more senior workers labored to dig into the packed ridge soil, whilst Rory and the more junior others did put down large basket-like vessels in front of them. In no time would those baskets be filled with the muck dug out. Accordingly, it was Rory's responsibility to see to it the two diggers he assisted always had empty vessels before them; once a basket was filled, he was to hoist it up onto his shoulders and carry it off into the swamp to dump as spoilage on lowlands the master did have designs on for the making of more and more money.

The farther the diggers dug, though, the muddier the soil became, until ultimately it was necessary that boards be put down for the spoilers—as Rory and his lot were called—to walk along so as not to bog down in the mud. Poor Rory did suffer immensely from the beating he had taken the day before, so his gait was not all that steady under the weight he bore. On more than one occasion did he incur the wrath of the big boss-mon when he staggered off the wood planks and bogged down in the mud. More than once had he lost a boot in the muck and been forced to stop and dig it free, causing a disruption in the rhythm of the digging. So wet and filthy did the boots Maggie had pilfered from his young lordship become, that in exasperation, Rory did stop long enough to pull them off and stow them aside, so he would not have to be stopping to dig them out of the mud when he bogged down. And once the ditch had been dug deep enough, it soon became necessary for the spoilers to climb up ladders to get to the top of the ground.

Unfortunately, too, the deeper the ditch was dug, the weaker and the more unsteady Rory did become. On one occasion, then, did the poor soul, there in his muddy, bare feet, slip off a ladder rung and drop an entire basket full of diggings, much to the moans and groans of the others.

By quitting time, he was worn out, to say the least, but rest was some ting not easily come by, there in the swamps. That evening proved to be a stifling one, yet Rory sat with young James around a roaring fire, where the smoke helped keep the mosquitoes from biting so much. Filthy he was, covered from tip to stern in the putrid smelling swamp mud. He had worked steadily that day, until the last rays of light made it impossible to dig any further. His every muscle ached, and several of the lacerations from the belt whipping had broken open and begun to ooze. But bad as his physical anguish was, it was nothing compared to the turmoil brewing in his soul. Again and again he would moan to his newfound friend, "James, I've gotta get outta here. I've gotta get back to me Mary. She'll not know what's happened to me. She'll be so upset."

And again and again Rory's new-found friend would counsel him, "If you know what's good for you, you'll be stayin' put. You say you ain't done nothin' to turn no one again' you, but I tell you, surely you must've. People just don't come at a man like they done with you. Not for no good reason they don't. You go and try to head back to town now and it might be a grave you're comin' back to instead o' a job. Them hooligan's is likely as not to go killin' you, lad."

Ha!" Rory laughed as he pitched a stick on the fire, sending a burst of amber sparks up in the dark, night air. "Yer're a sittin' there a tryin' to tell me that them hooligan's in town is any worse than this lot o' Celtic cut throats out here?"

"Desperate times do breed desperate men, that much I'll be grantin' you You watch your back around this bunch, but otherwise, they ain't so bad once you get to know 'em."

"But me Mary! What about me Mary?" Rory would moan, to which James would just shake his head in despair.

"Ah! I tell you for sure there ain't nothin' more pitiful than a dirt-poor mick in love. That there ain't. Look at yourself, there, lad! You ain't got a pot to piss in, nor a winder to pitch it out of. But you want to go runnin' back to town to see your woman. And lose the only job you got, in the doin'! Lot o' good the likes o' you'll be doin' this Mary o' yours. Whadda you think, then? There be fancy gentlemens just lined up there in New Orleans to give a mick like yourself a fine job? If you'll take me advice, you'll be a forgettin' that woman o' yours, you will. She'll be better off without you. And I know you'll be better off without her."

"And ain't ye the smart one, then. What is it ye would have me to do with meself, James, me friend. While me time away around here, digging in that muddy canal, 'til one o' you slaps a slab o' rock atop o' me, like poor old Gerald down there?"

Instantly did James grow most serious in tenor. "Now you ne'er heard me say nothin' 'bout makin' no career outta diggin' this canal, did you?" he shot back, slapping hard at the mosquito that had bitten deep into his neck. "Alls I'm a sayin' is you play it smart, like me. Work here just long enough to come by enough money to get yourself on over to Texas. That's whur there's a future. In Texas.

"Rory pondered over James' remark. "Texas? Where's this Texas? I ne'er even heard o' it."

"Texas, me laddie, tis a country independent of Louisiana and these American states. Just won their independence from Mexico, they did." And he stared off into space, like Moses looking out over the Promised Land for the first time. "Ah, but a big country it is at that. With plenty o' land for all. And free for the settlin', too." Rory thought about what James had said for a moment, then scoffed at him.

"Ye're a lyin' through your teeth, James, that's what yer're a doin'. Free land! Ain't no free land to be had on the face o' this earth."

"Is too! I tell you there is. O'er in Texas there is. Plenty o' free land. Alls a man has to do is get his self o'er there and claim it!"

Much of the rest of the night did Rory ponder his newfound friend's words about this strange new country, full of land free for the taking. Could it be? Could there be a place on earth where there was so much land they could just give it away? Or was this nothing more than the idle, wishful talk of some rag-poor Irishman, carrying on to make himself feel bigger. Rory was almost too scared to find out the truth, lest James' claims prove to be baseless. In his mind, he was sure he could survive all the belt whippings and knocks upside the head they could give him; what he wasn't sure of was could he survive having his hopes dashed many more times.

That night Rory and James slept in one of the canvas tents with four other men. Never could Rory remember being hotter or more miserable in his young life, for they all slept with door flaps to the tent tied shut against the swarming mosquitoes. Indeed, they all slept fully clothed, with scraps of old burlap over their faces to keep the bloodsuckers from draining them dry. It helped, of course. It helped some; but still were they bitten unmercifully. All of the heat and the mosquitoes aside, though, Rory would not have been able to sleep, anyway; that place called Texas held his mind hostage. No matter how tired he was, how much sleep beckoned him, he could not get Texas out of his mind. During the course of the night, he rolled over on his cot, nearer to his new ally. "James? James. Ye awake?" he whispered.

"And how might you be expectin' a body to sleep in heat and mosquitoes like this?" he whispered back.

"How far off is this Texas-place, anyhow?"

"Not more than ten days, maybe two week's ride, I reckon. Due west."

"They're really givin' away land there? For true?"

"On me mother's grave, I swear it. I was told by a friend o' a friend, on good authority."

"Well. How much are ye a thinkin' it'll be costin' to get from here to there?"

James rolled to his side to face Rory in the dark, his tenor suddenly growing very business-like. "I'm figgerin' around a hundred dollars American..."

"Hundred dollars!" Rory blurted out. "Jesus, Mary and Joseph, man. Ye might as well a told me it was going to cost a million."

The room stirred a little, and one of the older men offered a warning. "Pipe down you two o'er there, afore I come o'er there after you,!"

"Keep your voice down, lad. You want to wake the whole camp?" James cautioned. "Think about it. You'll be in need of cash to buy plantin' seed and a decent milk cow, once you get there. And on the way, you'll be a needin' some sort o' wagon. A buckboard and a mule's the only way to go, to me way o' thinkin".

"Ah, I hate mules. That I do," Rory said softly. "Only an Englishman could dream up somethin' as mean and ornery as a mule."

"Yeah, but they're strong and dependable. And you'll be needin' all the riggin' for the mule; some axle grease for the wagon wheels…"

"Bacon rind's work just as good as grease, an' cost a man nothin' to boot."

"Besides that, you'd need you a bedroll and piller…"

"Not me. I can sleep just fine usin' me arm for a piller."

"Then you'll be in need of a fry pan, good knife, water barrel—don't have to be too big a 'cause there's plenty 'o water 'tween here and there. A lantern—. Again, James was interrupted.

"I can see just fine by the light o' the fire." By then poor James' patience had begun to wane.

"Well you tightwad, hardheaded jackass, sounds to me like you can just strip down naked and walk all the way to Texas without no problem. Some o' the rest o' us like to travel prepared."

Rory grew defensive. "Ye needn't talk to me that way, James. I was only tryin' to think of ways to save some o' the cost. A hundred American dollars is a lot 'o money. It'll take a lot o' shovelin' mud to save up that kind o' money, and I was hopin' not to have to hang around here no longer than I had to."

"Then listen to me, lad. Serious as a stab-wound to the gut I am. If you be careful with your money around here—don't buy nothin' from the company store on credit, that's where they get you—you outta be able to save up twenty dollars a month, for sure. That's only five months! Them's not bad odds. Take yourself, you only got about two more really bad months ahead afore winter sets in. Come winter, you won't have to go worryin' about the deathly fever, or a poisonous infection from a mosquito bite, or even a snake a gettin' you. You can have the money saved up and be outta here long before spring. And ye definitely want to be long gone before the spring—that's when the yellow fever comes, you know. Besides which, you want to be in Texas early enough to clear a plot and get a decent enough crop in the ground to see you through the winter."

Rory rolled back over on his back and swatted at the mosquitoes swarming around his face. "Five months, James. That's a long time to spend in a place like this. If I thought hell was this bad, believe me, I'd be a mendin' me ways." He pulled the piece of cloth up over his face to keep the mosquitoes off and dared to dream about a place called Texas, as James, in turn, rolled over onto his back and sought that illusive mistress called sleep. Texas must be close to heaven if they are giving away land, Rory thought to himself. "Psst. James," he whispered in the dark.

"What now?" asked James, irritation registering in his voice.

"Ye reckon they have mosquitoes in Texas?"

Sunday, 8 July 1837

The heat this afternoon is most overwhelming. Just outside my chamber window, Mon. Isaacson sits alone in silence on the upstairs, front gallery, where any wayward breeze that may happen along might afford him relief, no matter how abbreviated. Always has he taken refuge from the heat on the front gallery, where he could be privy to all the goings and comings down in the street below. Always, that is, until that period when Mary Dunnigan did take up residence in this house. Soon thereafter, it was that I noticed he had taken to sitting on the rear gallery outside his bedroom windows. There he could sit and wait for his heart to leap within him each time Mary was to be seen coming and going about, I imagine. Now, with the courtyard and the outbuildings devoid of Miss Dunnigan's presence, the master has returned to his front gallery, where I keep watch over him through my chamber windows.

My room is all but unbearable, so heavy and still is the air. Sometime before four in the afternoon, if all goes according to the norm, thunderheads should build in the south, bringing with them a brief, but intense shower. Afterwards, the heat shall have been mitigated, although the stickiness will intensify. I would that I could avail myself of a seat out there on the gallery, next to the monsieur, but it is my writing that summons me and I find myself unable to resist. Thus, lest I should stir interest in my little project, I do my writing in the privacy of my chambers, where I jot down a quill's worth of words, then stop to fan myself briefly, before giving pen to ink and continuing on. Perhaps someday I shall share my writings with Mon. Isaacson. Perhaps. But as for now, I am sure no good could come from his seeing what I have put down within the covers of this daybook.

For the past three days have I thought of little but that afternoon after baby Thomas' baptism. I find the scene indelibly drawn on my mind, with old Marie sitting on her milking stool beside the big hearth, puffing on a cob pipe and nodding her head as she listened to Molly and Patrick's discourse. Much have I thought about what they talked about that day, and as I reflect over their words, I now realize that even I had taken note of the change that had occurred in Mary Dunnigan's temperament so shortly after her Rory's disappearance. Within a few days of her having fled the parlor in tears—that morning of Etienne's departure—she had grown most cheerful and agreeable. So remarkable was the change in her disposition that I had found it most puzzling, although I had dared to hope that perhaps she had gotten herself over Rory O'Kelley; that, or the two had found means to steal away up river somewhere. Little did I know, at the time, the truth behind what had precipitated such a change in the girl's emotions. What follows, therefore, is the essence of what I did hear from Molly and Patrick, that afternoon in the kitchen after master stumbled back to the house proper.

Having been given the unsettling news of her beau's fate, it was upon Mary's insistence that Patrick O'Bannion made his way through the swamps to the ditch diggers' campsite. There, he found poor Rory all filthy and covered with insect bites, still bearing the marks of his beating. Patrick was most appalled at his good friend's condition and did voice his concern, in no uncertain terms. But Rory would have none of his sympathy, and bid him to hasten back to Mary, there to advise her that the canal laborers were given Sundays off to go to church. For that reason, come Sunday morning, Mary was to tarry behind rather than going off to Mass. Rory would meet her behind Mon. Isaacson's mansion, beneath their big oak tree across the back street.

"Tell her I said not to go a worryin' herself none, Paddy," Rory charged him. And then he proceeded to tell Patrick all that he had been able to learn about this wonderful new place called Texas. It was with the admonition that he should tell Mary nothing of the squalid camp that Rory did send Patrick on his way back into the city. There, Mary did wonder—disbelief and hope wrestling for control of her feelings, as they did—as Patrick told of her beau's being a bit worse for the wear, but otherwise fine and eager to see her, come Sunday, to tell her of wonderful new plans he had for their future. "Me thinks he aims to be a marryin' you, Mary," Patrick told her.

"He said as much to you, did he?"

"Not in so many words, he didn't. But still, what he's got in mind for the two o' ye! It could only involve matrimony, to me way o' thinkin'."

Thus it was that Mary Dunnigan hoped against hope that her Rory would be there, beside that big oak tree. And as Sunday drew nigh, hope gave way to despair, then despair back to hope, as her anticipation orbited in her mind. Finally, the sun did rise on the Sabbath. With the first light of day, Mary sat herself in the window of her room overlooking the back street and that big oak that spread itself over it. The day was young, but there was no Rory beside the tree. Eventually, sounds of the house coming to life were to be heard all about, as the staff mulled around and wandered off to Mass in small groups; but still, there was no Rory to be seen. Clyde loaded Marie, Sonnier and me in the landau to deliver us to the cathedral, even as Mon. Isaacson mounted his fine steed and galloped off to his office. (Saturday being his Sabbath, he always spent Sunday's in his bank office where, there in the quiet, he claimed to get more done in one day than he did the rest of the week.) Ergo, just as Mary became most dejected, as the monsieur and we, the last of the household, did ride out of sight, she did notice Rory's head peek out from behind the great oak.

He pointed to the coach house with exaggerated motions and Mary did flee from her room. Across the balcony, down the stairs and out across the courtyard she ran, where she did rush into the carriageway and stopped abruptly. There was no Rory to be found. Around in a circle she did turn, until he stepped from his hiding place in one of the stalls and took her into his arms. Tightly did he squeeze her to himself; passionately did he kiss her. For the longest they stood there, locked in each other's grip, as if years, rather than days, had separated them. It was he who broke the embrace, urgency resounding in his voice. "Come with me," he whispered .

Up the narrow, winding stairs to the hayloft over the carriageway did he lead her. There they did take refuge in a dim corner where their love for each other overpowered them and led them to its natural conclusion, all their clumsy fears and anxiety notwithstanding. Afterwards, they were to lay intertwined in the hay, the soft, quiet breeze through the opened doors caressing their naked bodies. There, fully exposed to one another, with no secrets between them, Rory told his Mary about Texas, about his plan to save up a little money so they could be married and move off to that wonderful place of so much promise. There would they find themselves a little patch of land. During the day, he would work the land whilst she tended the house and garden. And in the evenings, the two of them would make love for hours on end. Rory and his Mary.

"It's wherever you lead me that I'll be a goin'. You know that don't you?" Mary asked of Rory. His answer was a soft kiss on her lips. "But I have to tell you, Rory, I worry so about you bein' in that swamp. The stories I've heard about them workers dyin' one after the other."

"Don't. Don't worry like that..."

"Maybe I could ask Mr. Isaacson to find you some work?"

"No. Don't ye be a doin' that. Promise me ye won't."

"But why?"

"'Cause it'll just take all the longer, don't ye see. There ain't nowheres the likes o' me can make as much money as I can workin' on that canal. We'll have enough money to get married and outta here in no time. Don't ye see that? That's what's important. You and me. Married! With a life ahead o' us that's all our own." Mary Dunnigan did see. She did understand Rory's urgency, for it was an urgency she shared with him.

Still, six months or so of his working in such hostile conditions gave her pause.

"Then let's us vow that you won't spend a minute more than three months working that canal," Mary pled. "I've a little money saved up. Not much, but every little bit helps. It's on deposit in Mr. Isaacson's bank where it's safe. Let's us vow to one another that three months from now we'll be a gettin' ourselves married and leavin' for this Texas place. No matter how much or how little money we got. We'll make it, one way or the other."

Rory looked deep into her eyes and promised her it would be no longer than three months. Then they'd be married in The Church and set out for their new home in Texas the very next day. There that afternoon, all intertwined in the hay up in the loft, they did dream together of their place in Texas, their place in the world. Together did they plan their dream house, with a big rock fireplace and long, wide porch. Full to the brim with little ones, in time. Together did they dare to hope that life might hold a future for the two of them, despite everything.

It was only when Mary heard the return of the landau below in the carriage way that they stopped their dreaming and returned to reality. Quickly they dressed themselves, lest they be discovered in shame. "Come, Rory. Let's us get away from this place. It's not right we hold ourselves up here like a couple o' desperadoes," Mary said. "Take me for a walk somewheres. Somewheres folks can see us together."

"Ye must know there's nothin' I rather do than be seen with ye on me arm. But we must exercise caution. For the life o' me, I don't know who I could have offended, but someone in this town's out to get me. Best that we just lay low for the time bein'."

So happy had Mary been at her Rory's return that she had put out of her mind the unfortunate situation that had taken place of late. "But who, Rory? Who could it be what's got it so in for you? Have you been a fightin', lately? Maybe it's someone you insulted in a fight. Or in a saloon. Maybe you could go and apologize to 'em?"

"Mary Dunnigan. On me poor Mother's grave I vow to ye—right here and now—I've not been fightin' and I've not been in no taverns."

"Then who? And why? Who could take such a dislike to you? And why?"

"I tell ye, I don't know who or why."

Much of the rest of the afternoon, they did argue over who was responsible for Rory's beating and banishment. Mary was certain there was some ting Rory was not telling her. Never did they suspect, even in their wildest imaginings, that it was Mon. Isaacson who was responsible. Eitenne and I were the only ones in this house to know how low master did stoop in his infatuation for that Irish maid—that Mary Katherine Dunnigan, the very one so in love with, and so loved by, another.

But my thoughts do wander...

Too soon did the sun begin to set, and as the house settled down and grew dark, did they slip away from the loft, to their tree where they bid each other farewell until the next Sunday. Then with a final kiss and long hug, Rory ultimately found the strength to pull himself free of his love's grip. "If I'm not back at the camp in time, I could lose me job. Until next week... And don't forget I love ye," he told her. Then quickly he spun and ran from her, down the dark street as fast as he could, lest he lose his courage, and his job, and remain the night in the arms of the woman he left in charge of his heart.

Looking back over it now, I can see it was that Monday-following that very Sunday that I first noticed the change in Mary Dunnigan. So carefully had her frock and apron been ironed. The color had returned to her cheeks, the sparkle to her eyes. Her dark hair had been laboriously brushed and combed and piled just so, high atop her head. There was life, there was optimism in her gait, and all the while she worked she hummed to herself. As I've already said, I had no idea what precipitated such a change in the woman. My own wishful tinking did give me hope it was a sign she was either over that boy, and could return to the proper discharge of her duties; or, perhaps even better, she and the mon were planning to run away together, somewhere—anywhere—away from this house. So had I dared to hope, but such was not to be. Days went by, then weeks, and still Mary Dunnigan remained in the house, just as cheerful as ever.

The staff all took note that she ceased to go to Mass on Sunday mornings, and although Molly Connelley made it her business to badger her about it, the rest of us made it none of our concern, even if the missing of Sunday Mass is a mortal sin. Apparently, Patrick O'Bannion was the only one to know what was taking place up in the hayloft each Sunday, and he kept the whole matter to himself—as was proper. No, most everyone noticed Mary's soaring spirits but thought nothing much about it. No one, however, appreciated her cheer as much as did Mon. Isaacson. To be sure, my initial hope that perhaps Mary's change in attitude would signal a positive change for this house soon gave way to the unsettling reality that it was only serving to stir tings up worse that they already were. Indeed, that very Monday after she and Rory spent that first Sunday up in the hayloft, I was to be confronted with the pitiful reality of the matter. Monsieur was in his library, preparing his poke to take with him to his office. I, too, was in the library, inquiring of him as to whether or not he thought the shutters and trim should receive a coat of paint before the winter weeks sat in. There in the midst of our conversation, Mary Dunnigan did waltz into the library, bearing her cleaning tray with her.

"Good morning to the both o' ye!" she sang out like a sparrow in springtime. "And how might you be this fine morning, Mr. Isaacson."

Even Mon. Isaacson was taken by surprise. Once I had recovered from the initial shock, I exclaimed with some volume, "Unacceptable! Unacceptable behavior to come parading into this room, speaking to Mon Isaacson before you have been spoken to! "

Never! Never in my entire life had I encountered an instance in which a lowly household servant had so addressed the master of a manse in terms so familiar. Yet while my astonishment remained, his shock quickly turned to amusement. "Oh, don't stand so on ceremony, mademoiselle," he chided at me, then turned to Miss Dunnigan in the sweetest timbre possible. "I am fine, dear. And how are you this morning?" he asked.

Humiliated, I hastened from the room without waiting for the monsieur's decision on the painting. Most of the rest of the day I spent at the writing desk in my chambers, composing a letter to Etienne, a letter I left unsent. In it, I expressed my outrage at my master for having spoken down to me in front of a humble housemaid, for his having allowed a servant to speak to him in terms so familiar. Sick to my stomach did the entire matter render me, until I feared I could not long endure remaining beneath the monsieur's roof, given such dire circumstances. I yearned for Etienne, much the way I suspect Mary Dunnigan did yearn for Rory O'Kelley when he disappeared. It was a burden my master had placed on my shoulders that was far, far too great for me to bear alone. And far, far too unfair for him to expect me to bear. Yet, what was I to do?

It was early when Mon. Isaacson returned home that same Monday-after. I heard the single peal of the dinner bell, the signal to Sonnier and Mordecai that their patron had returned. From my room I could hear Mordecai rumbling down the staircase, and I knew he would bear with him one of Mon. Isaacson's fine house jackets. I stepped from my chambers and made way across the upstairs hall to peer over the banister. There below, I witnessed monsieur's grand entrance. His tall hat and gloves he gave to Mordecai. Sonnier waited, holding forth the silver tray with some sort of message on it. Master took, opened and read the note, and tucked it into his vest pocket, before Mordecai exchanged his undercoat for the jacket. Normally, then, our monsieur would retreat into his library until dinner, but this afternoon I was to witness him follow in after Mordecai, who was ascending the stair. My heart raced, and I turned and rushed across the upstairs hall as quickly and as quietly as possible, to the sanctity of my quarters. I had no desire to set eyes on Mon. Hiam Issacson that afternoon. Shortly thereafter, I would be drawn back out of my room by a boisterous commotion out on the rear gallery. For the second time that day was I to be astonished at the lack of decorum pervading this house. As I stepped slowly forward, wondering what the racket could be about, at the end of the hall I did encounter Mordecai, standing, peering out the rear hall door. Quickly, he turned and retreated, and as he did, I motioned him to me.

"What is happening out there?" I asked him quietly.

Under his breath, he told me. "Massah Isaacson an' Missy Dunnigan's out dere carryin' on like a couple school kids at recess. Laughin' and all. Downright scandalous, if'n you ax me, Miss 'Manda."

I knew not what to do or to say, I merely shook my head in disgust and returned to my quarters. But I vowed to have as little to say and do with monsieur as I possibly could in the days to come. Soon enough would Etienne come calling. Then

I would consult with my love as to what direction I should take in all this, I remember tinking. As it turned out, I would not have to wait that long.

The frivolity and gaiety between Mary Dunnigan and Mon. Isaacson quickly reached a climax, and over the course of the next several weeks began to decline rapidly. I suppose the first splash of cold water over the whole, unfortunate situation came when the monsieur began to ask Miss Dunnigan to take buggy rides with him down to the docks where his cotton was being loaded on the ships. Or down the river to one of his plantations. From what I know now, master's advances must surely have startled Miss Dunnigan as much as her behavior had startled me, she being so in love with young O'Kelley as she was. I am told it was to Molly that she unwrapped her fears that, in the giddiness her love brought with it, she had failed to keep a proper distance with her employer; now the attention and invitations he showered upon her gave her reason to assume he was pursuing her. It was a deep hole she had dug herself into, a hole that she could only hope would not cave in around her before she and Rory could set out for Texas and their better life together. That, after all, was their destiny; of that Rory had assured her.

Thus, over the course of the next six weeks, as the balmy days of fall gradually began to replace the oppressive days of summer, so too was there a discernible cooling of communion between Mary Dunnigan and Mon. Isaacson. I can only surmise that he noticed Mary's pulling back away from him. Certainly, it was evident to me that, seemingly overnight, she returned to her more formal, infinitely more proper, comportment, at least where he was concerned. Perhaps, then, it was her distance that so panicked him, that led him to make such a bold and blundering move. Whatever the reason, one ting remains for sure; his next course of action would leave him looking like a tactless, irresponsible old fool.

At the start, I had no idea of what had taken place there in his library that one particular Saturday afternoon. To be sure, it would be several days later before I knew any ting had transpired at all and only then because of Sonnier's sudden, sullen ways. Certainly, it did not take someone gifted like Mme. Laveau to see the anger and bitterness percolating through our steward. That was evident to all. Even Mon. Issacson had sought me out to inquire as to what the mon's problem could possibly be. For days on end, to ask him a question was to receive, at best, a curt, one-word response. The slightest, most inconsequential annoyance would all but send him—a mon fully grown—into tears. A sight he was, I say. A sight! Finally, upon the monsieur's insistence, I did approach Sonnier in his pantry early one morning.

"Sonnier," I began, "We need to make the talk. I need to know why you're so put out around here lately. Some ting's bothering you, no?"

"No," came the curt reply, not the least unexpected, I might add. I gave him a few minutes to volunteer some ting, any ting, but all he did was wash and dry the breakfast dishes with all the tenderness a mother would wash and dry her newborn. Finally, I could endure the silence no more.

"Mon ami, we been knowing one another way too many years now. You need to tell me what it is that bothers you."

Down he threw his dishtowel and up he threw a look at me, with the whites of his eyes, usually so pretty and so prominent against his deep, dark skin, now red and turbulent. "Why you don't jist go an' ax Miss Dunnigan that? She tell you. She show you. Show that pretty neck-jew'ry Mast Isaacson done bought her." So that was it. monsieur had gone crazy and bought that Irish girl a pretty piece of jewelry, and I was the last in the household to know about it, I remember grumbling to myself.

"What you telling me, Sonnier? Your monsieur's gone and bought a pretty necklace for that girl? Is that what you're saying?"

"Sho is. Dat whut I'm sayin', aw right."
"Well, is that any ting for you to go worrying your head over," I reasoned. "It's the monsieur's own money, is it not? I tink he can do with it what he wants."

"You kin say that again. You kin sho sure be sayin' that again. Yas'am! It's the mast's own money aw right. Don't make a damn what ole Sonnier works his fingers to the bone for the mast. Give that pretty white girl all them 'spensive presents. Don't go worryin' 'bout old Sonnier. He don't deserve the time o' day."

That was it alright. Sometimes Sonnier could be downright silly in his jealousy over our monsieur. I am sure he knew the common thread the master and I shared. (I am sure the entire staff knew of it, so unwavering was their interest in all Mon. Isaacson's private matters.) Yet, nonetheless, on more than one occasion had I found myself on the receiving end of one of Sonnier's fits of enviousness over affections the master would bestow on me. Yes, Sonnier could be difficult at times, but knowing there was nothing I could do to soothe his hurt feelings, I quietly left the room, leaving him to his seething and simmering. My own anger I found to be directed toward the monsieur and Mary Dunnigan. How could the master expect me to keep an orderly household for him, if he was to show such outright partiality to one of his servants? It was improper, that's what it was; unbecoming that the master of the household should be seen openly cavorting with a servant girl, buying her gifts of any sort, much less something so personal as a necklace. To be sure, so infuriated did I find myself that I was soon forced to my daybed with a headache. And there as I lay flat of my back, with a cool cloth across my eyes while my temples pounded, whose voice do you suppose should disturb my peace but that of Mary Dunnigan herself. It was the last voice in the world I wanted to hear at that moment in time. "Miss Maneau?" she asked so meekly it turned my stomach. "Am I disturbing you?"

"You are, indeed," I heard myself reply coldly, callously. I slipped the cool cloth from off my eyes and tossed it aside, as I struggled to sit up. "What do you want?" I asked, noticing, as I propped myself up with a pillow, the black case Mary held in her hands. She said nothing, but advanced toward me, handing me the case as she did. I looked up at her questioningly, but still she said nothing. I took the case and snapped it open, revealing within a large brooch, carved from the blackest of onyx stone, decorated with a bejeweled bird and hung on a twisted gold rope. It was, to be sure, a lovely piece of jewelry, although candor dictates I admit I have many pieces far, far more impressive in my own collection. I, however, was not a common servant.

"Yes, I've heard about this necklace of yours," I said. "I am sure you will enjoy wearing it. Although not around the rest of the staff, I hope." The anguish I heard in her voice I found loathsome.

"O' Misses Maneau, I could never be seen wearing something as grand as that. Me Rory would never understand. I don't know what to do with it? I ne'er asked sir to give me nothing like that. What shall I do, Missus?" I could feel my very backbone stiffening within me as my anger grew. Already was my head throbbing and now this woman had the audacity to stand before me, pretending to be the humble little princess of the manor, unworthy of our monsieur's fine gift. I tell you I could not help myself, I exploded in rage.

"You dare to come into my chambers like this? Whining and sobbing like a spoilt child. What do you tink? That I have no eyes to see how you've been carrying on around Mon. Isaacson? Do you suppose, I've no ears to hear all the sweet talk you've been making with him? What were you tinking? That he was not a mon, with mon's feelings down inside his britches. And you parading around all happy and gay, talking to him like you were his equal. Shame on you, I say! Shame on you! You want to know what to do about this pretty present of yours?" I thrust the case out toward her. "Let me tell you! Take your fine necklace and leave! Leave this house and never come back. You've brought it nothing but trouble since the day you came."

There, I'd said it. I'd allowed my anger to get the better of me and I'd said what I thought. Tears welled up in Mary's eyes and she slapped her hand to her mouth in an effort to stifle her sobs. She wheeled around and ran from my room, leaving me sitting up on my daybed, holding her jewelry case as my head felt as if it would split in two. There would be the devil to be paid, I knew, if she were to tell the monsieur what I had said to her, but for once I did not care. Maybe it was my head; it hurt so badly. Whatever the reason, I snapped the case shut and threw it out into the hall with all my might, then slid back down on my bed, closing my eyes tight against the intruding world.

"My necklace." Susan breathed out. "That's where the necklace your grandmother gave me came from. T.K.. She had to know that. She had to know where it came from. How it got into her possession."

"Probably. But grandmother always plays her cards close to her vest. What did she tell you about it?"

"Just that it was the oldest piece in her collection. That it'd been in the family for over a hundred years."

"Well, now we know. Don't we?"

"It's not what she told me about it. It's what she didn't tell me. I was given the impression it was your great-great-great grandmother's. Only it's not. It belonged to some woman I've never heard of."

"Yeah. I keep getting the feeling there's more to the story than the family's been led to believe. Let's read on and see if the mystery gets solved," T.K. replied, handing the journal to me. "Here. It's your turn."

Monday, 9 July 1837

That was the last I would hear of that necklace for a while. When I awoke from the nap I had taken, I found my headache gone, along with the black case I'd tossed out into the hall. I know not who it was that picked it up, I only know it found it's way back to Mary Dunnigan's room, where it was kept hidden in her bottom chiffonier drawer, except for the one time I was to know of her putting it on. I remember having taken refuge out on the upstairs front gallery, there to gather my thoughts together. With the throbbing pain in my head now gone, I was able to tink clearer and doing so realized I had taken a dangerous position—if not an unfair one—with Mary. She had come to me for help and I had turned her out. What was I to do to make amends? Truly I did fear that if Mon. Isaacson were to get wind of all that I had said to his fair one, I might well find myself on that same auction block my mother had stood, those many years ago.

After a fashion of collecting my thoughts, I determined that, at the least, I owed an apology to poor Mary for having spoken so harshly to her. Servant or no, she deserved a tongue more civil than I had offered her. On the other hand, I could, at best, hope my apology would soothe any hurt she might feel toward me, and thus ward off her turning to the monsieur in retaliation. I retreated from the gallery and made haste to Mary's chambers, where I did find her sitting by the window overlooking the great oak across the street. I tapped softly at her door, only to have her turn her face from me in a pout. I refused to ask permission to enter a mere hireling's room, so it was with all the contrition I could muster that I stepped just beyond the threshold.

"I am afraid you caught me in bed with a swimming head, Miss Dunnigan. I do apologize that my behavior was so coarse a while ago. I hope you took no offense?" Mary Dunnigan looked around to me and I could see her emerald eyes were as red and puffy as Sonnier's had been earlier in the day.

"I've no place to go, straight aways. I pray you won't go a turnin' me out to the streets afore I do."

"No. Of course not. Put such as that out of your mind."

"You should be happy to know that I am to be married. Just next month. Right afterwards, me and Rory aim to be movin' on to Texas."

Her words took me by surprise, but I tried to sound joyous in the news. "You're to be married, then! How wonderful. You and that handsome Mr. O'Kelley of yours?" But Mary Dunnigan was in no mood for small talk.

"So you won't need to go a worryin' 'bout the likes o' me bein' 'round here much longer. That should settle your mind for you."

"Miss Dunnigan, I meant no—" Mary would not let me finish my sentence, however.

"I know full-well what you meant, ma'am. You made as much perfectly clear. Married women do not work in your household. And you blame me for the way Mr. Isaacson has been actin' o' late."

It was a streak of the irrational I detected in the girl, so I studied the floor in quiet for a bit before attempting to go on with her. "This is not the first house where you've been employed. You must know that housekeepers simply do not bring their husbands to live under another's roof. As for Mon. Isaacson... I'm afraid he's grown enamored with you. I could see it coming, I'm just surprised that you couldn't."

"I'll have you to know, Missus Maneau, that I ain't the kinda woman who'd lead a man like Mr. Isaacson on! Him or any man for that matter!"

I could see there was nothing I could say that would do away with the foul cloud hanging over her. Better to leave the situation well enough alone for the time being. "No, certainly not. No one harbors thoughts such as that about you," I said, then turned and left her room as quietly, as contritely as I had entered it.

And thus did I return to the house; and thus has old Dr. Penney come to check on Mon. Isaacson this late afternoon He spent only a few minutes in the chambers with master, then as I saw him out, he hesitated at the front door and motioned to the nearby seats, as if to ask permission to sit. "S'il vous plait," I said to him with a sweep of my hand and we sat ourselves upon monsieur's modern, wrought iron chairs. The old physician seemed to gather his thoughts together before he spoke.

"A dose of fresh air should do him some good. See if you can't get him to sit a spell outdoors in the mornings. It's a peculiar thing, the human mind. You're never sure what to expect with these nervous conditions. Don't get me wrong, Miss Maneau, I can see some improvement. At the same time, though, this seems to be taking a little longer than I would have expected." He gazed off across the street and I left him alone to come back to me when he was ready. Finally, did he look down between his feet, never looking back to me as he went on. "A group of my colleagues and I were supposed to meet with Mr. Isaacson today. Did you know that? It'd taken me weeks to get him to consent to such an audience and now... I had to send messages to them all telling them he was indisposed and unable to meet with us. Damn that canal anyway! We'd all be better off if he had never come up with that notion in the first place."

Thereafter did it seem the words just rolled off his tongue like sweat off the brow of one of those Irish diggers and he did explain how he and his colleagues felt most put upon by the master and his canal confederates. Permit me to elaborate, if I may. It does seem that in the progress of digging the canal more than just a few workers have screamed aloud in abject terror, then disappeared beneath the black swamp water, a meal for some monstrous alligator, many of which can reach lengths of seven to eight feet, nose to tail. Far worse for the physicians of town, however, are the sheer numbers of men suffering from the bite of poisonous snakes. Most, it seems, are bitten but a single time upon the foot or leg. They are the ones more likely to survive the ill-effects of the venom than those bitten on the hands or arms, which are much closer to the heart and by reason much deadlier; or those bitten multiple times who seldom survive for more than a few agonizing hours. Far, far too often, however, the snakebite will cause a worker's foot or leg to swell so awfully that that the flesh will go bad. Ultimately, then, it will be necessary to amputate the limb lest gangrene should set in. It is in such instance that the physicians of the city come into play, for such unfortunate workers are carted into town to the good doctors' offices, where slaves are brought in to hold them down whilst the doctor cuts their limb from off the body.

A good number of those undergoing such surgery die from the shock of it, or from infection. Yet, even those who survive the ordeal are so maimed as to be good for little more than begging off the good conscience of the city's populace. Certainly, they are no longer sufficiently productive to ever be able to adequately repay the doctors for their services," he continued. And so it was that the good doctor, as neighbor and physician to Monsieur Isaacson, had been prevailed upon to arrange an audience with him. It had been hoped by the doctors that some arrangement might be made whereby they could receive some remuneration from the canal associates for the treatment of such unfortunate canal workers

So taken aback had I been at the old man's description of the plight of the laborers that I must confess to a social faux pas. So heavily did the doctor's tale weigh upon my mind that it was not until after he had left that I realized

I should have offered to poll the canal principals—in proxy given Mon. Isaacson's absence—to see if some relief could not be arranged for the doctors. Thus, it was just such a message I sent to Dr. Penney, along with my apologies and I do vow to poll the others without undue delay. And yet, right now it is Dr. Penney's tale that holds hostage my thoughts, vis-à-vis some ting that Patrick O'Bannion had told me.

From what I have been able to piece together, the digging of the New Basin Canal has been a highly scientific and most organized process—nothing less than a modern marvel, a testament to mans' ultimate triumph over nature herself. Now, Mon. Isaacson owns almost all the land fronting on either side of the canal and it has always been his scheme that once the canal has been dug, a series of channels crisscrossing his land will serve to drain the swamps into the great canal. Afterwards, the spoilage piled up as a levy can then be spread out to create buildable dry land, which should turn him a fine profit one day very soon. It is indeed a most astute business scheme, and yet the more I do learn about this canal, the more I do wonder if Our monsieur has been kept fully informed as to the cost in human terms. I do search my mind, and it is there I believe—I pray—I have found the answer: surely the master I know and love would have naught to do with a venture as odious as this one appears to be.

Perhaps what young Patrick O'Bannion told me will afford you, who may chance to read these words, the opportunity to appreciate my concerns. Patrick tells of a story told to him by Rory O'Kelley, about late of an afternoon when he was standing almost to the knees in water, digging out the last few inches of mud from the canal bed. He stopped long enough to wipe the sweat from out of his eyes when the shouting of his friend James up on the bank did beckon his attention. Looking up, the salty perspiration in his eyes blurred his vision, but he could tell by the tone of his voice that James was most agitated. It was at that moment that he heard a commotion in the water behind him, a hissing noise like none he'd ever encountered before. Quickly rubbing his eyes, he turned to face the noise just as a gunshot rang out loud and close from the bank. Instantly did Rory wipe his face on the bottom of his shirt only to discover that he was about to be eaten alive by a most ponderous alligator.

Even before he could catch his breath again, a rope was tossed down to Rory from the bank. Looking up, there he discovered his savior was the Arcadian sentinel hired to guard the laborers. His aim had been quick and on the mark, saving Rory in the process. Now, he was most animated, waving his arms and shouting in his strange French tongue, none of which Rory understood. He stood in the murky water, dazed and confused until his friend James came to his aid.

"Don't let that 'gator sink there, Rory! Get in there and get that rope on 'em quick like!"

"I ain't touchin' that thing! Damned near ate me alive as it was!" the boy protested.

From the bank, the Arcadian had had enough as he did watch the alligator begin to slip under the murky waters. Into the ditch did he jump, where he proceeded to tie off the abominable creature's body. Once he had it tied and the rope tossed up to James and the others on the bank, he turned to Rory. "Stupide! Perureux! Louis Verret non rater!" he growled as he struggled up the muddy ladder to help hoist the creature up to the bank.

"He just called you an idiot and a coward," James taunted Rory. "Said he never misses when he shoots."

"Aye? Well you just tell him that I ain't no coward and he better think twice before he says such as that again. If he knows what's good for 'em. I'll not be a caring if he's got a gun or no."

"Ah! He don't mean no harm. The only pay he gets for keepin' us from gettin' eat alive is the money he makes off them hides. Alligators make a fine strong leather. He just didn't want the thing to get lost in all that black water down there. That was all. Besides which, he'll makes us a salve from that there 'gator's innards that'll keep the 'skeeters off us tonight."

And he did. The Arcadian Louis Verret did just that. Once he had the alligator on the surface of the ground again, he went about dressing it out. Most cautious was the mon to make sure the hide was not damaged in anyway in the skinning process, and once he had the prized hide salted down he went about rendering the meat for its fat. That evening, did Verret take the alligator fat and mix it with a small amount of swamp mud. To each of the men in their gang he did offer a small portion of the salve, just enough to smear over their faces, hands and arms. As usual that night, the air hung still and heavy, but at least there was no need for the smoky fire to drive away the mosquitoes and other insects that preyed upon them. All sat around the spot where they usually built their fire. which they covered with palmetto fronds to create the thick smoke the mosquitoes could not abide. And as they sat there, James told Rory of the time Verret had saved him from a provoked cottonmouth.

"I tell you lads," James finished his story, "it's times what I think ever snake St. Patrick drove out of Ireland must've swum straight over here to this swamp."

"The snakes I can handle," Rory said. "They don't scare me all that much. I've too much respect for 'em. Give 'em too wide a berth. Tis them god-awful bitin' bugs that I can't handle. Least ways a snake don't go lookin' to bite you if you leave 'em alone. And on top of that, I don't know what I hate worse: the smell of this alligator salve or the wind comin' up from the south."

Once again, you must allow me to explain: those poor souls digging in the swamps, I am told, have only three options available to them to keep the swarms of mosquitoes from carrying them off. In the first instance, the smoke from the fire will keep at least some of them away, even if the heat of the fire makes the humid night even more unbearable and the smoke irritates the lungs. Then, there's the salve from rendered alligator fat that smells so repulsive even an insect won't come near. And finally, there are the strong southern breezes blowing up from the Gulf of Mexico, from time to time, which sends them away. Unfortunately, I am told the wind only serves to blow the stench of the open latrine over the camp. The worker's only facility, you see, is a short trench dug in the ground that gets burned off with a little coal oil every once in a spell, the odor from which is most repulsive. There that still evening, besmeared with the Arcadian's concoction of reptile fat and mud, the men argued about which of their mosquito options was the least desirable. And when the conversation settled down again, Rory did speak up to voice an opinion on another topic. "Ye ask me and I'll tell ye this: it ain't right, our employers expectin' us to live out here like this. And I ain't just talkin' 'bout them mosquitoes neither." He stuck out a finger toward town as he leaned forward for emphasis. "Ye go and ask any physician or any chemist there in town and what'll they tell ye? That ye can catch any disease known to man bein' out here in this night air, what with all the rottin', decayin' plants and creatures and who know what else all around you. That's what gets a man sick in the first place: breathin' in foul air such as that. It's just a wonder more of us don't die out here."

"And what might a man be doin' about all this injustice, young O'Kelley?" one of the older workers taunted him. "Insist that them gentlemen payin' us to work out here buy us each a fancy home in town." Laughter arose from the group and the older fellow did grin and nod in satisfaction as he looked around to the others. "Drive us out 'ere to work eve day in a sedan and matched team?"

"I ain't expectin' nothin' of the kind and ye know it. Still, seems to me twould be little enough for them gentlemen to provide a little better for our livin' arrangements than this," he defended himself, looking around at the camp. "It wouldn't take no food off their fine and fancy tables for 'em to find someplace in town where we could be put up. Nothin' fancy. Just someplace where we could get in out of the night air. They could haul us in and out ever mornin' and evenin' with the wagons and teams they already got out here. What's the trouble with that, I ask ye?"

"Trouble with that, young O'Kelley, is there ain't no one of them gentlemens in town, or no one else, goin' to give the time o' day about an Irishman like me or you. And the sooner you figure that out for yerself, the better off you'll be. 'Cause there ain't a thing on God's green earth you can be a doin' about it. That's just the way things is."

"But men, there is somethin' we can be doin' about it," Rory protested, "There's lots we can be doin' about it."

"Like what?" James scoffed.

"Like the last thing any o' them dandies in town wants is for the diggin' o' this canal to drag on any longer than it takes. The quicker we get it dug for them, the quicker they'll start makin' money off it. I say if we all just laid down our shovels and sat down on our backsides—refused to do any more work until they provided a little better livin' arrangements—well, then they'd have to give into our demands."

"Rubbish," grunted one of the men. "They sack us all on the spot, that's what they'd do."

"And replace us with who? They sure aren't goin' to put none o' their slaves to work out here. They're worth too much money to go a riskin' 'em to this kind o' air. Not to mention the snakes and alligators. No, laddies, they'd have to bargain with us if we was to sits down. They'd have no choice. It'd take 'em a good six months just to send over to Ireland for our replacements," Rory argued, even as the big boss mon beside him began a series of deep puffs on his cigar. "And even then, that would cost 'em more to import replacements for us than it would to put us up somewhere decent. Somewhere we could shut ourselves out from all this poisonous air."

No sooner had Rory finished what he had to say, than the boss took his cigar out of his mouth and looked at the fat, glowing hot end. Then, quite calmly did he lean across and jab it hard into poor Rory's cheek. It was a horrible scream the boy let out as he fell to his knees holding his burning cheek. All looked up in horror as the boss mon slowly got to his feet and stood towering over Rory.

"It's a nice scar you'll be having there on your pretty face lad. Now ever time you look at yourself in the mirror you can be reminded of how little I think of you and your big ideas." He reached down, snatched a handful of Rory's hair and lifted him up by it. "Now let me make me self clear to you, just in case I ain't already. Ain't nowhere a man like me can get a job what pays good as this one. Now I got me a wife and family o'er in County Cork and I aim to bring 'em o'er here to be with me. Am I clear so far?" Rory tried to nod his head but the pain of his burn and of being held by his hair proved too much and he only grimaced even more.

"Good. Maybe we'll come to an understandin' after all. Now pay attention to this the lot o' you! You go tryin' to stop work around here and them very powerful men in town will just send their goons out here bustin' heads and breakin' bones. And I don't fancy getting' me head busted or no bones broke." He shoved Rory to the ground and kicked him hard in his side. "So you just get all these fancy notions outta your head, boy. I hear any more talk like that comin' outta you and I'll send you back to town and let that bunch that got hold of you in the first place finish you off. And that goes for anyone o' the rest o' ye who might be harborin' sympathies for young O'Kelley's highbrow notions."

He looked over his shoulder toward the east where the foreboding swamp lay cloaked in the darkness of night. "A man could get his throat cut and end up 'gator meat out there in that swamp. And no one would be the wiser for it." Then the big boss mon did look around most menacingly at his audience. "I make meself clear?" he asked of them. Needless to say, no one challenged the bully.

As he did later relate the story to Patrick O'Bannion, Rory did allow that ever after was he most afraid for his own personal safety. He had struck a bad chord with the big boss mon, who had the power of life and death over the boy. Rory related that thereafter was he headset upon working his hardest and keeping his profile low, lest something sinister should come of him. And thus it was that my concerns over what was taking place out in the swamps did grow, when coupled with Patrick O'Bannion's story and that which the good doctor told me this evening. The tale Rory O'Kelley related to Patrick O'Bannion I could have easily enough dismissed as so much sour grapes and exaggerations of a lazy young mon, but what Dr. Penney had to say seemed to lend credence to Rory's claim. I now find that I have spent most of my evening churning all this over inside my stomach and have come to the inescapable conclusion that Mon. Isaacson is either uninformed or misinformed as to the conditions under which the Irish are forced to work. Were he fully cognizant of what all is going on out there, he would surely be most outraged and would wash his hands of the whole affair. Of this I am certain, and I realize the importance of bringing all this to his attention, once he has regained his faculties.

For now, however, there is little I can do on my own, other than wait for him to come back to us and right this wrong.

There was something T.K. Needed to know: "So how much of this do you think is fact and how much exaggeration? I mean did those men working on that canal really die in droves?"

I bit my bottom lip as I pondered his query. "Well, nobody knows for sure how many died. No records exist. At least not today. But it was a lot. No doubt about it. Numbers I've been told range from six to over thirty-thousand."

"Unbelievable," Susan gasped. "And they just buried them where they dropped. No headstones? No nothing?"

"Pretty much. The only recognition the poor souls have is a little Celtic cross the local Irish heritage society erected out where the canal used to connect to the lake."

"I think I know now why my grandmother doesn't want to talk about our family's New Orleans connection. Not exactly something a family like ours would be proud of."

T.K. just shook his head, then suggested that we keep reading.

Tuesday, 10 July 1837

For the remainder of that week in which Mary and I had had our falling out over Mon. Isaacson's necklace-present, she did present in a most low mood. And she did avoid the master like he was some creature that had crawled straightaway out of the swamp. In turn, then, the more she avoided him, the lower his mood fell. And the lower his mood did fall, the more I sensed the staff picking up on it, until all, it seemed, grew demoralized—so unhappy was our lot those days; so downcast had that necklace left us all. Yet, there was nothing that could be done about it. The unfortunate fact was the seeds of our dissatisfaction had been sown and this was the beginning of that drought of tranquility from which this household has never recovered, even unto this very day.

Of course, by the time Sunday had arrived, Mary's mood had improved in anticipation of being with her Rory, even if everyone else remained most dispirited. As she had every Sunday since their first encounter up in the hayloft, she rose with the chickens and positioned herself by the window overlooking the great oak across the back street, there to wait for all to leave for church and her Rory to come forth for her. Only this Sunday would be different. It would be all day she would sit and wait, with never her love to present his person. With no message from Rory explaining his absence, no word of his condition, Mary did worry herself frightfully the entire following week, rendering the house all the more crestfallen. Only when the next Sunday came around was her heart lightened, for there, beside the oak, after the landau had left for the cathedral, stood her Rory. Out into the street she did rush, whereupon she did leap into her love's arms to hug him tightly in delight at his being well. Then, as quickly, her delight did turn to anger as she let go her grip of the boy and demanded to know why he would leave her so worried sick, not knowing what was the matter with him—whether he was dead or alive. Rory sought to explain: "Twas such a bad humor I had last Sunday, I could not even raise me self outta' the bed."

"What was it that ailed you?"

"Me head felt like someone had hit on it with a hammer, it did. And I was sick to me stomach, to boot. Thought I was goin' to die right then and there, I tell you. Till one o' the men by the camp give me a good dose of tonic what knocked whatever it was a botherin' me straight out o' me system."

"Good for him. Good for whoever it was that got you the tonic. But you must learn to take better care o' yourself, Rory, until we're married and you have me to look out after you.

And so it was they passed yet another Sunday up in the hayloft, a Sunday made all the more gratifying by their absence from one another the previous week. Those were, indeed, their good times, those Sundays the pair had alone to one another. Still, no one knows better than I do that the good times must always be fleeting, and that's what happened with Rory and Mary. You see, the very next Sunday did Mary perceive her love to look poorly. His color was blanched; his appetite meager and he lacked even the energy to be intimate with the woman he so loved. Mostly, he slept in the hay, cradled in Mary's arms. Thereafter, did it appear to Mary that the boy would be fine one Sunday, only to be sicker than ever the next, and she began to worry herself about his soundness of body. Then there came that Sunday, that awful Sunday, a day I tell you I shall never forget as long as I live.

Now Rory and Patrick were men secure enough in their friendship that they could easily enough share their hopes and fears with one another, which is some ting I guess most men must find awkward. But what took place in up in the hayloft that awful Sunday, Rory was never able to share with his good friend Patrick. Time, for them, had rapidly run out for that kind of camaraderie. Were it not for Mary's confiding in Molly some days later, neither Patrick nor I, either one, would have never known what happened that Sunday when Rory showed up uncharacteristically late. And when he did finally get there, Mary was fully prepared to lash out at him for leaving her so worried, until she beheld the strange golden radiance he had about him. Once again, he was in terrible pain with an aching head. Mary Dunnigan did her best to ease his suffering, cradling his head in her lap and bathing his face with cool water until he did quickly fall asleep, slumbering well into sundown.

I suppose she must have felt like the sky itself was closing in on her: I know she had been distressed at the monsieur's advances and she had to be near out of her mind with worry over her Rory's malady. What none of us were to know, until months later, was that no one else could she turn to that awful Sunday but Rory, yet he was in no condition to attend to her.

"Rory. Tis somethin' I'm needin' to be a tellin' you," she would tell the mon, over and over. Yet over and over the only response she was to get from him would be the most pathetic of moans, until, ultimately, she did give up trying to make the talk with him. To be sure, such was his agony that he soon grew delirious and began to make noise about needing to return to the digger's camp. Poor Mary must have been beside herself; she needed Rory to ease her own pain but found herself, instead, called upon to ease his. Moreover, as he grew more and more restless, she grew more and more terrified Mon. Isaacson would find them out. Rory, it was most obvious, was in no condition to get himself back to the camp. She thought about turning to Sonnier for aid, but thought better of it: her old confrere had been most cold and uncivil toward her of late. Finally, in desperation she turned to Clyde the coachman.

It was a friend, indeed, that Clyde turned out to be that night. Recognizing Rory was seriously afflicted and realizing the rancor that would be gotten up if Mon. Isaacson were to find the couple alone up in his hayloft, he schemed to get the mon on horseback. There, tied to one of the grooms to keep him from falling off, he was secretly ferried back to the digger's camp.

The groom tells of a young Irishman named James who stood aside to watch in dread as two strapping men untied Rory from him and laid him out on the muddy ground, just as the rain began to fall. For most of the way to the camp, Rory had been seized by the rigors and the groom could feel his burning fever even through his own shirt, as Rory rode slumped over against him. Once they had him laid out on the ground, an oil lantern was brought over and the foreman did examine Rory closely, pointing out the trickle of blood oozing out of his ears.

"Well, I'll be damned, lads," he said to no one in particular as he rose from Rory's side. "Here it is this late in the season and look what this one's got. Tis the malaria, sure as I stand here. See the blood a comin' out o' his ears. Means his brains 'ave taken to bleedin'. He'll be dead afore the mornin' I fear. Too bad, he was a good lad, even if he was of peculiar opinions. Well, nothin' we can do for 'em now. Go on ahead and drag 'em o'er there beside the ditch, men. T'will be easier to get 'em buried come the morn." And as two men did take Rory O'Kelley by the arms and legs and drag him away in the falling rain, James rushed to the groom's side. "For God's sake, man. Get on that horse and ride! Bring his woman Mary out here before he's gone!"

"Bring Miss Mary Dunnigan out to dis place?" the astonished groom asked.

"Would you have 'em die without so much as a good bye? Now, ride boy, ride!" James shouted at him.

The groom could not have mounted the horse and galloped off down the narrow road any faster if a rabid hound, itself, had been nipping at his heels. By the time he got back to the mansion the rain was falling in torrents. I had been sitting at the piano in the music room, when I first heard the commotion outside. Unaware that the monsieur was seated on the rear gallery just above me, I stepped out onto the lower level to see what was the matter. It was dark and difficult to see in the pouring rain, but I could make out there was some fuss going on in the coach house. Several lanterns were to be seen flashing about, and the chatter, although not understandable, was markedly excited. Soon I was surprised to see Clyde run across the courtyard, fast like a ghost was chasing after him. He bounded up the outside stairs, two treads at a time, and owing to the noise of the rainfall I could not understand what was being said up there in the yellow glow of candlelight spilling out of Mary Dunnigan's room. I can remember being startled when I heard her scream. In an instant, the entire compound came to life, as the staff hurried from their rooms to congregate near Mary's door.

Monsieur, I did notice, scurried across the balcony to her door, as she wailed at the top of her lungs, loud enough to be heard over the falling rain, "Oh, God no! Not me Rory! Not me Rory! Take me to 'em! Somebody take me to 'em."

Clyde and old Marie took Mary by her arms and lead her down the stairs, where I ventured out into the pouring rain to meet them. Mary was sobbing and moaning uncontrollably, "Help me get to 'em before it's too late. Please help me get to 'em." I stood on the lower step blocking their path and took Mary's hands in mine. I looked to Clyde and he explained, "It's her beau, mam'ouselle. He done gone and caught dat ole malaria down at dat canal. He ain't long for this world I 'fraid."

I looked to Mary in disbelief. Only a few weeks earlier had she told me of their plans to marry. Now this! I squeezed her hands, not finding words to comfort her, and she looked to me pleadingly. "Please, Ma'am. Lend me a ride to get to 'em."

"Oh, my Child," I heard myself saying, "it's dark and the weather's gone bad. There's no way you can get to him tonight."

She tilted her head to one side and the rain dripped off her hair and ran down those pure white cheeks of hers. "Please. He can't die alone like that. Please," she begged, her sorrow tearing at my very soul.

For once I was at a loss; I knew not what to do nor what to say. Up I did look and there spied the monsieur standing at the top of the stairs. His eyes caught mine and with my gaze I told him that this vile business was all his doing. "How quickly have you gained what you've schemed for. Now what will you do about all this?" I hissed at him with my eyes, all the while he stood looking down at his precious Mary Dunnigan, weeping and wailing in the falling rain. He stared at me momentarily, anger flickering in his eyes, too. Yet when finally he spoke up, I was to be most astounded by his words.

"Hitch up the carriage, Clyde. Somebody go fetch Dr. Penney," he ordered, authority ringing in his voice. "Marie, bring some quilts from the house to keep Miss Dunnigan warm. You!" he shouted at me, "Help her to the coach house!"

Perhaps the relief was too much for her to bear, for Mary Dunnigan collapsed into Clyde's arms. Down the stairs the monsieur dashed, taking her up in his own arms and directing Clyde to go on to the coach house to tend to the landau. "The rest of you go on back in your rooms," he shouted at the gawking staff, then turned to me. "Will you come with us? In case she should need attending?"

I nodded and fell in behind my master, as he carried poor Mary Dunnigan to the waiting carriage. By the time we had her loaded in, the groomsmen had both tops up and the side curtains in place. Clyde was about to whip the horses off, when I called for him to stop. I pointed to the older of the grooms. "You! Go as fast as you can to the rectory. Tell one of the priests what has happened. That they may need to perform the Last Rites." Then off we bolted.

The interior of the landau was dry enough, and it made good time along the board road leading to the campsite, considering how slippery cypress wood can get when wet. Carved through the swampy terrain, as it was, the road was like a giant snake's rut and the silhouette of the black, foreboding swamp surrounding, closing in on either side of us, caused my blood to run cold. I forced myself to stare at the carriage floor, and fought to put out of my mind the fact the canal site could be no more than two or three miles from our residence. It seemed it took an eternity for us to get there. Once we did, however, the arrival of a fine carriage bearing two women, so late of the night, did cause a stir. The big, burly boss-mon rushed out of a nearby tent, holding up a lantern and calling out, "Who's this comin' in here this time o' the night!

Monsieur did jump forthwith from the carriage and approach the foreman. "Hiam Isaacson, here. You have a young man among you that's sick of the malaria?"

The foreman seemed astonished to confront his employer and ladies at his campsite on such an inhospitable night. "On my word, sir! Tis not a fit night for a gentleman like yourself to be about!"

"The young man—" Monsieur started to demand of the boss, but Mary interrupted.

"Rory O'Kelley! Is he here?" The giant of a mon looked completely dumbfounded as to why Mon. Isaacson and this woman could be inquiring about one of his laborers. Wordless did he stand, looking first to Mary, then to the master. Monsieur, however, did look to the boss with insistence, "Well? Is he out here or not!"

"Aye. That he is. Though I should hope he's dead by now, me lord. All the sufferin' he's been through."

Monsieur turned to the carriage and took Mary's hand to help her down. Clyde did help me from the other side. No sooner had our feet touched the ground than, mercifully, the rain let up. Master demanded of the foreman that we be taken to Rory, although none of us had been prepared to be led by lantern light to the side of the muddy ditch. There, Rory O'Kelley did lay upon the bare ground, soaked through and muddy as a discarded melon rind tossed out in the street to keep down the flies. Mary Dunnigan did drop down in the mud beside him, taking his head into her lap where she sobbed and brushed at the hair in his face. And, oh how grotesque did the mon look.

I tell you, he looked nothing like that robust young mon who had come knocking at the rear hall door at such an unfortunate hour. In the dim glow of the lantern light, I could see his breathing was shallow and noisy, that his big, round eyes were sunken back into his skull, his gaze fixed overhead, leaving them looking all the bigger. Already had his lower jaw relaxed. But mostly I was appalled that these men of the camp could be so hardened as to have put poor Rory out in the pouring rain to die. Had they no sense of decency? Had they no feelings left inside them?

Apparently, my thoughts mirrored those of Mon. Isaacson, for he demanded of the boss, "Why is this man laid out in the mud and the rain like this? What manner of man are you that you couldn't find him a dry pallet?" The boss-mon, though, seemed unimpressed with our monsieur's sense of decency. He stuck out his big, bottom lip and kicked at the mud.

"I mean you no disrespect, sir. But you want that we should get this here canal dug inna timely fashion, then you just don't go a mixing the dead in with the livin'. They won't stand for it, they won't. Reminds them too much of what lies ahead for most o' 'em. You want a good, hard day's work outta this lot, it's better you leave the dead to themselves. Believe me on this. I know what I'm a talkin' about."

Neither the monsieur nor Clyde, nor even I, knew what to do or say. Awkwardly did we stand over Mary Dunnigan, seated in the mud whilst holding her dying beau, until the boss ordered camp stools to be brought for us. Mary refused to let go of Rory, so the rest of us took seats, our heads bowed as we waited for the inevitable. Soon, however, faithful old Dr. Penney did arrive astride his horse. It was the big boss that escorted him to Rory's side, where upon the old gentleman did hurriedly kneel down in the mud to examine the boy. It was from his bag that he took a vial and pulled out the cork by his teeth. "Here," he said to Mary, as he spat the cork aside, "we must get him to drink this. All of it."

Gently, then, did Mary lift Rory's head up to receive the remedy; gently, then, did Dr. Penney lift the vial to the boy's lips. But, alas, the first drop of the drug that did pass down his throat sent him into a reflex of coughing, so far gone was he. Dr. Penney stretched the poor boy's arms up high over his head, until his body had expelled the medicine from his lungs. Then his head collapsed down on his chest, and I took note of Dr. Penney's head drooping, as well. He helped ease the boy back down into Mary's loving arms, and there was nothing more he could do. The anger the old doctor felt inside registered upon his face, as he arose from the mud and stumbled over to one of the stools beside Mon. Isaacson. There, he held up the vial for master to see. "Quinine," he explained.

Involuntarily, I heard myself gasp, "Poison!"

Was the only thing that could've saved him, but he's waited too long now. He must've been infected weeks ago. Now his brain's too swollen for me to do anything for him. Why! Why won't menfolk avail themselves of my medicine before it's too late? Especially these worker-types. Why, when I can save them?"

The kindly old soul could do nothing more than look down at his muddy boots and shake his head. A little while later, he would rise and without a word to anyone, he would take up his bag and go mount his horse to return home, lest someone else in town should be in need of his healing art.

Master, Clyde and I did remain there by Mary's side, however, waiting for death to put an end to that unfortunate boy's ghastly suffering. When I could stand the gasping rattle of death no more, I took my rosary from my pocket and Clyde joined me in prayer. It seemed the least I could do, and it drowned out that awful death rattle.

All through the night—the wettest and most miserable I can remember—did we sit beside Mary and Rory, even as the big boss and the rest of the camp slithered back into their tents to sleep away this unpleasantness, all snug and dry on their cots. There toward the end, the rigors did once more seize Rory O'Kelley and he shook most violently and sweated most profusely. At last, blood did ooze and bubble out of his nose and soon thereafter did he breathe his last, as his beloved clutched him tightly and wailed in a shrill singsong way.

It would not be until near sunrise that we would notice the young priest—the one I would come to know as Fr. O'Donnell—who had ridden into camp on a most unfortunate mount; nor the dirty young mon named James sitting off all alone, a little distance away. "Fine time for you to be a showin' up, Father," young James scoffed at the priest as he passed by him. "He died hours ago. Where might you have been when me friend could'e used your fancy prayers? Asleep in your fancy rectory house, I imagine?"

I remember asking myself what could have brought such a young person to harbor such disdain for a mon of the cloth. With the coming of the morning, I would have my answer.

The priest, on the other hand, just ignored the bitter young mon and walked right past him without a glance. Down in the mud did Father kneel to take Rory by a hand still holding a hint of warmth. His head fell as he slowly shook it, like a mon fairly beaten. Eventually, he lifted his eyes up to Mary, but her gaze was fixed on Rory, just as it had been for lo' those many hours. Up out of the mud the Father then stood, only to stare as deeply and coldly into the monsieur's eyes as ever I could picture. A mon of God or not, I did get the impression he could beat him to death with his bare hands. Fear reared itself up inside me and I did look to my master for his manly protection.

What I saw before me, though, was not a brave mon ready to stand his ground, but one consumed with guilt and grief. He had to look away from the priest and the priest, in turned, turned from him to the muddy canal, just now revealing itself in the morning light. I was exhausted with the tension of situation; I had not slept all the night long, so I do not remember how long it was Fr. O'Donnell stood staring off into that canal—horrible ditch of death that it was. All I now remember is his turning back to Rory O'Kelley's body. From his cloak the Father did take his stole and kiss it, then hung it around his shoulders. "Hail Mary, full o' grace, the Lord is with ye," he began in his heavy brogue, as he went about anointing the body: if the fluid from Dr. Penney's bottle could not save the boy's life, then surely the Holy Water from Fr. O'Donnell's vial could save his soul.

Two men bearing shovels passed silently by and dropped down in the ditch, where they commenced to dig at Rory's grave, their shoveling in the mud keeping cadence with the Father's drone: "Blessed art Thou among women and Blessed is the fruit of thy womb, Jesus. Holy Mary, Mother of God, pray for us sinners now and in the hour of our death. Amen."

And by the time the young Father had finished the anointing ritual, a crowd of the diggers stood milling around over the dead mon's body, until the foreman spoke up. "Excuse me, Mr. Isaacson. We'll need to be gettin' 'em in the ground 'fore he goes and turns on us," he said gently. Monsieur merely nodded in resignation, and as he and Fr. O'Donnell stooped to take Mary by the arms, the foreman turned to the crowd standing around. "And the rest o' you be a gittin' yourselves on to work," he commanded. "Ain't nothin' here none o' your business. You act like you ain't ne'er seen a dead man before."

Lifting poor Mary was like struggling with a wet sack of salt. "Come, Mary, me child," Fr. O'Donnell said. "That's not your Rory a layin' down there. Surely he must be up in heaven with the angels by now. Let's us go on home." And as the crowd slowly began to disperse, the young lad James rose to his feet to confront his boss. "You kin be a kissin' me filthy boot, you sorry..." he hissed, glancing at Mary and me before he said some ting indelicate. "It's a belly full o' this place o' death and mud I've had. I'll be a makin' me way to Texas and I pray I'll never set eyes on Louisiana again!" And with that he merely wandered off, without so much as another word to another person. And as that young mon called James wandered away, reluctantly did Mary allow herself to be led back to the waiting carriage, looking back over her shoulder to that horrid canal all the while.

Once we had her settled in the landau, no sooner were we about to start on our way than I did witness the two gravediggers as they climbed back up on the bank. I shivered like it was cold, as I watched them take Rory's limp, lifeless body and fling it over the side, down into the filthy canal bed, even as Father O'Donnell stood with head bowed, praying over his open prayer book, his stole dancing in a idyllic morning breeze. And how well do I remember looking up to the sky that sad morning, as the carriage wheeled away from that place of so much death and desperation. Swirls of rose and gray and yellow colored the heavens like some ethereal church window. It was indeed a glorious morn, and somehow, for some reason, in my mind there came the refrain from that old Negro spiritual I so often had heard the slaves sing:

> My Lord, what a morning!
> My Lord, what a morning!
> When the stars began to fall.

Wednesday, 11 July 1837

The single peal of the dinner bell in the belvedere above the coach house rang out, as Clyde skillfully directed the team and landau into the passageway. Long ago, in sheer exhaustion, had Mary collapsed against monsieur; now, back at home at last, master did take her in his arms to carry her to her room. I had fully expected to be greeted by Mordecai and Sonnier as we stepped into the courtyard and there they stood, indeed, just outside the back hall door. What surprised me somewhat, however, was the presence of the entire staff, assembled and waiting anxiously. The bell's call to Sonnier and Mordecai had summoned them all. The tired looks on all but Sonnier's sullen face told me they had not slept well, if at all, last night. I followed our monsieur silently, trying not to catch the eye of any of my staff. At the rear stairs, however, Marie stood with Molly Connelley and Patrick O'Bannion. As I reached the stairs, the old cook reached out to me and I saw the supplication in her coal black eyes.

"Mam'oselle, kin it be true?" she implored. "Kin that po' boy be dead this young?"

I chose to answer her with nothing more than a slight nod of my head and old Marie instantly made the Sign of the Cross. Molly gasped and clasped her hand over her mouth as if to keep herself—for once in her life—from uttering so much as a sound. But what I remember most vividly was Patrick O'Bannion's reaction to the news. I wonder, how is it we can be so alike and yet at the same time so different—we mens and womens. Where Marie and Molly reacted to the news with tears and cries of emotion, poor Patrick stomped angrily away. Off across the courtyard he went, his jaw clamped shut, his hands balled into fists of rage. How much did he look like a punch-drunk prizefighter, ready to take on the whole world that morning.

Already was Mon. Isaacson stamping up the stairs with Mary in his arms and I reached out and took Molly and Marie, both, by their arms, turning them toward the stairs. Up we three climbed, behind him. At the top of the stairs, he turned and shuffled sideways as the balcony was so narrow and he did not want to risk striking poor Mary's head against one of the posts. We followed behind and went with him into Mary's room, where he deposited her as gently as he could upon her bed. He stood bent over her, tenderly brushing her hair from her eyes, until I took him by the hand and led him to the door. "Let the ladies get her into her sleeping clothes," I bid him. He nodded and quietly left the room, while I, seeing that Molly and Marie had already begun attending to Mary, followed close behind him.

As we made our way down the balcony to the rear gallery, I could see the stable hands still mulling about down below and I waved them back to their work. Just outside the upstairs hall door, monsieur had collapsed down in his planter's chair. Almost before he hit the seat did Mordecai materialize, extending out one arm of the chair and lifting Mon. Isaacson's leg up on it to remove his mud-caked boots before he entered the house. I warded the valet off with yet another wave of my hand. "Allow us a moment's privacy, si vous voulez." "I'll attend to the monsieur's high shoes. See to it one of the grooms cleans the mud off them, please. They'll no doubt need a fresh coat of boot-black, as well." And as Mordecai left as quietly as an apparition, I knelt before my monsieur to remove his boots for him. "It was you, was it not?" I asked of him, meekly enough I prayed.

At first I thought he was to ignore my question, as he did not answer me forthwith. As I looked up to him, I saw he was rubbing at his eyes with the palms of his hands. Only when I yanked his boot off and he noticed me looking to him did it dawn on him that I had spoken. "What is it?" he asked absently.

I turned my attention to his other shoe, extending out the other chair arm and resting his leg thereon, before I replied, "I know it was you who sent that poor boy to work in that awful swamp." Not a word did he breathe in his defense. Not a sound was to be heard, save my fiddling with his footwear. "But you needn't worry yourself on my part," I went on. "I know my place in this house. Can't anyone say I don't. Still and all, I know what I know."

"Are you suggesting I am responsible for that man's death? Do you actually think he caught the malaria from me?" he responded, most defensively.

"That poor girl in her room back there did so love that boy. I know this for a fact. This is going to take her a long time to get over, I tink. But she'll be getting over it. Sooner if not later." I tugged off the left boot and neatly placed it with the other beside his chair. And before I stood back up, I did look up to him as I wiped the mud from my hands on my dress. "And once she be over all this misery, I reckon it would be good for you if you were to find both those Irish girls another house. I hate to say so, but I told you there would be no good to come from them being in here with the rest of us. Now it's come to pass." For a moment there, Mon. Isaacson said not a word, not a syllable to me, he merely sat with his leg propped up on the long chair arm studying me. Then his gaze did drop down to my dress and muddy hands.

"Look what you've done there. You've ruined your dress, Amanda."

I looked down at my muddied frock, then stood and looked him straight in his eyes. "Some tings, monsieur, are easy enough laundered out in the wash. Still other tings aren't." Then, I turned and walked away from my master with my dignity intact. Subservient though my position here may have become, some business just needs to get said sometimes. At the hall door, I hesitated a moment, then turned back to the monsieur, still sitting in his planter's chair, staring at his damp stocking feet. "You expect me to see to it your house runs smooth. Please don't go showing partiality by hanging 'round that poor girl anymore. Even darkies got eyes. Causes too much grumbling and mumbling when a master goes to showing favor. Besides which, that young girl's not going to be interested in the stars in your eyes any time soon. Not with what she just been through." And as I stepped through the door and made my way down the upstairs hall, whilst passing the monsieur's room I spied the oil lamp on his bureau, taking notice how the glass was all dulled with soot. Exhausted though I was, I knew sleep would not come that morning so I snatched it up and hurried down the stairs. Here was a little chore that could occupy a small portion of my waking hours. Here was a little chore that perhaps could dilute the hard feelings toward my master that were fermenting in my mind that morning.

To Sonnier's pantry did I take the oil lamp. There I sat myself at the tiny table where I cleaned the globe and took a pair of scissors to the wick. Only the day before had I cleaned that lamp and given it a new wick; but Mon. Isaacson did read for so long at a time by that lamplight, that the glow that had once danced so brightly in the dark, soon grew dim and wavering. Only would the trimming of the remains of that which had once glimmered so brightly return the radiance that had been. As I sat there, clipping at the wick, Sonnier did crawl into the room. He was as cross as cottonmouth; that I could tell by his walk, and I vowed to myself to give him none of my attention.

From the silver drawer did he extract master's set of pearl-handled carving knives. He laid them on the table and took a seat across from me where he went about sharpening the blades with his whetting stone. I had just finished with the wick and was in the process of replacing the globe when I heard him speak up, to mumble as if to no one in particular. "She layin' up there plumb prostrate with the grief!" he griped. "You ax me, she so in love with that boy, why she always be carryin' on so around Mast Isaacson?"

I took a deep breath and tried to calm myself, but I was tired from lack of sleep. I could no longer overlook Sonnier's sourness. I would no longer overlook it. "Sonnier, whatever it is between your monsieur and Miss Dunnigan is their business and their business alone. I would remind you that you are naught but a slave hired out to this house. If you are so unhappy here, I shall be pleased to arrange for you to be returned to old man Duffosat. Otherwise, you shall keep a civil tongue in your mouth. The choice is yours."

Down did he slam his whetting stone; out of the pantry did he storm. I so hoped I had made my feelings on the matter clear, for among slaves in New Orleans, Sonnier was most fortunate, being contracted out to one who had been as kind and compassionate to him as Mon. Isaacson. To be returned to old man Duffosat would be to know a severe whipping at having interrupted the income on his investment the old fellow did so enjoy. Such was a threat I took no pleasure in issuing, but it was high time Sonnier was put in his place. Matters had gotten unsettled enough around this house without his making tings all the worse.

And mon Dieu! What a miserable time the next three weeks would prove to be. Many were the moments I thought I would explode or go screaming berserk, one of the two. How we all worried that the melancholia had so overtaken Mary Dunnigan that it had touched her mind, for she kept to her bed those three whole weeks. Little more did she take than an occasional bite of food or sip of water, and only then when I or Molly or Marie had begged ourselves hoarse to get her to do it. Monsieur did keep his distance from her door, but the longer she lingered in her room, the colder and more callous he grew towards me. By that third week he had grown as sullen and withdrawn as Sonnier himself. And to make matters worse, I could see the effect all this was having on the rest of the staff. To be sure, even the drummers selling their dairy and eggs and vegetables at the back gate appeared so wary that they could not wait to get away from this house. Tings that had never looked brighter had never looked darker.

Or so I thought.

With the passing of the third week, though, circumstances did gradually seem to get brighter again, though not for long. At last did Mary venture forth from her room, on her own, to go straightaway to the Negro kitchen where old Marie did feed her heartily. From that day forward, she was most reserved, yet at the same time pleasant enough, in a strange, subdued manner. Her duties she performed most admirably and without complaint. By and large, though, she kept to herself and made little effort to enter into the ordinary discourse of the household, even during the boisterous meal times in the kitchen. Strangely enough, never once during this time was anyone to hear her even mention Rory O'Kelley's name in passing. Never once! I was relieved enough to have her up and about, yet at the same time did I still harbor concerns over the soundness of her mind.

To be sure, there was nothing wrong with her appetite, for old Marie remarked to me that she had trouble filling the child up at times. Still, it was plain there was a great suffering she was enduring in self-imposed isolation. To Dr. Penney did I turn for advice, and he explained that the melancholy oft times works on people like that: they eat to forget, and the more they do eat, the more they gain weight. The more weight they gain, the sadder they become. In turn, the sadder they become, the more their appetite does increase, until they find themselves caught up in an awful downward spiral.

Like a drowning person caught in one of the Mississippi's whirlpools, they just get overpowered and pulled under by the intensity of the situation.

That same Saturday that Mary ventured out of her room for the first time in those three weeks, she came to me, once her chores had been completed. Humbly, she inquired if she might have a lift downtown to take some money from her bank account and do a bit of shopping. Inasmuch as I, myself, had fancied some buying that same day, I invited her to ride with me and together Clyde chauffeured the two of us to Barrone Street. I went with Mary into the monsieur's Canal Bank and Trust, where she withdrew a bit or two from her account. As we turned to leave, my eyes did spy him, standing in the door to his big, handsome office, in discussion with one of his underlings. Mary never acknowledged his presence. I know not if she even saw him standing there. Monsieur, I was to notice, did discreetly flash several glances in her direction, but otherwise made not a move, said not a word to either of us.

It was into Miss Julia's boutique—an establishment clearly catering to the carriage trade—that Mary followed me, but I said nothing about it to her; surely she would learn soon enough that the merchandise in such a top-drawer store as Miss Julia's was far too expensive for a housemaid's purse, I thought to myself. Once inside the store, we parted company and went about our own shopping. For some while did I wander the aisles, admiring and picking out the latest accessories that caught my fancy. And once my account had been signed, I was surprised to find it took two porters to carry all my purchases out to the carriage. Clyde helped load my many totes and boxes up front near him, then helped me aboard, where I was further surprised to find Mary Dunnigan holding nothing more for her shopping than the tiniest of paper sacks.

"Miss Dunnigan, what is it you've spent your money on in such a little sack as that? Diamonds?" I teased at her. For the first time in so long was I to see that child smile.

"No. Corset laces," she said shyly.

"Corset laces!" I laughed. "Why in the world do you need corset laces?"

"Because your waist is tinier than mine," she replied, looking away from me as she did. "The laces to the corset you gave me are too short."

"What corset?" I asked, somewhat confused. "The one I gave you to wear with that opera gown Mon. Isaacson had made for you?"

"Yes."

For once, I guess I must have understood how it was poor Molly Connelley must so often feel when I heard my response flow off my tongue, as involuntarily as my heart does beat. "Sacre blur!" I heard myself declaring, "You've only worn that dress once in your life. I can't imagine why you'd worry about coming to town to buy new laces for a used corset!"

"Well.... One never knows. Maybe I'll be a wearin' it again someday. Before too long." It was all she was to say, and so softly at that. Instantly, I knew I must have offended her. I wished for the world I'd not said what I did, but I had. There was no taking it back now, though. Mary Dunnigan had neither the fancy wardrobe necessitating a corset, nor the prospect of ever having one, and I had thrown it up in her face. How I wished I had not said what I said.

We both jerked a little in our seats as Clyde pulled the team away from the curb, and I can still see Mary Dunnigan sitting there on our monsieur's fine leather upholstery, in her plain little frock, holding her little bag in her bare hands. It was a fine fall afternoon, that day. Sunny and pleasant. I raised my parasol to shade my face from the sun. Mary did not have even so much as have a sunshade to keep the sun off her porcelain white nose, not even a proper pair of gloves to cover her hands in public! And here she was wasting her precious money on corset laces—and in a shop as fancy as Miss Julia's, at that. What a peculiar bunch they are—these Irish ones—I remember tinking to myself. All that way to town had Mary gone, and for what? A sack of corset laces!

Now what do you suppose, you who perchance may be reading these words of mine? The very morning of this entry had I gone to Mary's room, just to check on tings, to see nothing was disturbed. Nothing was, everything was in order. Yet, on the sunny sill to the window overlooking the great oak across the back street was that necklace, right where Mary had last left it, boxed up in the black velvet case. And up there atop her chiffonier what should I spy, save a little dish full of corset laces. I tell you, the place left me feeling all empty inside, and so, with nothing left to build on in that room, I did summon Clyde from the stables to install a lock on Mary's door, that her room might remain just as it was. I know not what it was that drove me to have her door secured. Somehow this morning, it just seemed the fitting to do so.

Tuesday, 18 July 1837

I tink the climate in New Orleans must be ideal for every living creature except the human being—except in the fall.

In the fall the rains cease, the air dies out and the temperature lingers most comfortable. I love the fall in New Orleans; there is no other place on the earth I'd rather be that time of year. Maybe it was the weather that made tings around the house a little more settled, a little less disturbed; maybe it was the pleasant weather, then, at least in part. Mary Dunnigan continued in her quiet ways, but at least we were subjected to no outward displays of anguish on her part. That, in itself, was a blessing. And the untimely death of pitiful Rory O'Kelley, by then, seemed to have died out of most everyone's mind.

Oh, but how it grabs hold of you, when death comes calling that close to you like that. But I suspect people are formidable in that respect, and even death cannot hold us in its woeful grip for too long at a time. Too much is the worry life gives us in our day-to-day existing, for us to go on and on, moping over the passing of someone else. No, death throws a splash of cold water over our nice, warm nest; wakes us up to that we would rather sleep through. But in the end, our cocoons soon dry out in the dependable old sun, and we quickly get back to our slumbering through this life. Another's death is never as significant to us as the thought of our own, I suspect.

And so it was those fine days of the long shadows that Mary Dunnigan, to all outward appearances, did seem to be coping remarkably well. Trouble is, fall too soon gives way to the winter, and winters in New Orleans—though blessedly short—can be dreary. With the shorter and shorter days came the rains and biting, wet winds howling down out of the north.

It was about that time that I was to notice a change come over Mary; not a change in her emotions but a physical change. I would catch her struggling to get to her feet after scrubbing the floor, so low was her stamina. Her appetite remained fine, yet she was susceptible to waves pf nausea. And her back seemed to always be bothering her. Marie and I determined she was just run down and did need a good cleaning out of her system and a dose of tonic. We sought to have her partake of one of Marie's remedies, but she would have none of it.

Even Dr. Penney did send her a bottle of the latest tonic he made up special for her—made from the tomato, of all tings! Now, everyone knows tomatoes to be highly poisonous, but the old physician made up a dose of medicine called catchup and sent it over for Mary to take, anyway. I tell you, sometimes I question Dr. Penney's propensity to prescribe poisons; I, myself, am much more comfortable with old Marie's remedies than his modern ones.

Naturally, Mary wanted nothing to do with the stuff, it having tomatoes in it and all. Still, we wished she would at least let the doctor take a look at her, but she would hear nothing of it and we did not press the issue. After all, maybe it was nothing more than the despondency brought on by all she had been through of late. The melancholy can do that to you if you let it stay inside you too long. Or maybe it was just the dreary winter weather: I tell you, the lack of sunshine in the winter is enough to put a bad cloud over any soul. So I thought not much more of it, then, there being no change in the quality of Mary's work. What of it, if it took her a little longer some days to do her work? When she left a room, it would be as immaculate as ever. Better still, the monsieur seemed to have found the proper place to put her in his mind. Fewer and fewer were the little glances I was to see him toss at her. Less and less did he even acknowledge her when he would pass her in the halls. Of course, I would have preferred he had sent she and Molly packing by then, but such was not to be, I could tell. So, we all went about our lives, doing that which we had been placed on this earth to do, within the time we had been allotted to do it. One day had a way of melding into another, but at least all was mostly quiet and ordered around the place for a change.

Before I knew it, Christmastime was upon us, and that Christmas Eve when we returned from Mass, the entire staff gathered—as was our custom—out in the Negro kitchen, where we shared a feast of wild ducks, sweetbreads, stuffed merletons, dirty rice dressing, and candied sweet potatoes. Monsieur allowed no Christmas festivities to spill over into the main house, but he was kind enough to allow us to celebrate in the kitchen. There, in the corner, we would gather to sing our carols and laugh. Always there would be a big fire roaring in the massive fireplace and old Marie would shovel heaps of hot coals out onto the hearth, on which she would put vessels of foods to cook, and everyone would fuss at her not to set the helm of her dress afire. The old kitchen was always warm and smelled of smoke, especially in the dead of winter. Packed to the brim with the staff, it could get so stifling we would open all the French doors onto the courtyard, our laughter and gaiety spilling out the doors with the smoky warmth.

Outside, a cold and heavy fog hung low to the ground, while inside the kitchen all was warm and cozy and joyous. There, in the midst of our celebration, I found my mind wandering to my Etienne, and I did long for the morrow that would bring him knocking at the front door, bearing me gifts and bidding me a Happy Christmas. Right then and there I did daydream of that knock at the door, until a ringing at the back gate interrupted my musings. The younger of the two footmen jumped from his stool and hurried out into the cold and damp to tend to the call and I thought not much more of it until a short time later when I did notice Mary Dunnigan's face light up.

Throughout the night, I had glanced at her, from time-to-time, sitting to herself in the corner. I had been pleased to see she could smile and laugh with the rest of us, even if she was far more reserved in her enthusiasm. Now, her face fairly radiated with delight. I looked to see what could be causing her such joy and there I did see skinny Patrick O'Bannion standing in the open doorway and shivering, a pad of drawing paper clutched under his arm. Amid all the commotion of our frivolity, he did unceremoniously make his way to Mary at the back of the room, beckoning Molly on with him as he did. Over the clamor of the room I could not tell what was being said amongst the three of them, but I saw Patrick take out a sheet of paper and present it to

Molly. Her squeal brought a hush over the room, as she and Mary studied the paper as attentively as if it were a holy relic. "Look what Patrick's given me fer a Christmas present!" Molly shrieked, holding up for all to see a drawing of her as real as any I could ever hope to imagine.

The room burst into babble, as everyone vied to see Molly's drawing up closer. To Mary he handed a similar sheet and she threw her head back and laughed out loud. Holding her present aloft, she showed to all the picture of her that Patrick had drawn. I remember being struck by how beautiful she was in his drawing, as the staff clamored to see Mary's picture as well. During all the commotion, I tink I must have been the only one to see Patrick pull a chair up in front of Mary. He swung one of his long, lanky legs over the back and plopped down directly across from her. The slightest of smiles occupied his face as he stared at the girl, all the while fumbling in his cloak pocket. He took out a tiny package wrapped up in newsprint and tied with a red ribbon. To Mary he handed it and she did look questioningly at him, before tearing into the package like a little child would. Instantly, the content of the package brought a well of tears up in her eyes, as she looked up to Patrick with trembling hands. Even Molly Connelley could not conceal her emotions, as Mary showed her the tiny oil-on-porcelain painting of Rory O'Kelley that Patrick had done for her. When I finally got to examine it, I tell you it did make my blood run cold, so realistic was it, and thereafter I had to move my chair nearer the fire to warm my very bones.

For a while, I was afraid Mary Dunnigan would flee the room in tears once again and ruin everyone's Christmas celebration, but Mordecai did save the day when he stood and shouted over the roar. "Looky here, Mr. Mon," he said to Patrick, "why ya don't draw my picher?" Goaded on by the others, Patrick thankfully obliged, flipping open his pad and sketching away in broad strokes with a charcoal pencil.

And the roar that went up from that room! The laughter and hollering that went up when he held up his sketch of Mordecai was deafening, for what he had drawn was a most stylized, humorous and simple sketch of the mon. Few tings have I found as funny as that picture of Mordecai, with his most prominent features so exaggerated like the political cartoons in the newspaper Mon. Isaacson does read. His skinny neck was all the longer, like a chicken's. His big ears were huge and he wore a smile that covered most of his face. Pandemonium broke out, as each one beseeched young Patrick to sketch him or her. Of course he obliged, and the whole event soon turned into a big, wonderful game, as the one being sketched would sit in front whilst the others would congregate behind Patrick and squeal and horselaughing with every stroke he took. I did say to myself how I did pity those poor, stubborn protestants who steadfastly refused to celebrate the day of our Lord's birth, for I tell you I cannot remember the old kitchen ever being merrier than it was that evening; that is until Patrick was showing off his sketch of old Marie bent over the fireplace, stirring a pot, her backside most prominently displayed.

As I was wiping tears of laughter from my eyes, I looked up and did happen to notice Mon. Isaacson standing in the doorway bearing a huge basket of the freshest and most luscious fruits fresh off the boat from Central America. On his arm, he did escort Miss Myna Goldstein, dressed to the nines in yards and yards of deep green velvet and gold tassels. On her head she wore a fine bonnet sporting some of the rarest and most beautiful bird feathers I have ever seen. It was a most stylish couple they made, and Miss Myna did look to me and offer me a long, low bow of her head, which I returned to her. It did my heart good to see my master there, in the presence of a fine woman of his own status in life. Was it too much to hope that he had gotten over his lusting after poor Mary Dunnigan? I wondered.

He held high the basket of fruit he carried and cried out, "For your enjoyment! Happy Holiday to you all!" And as he sat the basket on the table, all scrambled to claim a piece of the precious fruits of winter. Everyone, that is, except for Patrick O'Bannion, who quickly scooped up his pad and pencil and slipped quickly and quietly out of the room. He did not even take the time to bid Mary farewell, he merely hurried forth, stabbing the monsieur through the heart with a cold and hateful glare I caught from out the corner of my eye. Could it be that skinny boy I had seen hanging around the great oak across the back street; that skinny boy who had brought Mary the news of her Rory's abduction; that skinny boy I'd encountered loitering in the courtyard the morning we brought Mary home from the digger's camp—could it be that skinny boy knew of Mon. Isaacson's role in that whole sordid affair? Or, could it be the skinny one was merely displaying petty jealously over master's higher class? The answer I would have in due course, but that Christmas Eve, Patrick O'Bannion—who had brought the room such delight mere moments before—slipped out and disappeared in the dark, misty night. Alone. Unnoticed.

And when I noticed him gone, I hated it, for I did fear he had left on an empty stomach, to return home to cold and empty room. It was Christmastime, and the bounty of our table had hardly been touched; surely if ever there was a night when even one who had entered this kitchen as a pauper should have feasted like a king, this was it. Now, it was too late for that. The opportunity to turn a good deed had been lost, overshadowed by the grand entrance monsieur and Miss Myna did make.

So, it was that Christmas came and went. A few days after the first of the year, a killing frost came our way. The banana trees—brought back by monsieur from one of his plantations in Jamaica—which had shaded that corner of the courtyard adjacent to the Negro kitchen, turned to mush and collapsed to the ground. We cut the stalks off at the ground level and burned them out in the back street. As stark as the grounds did look then, in four weeks, the world once again turned green, and even the banana trees began to send forth a new generation of shoots, from roots buried deep in the warm, friendly earth. At long last did the very air smell fresh and clean, most pleasant to breathe. Yet, amid all the joy and anticipation only rebirth can offer, our contentment was to be disturbed by Mary Dunnigan's deteriorating condition. By spring, even her work had begun to suffer as her endurance waned. Although she did protest to the contrary, it was evident to all she was in pain most of the time, yet she would have none of our offers of help, and spent much of her time in bed, sobbing and talking to herself like she had left her mind.

It would be on the morning of the first of May that all would come to a head, for on that day Mary's deep, dark secret—indeed the very one she had sought to share with Rory his last day on this earth—could be hidden no longer.

Friday, 21 July 1837

It had started out a quiet enough spring morning, a morning not the least exceptional in any outward respect. A breeze as gentle as a baby's breath played with the lace in the opened windows. Outside, Carondelet Street was just beginning to show signs of life and the blue jays fussed at the passers-by who strolled too near their nests in the sweet olives. Monsieur and I stood conferring in the library about plans for the Seder meal that evening. Sundown would mark the beginning of the Sabbath, and since Miss Myna Goldstein and her parents were to be guests at his table, master was most eager that all should go well. Out in the stair hall, unbeknownst to either of us, Mary went about cleaning one of monsieur's costly crystal oil lamps—imported from Germany, no less—but otherwise, our world was as quiet as it usually was, early of a weekday morning.

Then, just as the monsieur had finished promising me that before he left for the bank he would visit the wine cellar and set aside the selection he wished to serve that evening, suddenly there came a loud crash out in the hall. We did look up at each other in surprise, each asking with our eyes what such a clamor could have been. Silence preceded the crash for a brief instant, followed close by an unmistakable cry of pain. Monsieur and I both hit the door at the same time. There at the far end of the hall lay the crystal oil lamp, shattered in a million pieces on the floor, the expensive whale oil from it spilt all over. My first reaction was that the oil had ruined monsieur's beautiful Persian carpet, but before I could react to admonish, my eyes found a most ghastly expression on Mary Dunnigan's face.

Indeed, she did lean unsteadily against the console on which the lamp had rested, clutching at her stomach and trembling. Even more to my horror, I was to notice that she appeared to have wet on herself and she did look most pitifully and imploringly to me, before being overcome with yet another fit of the moaning, then collapsed to the glass-strewn floor. The blink of an eye caught us hovering over her, begging her to tell us what ailed her, but Mary was incapable of speaking, so bad was her distress. From the dining salon, Sonnier rushed out into the hall to see what the matter was. "Go!" I shouted to him. "Bring Dr. Penney!" Without so much as a word, he ran full speed from the house and down the street to the old doctor's residence three blocks away. Monsieur did move to take Mary in his arms as I directed him to the library. "On the divan," I told him.

Soon the hall outside the library was filled with the staff, standing about and asking to what the commotion could be. Spying poor Mary laid out on the couch, old Marie prayed aloud in a singsong chant until finally, Sonnier returned with Dr. Penney. Quickly was the old mon at the stricken Mary's side, his black bag popped opened and placed strategically by his side. "What seems to be the matter?" he asked, looking directly at me.

"We found her clutching her stomach and moaning. Then she fell out. I don't know…"

Dr. Penney rolled up his sleeves and made to palpitate Mary's stomach, only to recoil in astonishment. "This woman's stomach is hard as a rock!' He exclaimed, then looked to the monsieur: "Leave us, sir. I must examine her. Mademoiselle, you stay and help me," he said to me. As Mon. Isaacson left the room, I beckoned Marie inside to help and closed the door behind us. Dr. Penney rose from Mary's side and turned his back. He snatched master's lap blanket from off a chair and handed it to me.

"You ladies remove her dress and put this over her," he ordered.

It was with some difficulty that Marie and I were able to get the dress off the girl, so uncooperative was she. Once we had overpowered her, however, and pulled it up and over her head, we could not contain our surprise. Our gasps must have given us away, for instantly did old Dr. Penney turn to see what could be the concern. "For God's sake!" he exclaimed, for without her simple work frock what were we to find but her corset bound up tight around her, cutting sores into her flesh in places. The physician quickly knelled at her side where he looked in wonder at her breasts, examining them from every which direction. Then he looked up to me.

"This woman presents with labor!"

So that explained it. That was why Mary had been feeling so poorly. Now, at last, was her deep, dark secret out in open light. I tell you I could not believe my own ears. And as I looked closely at Mary's swollen, vein-lined breasts, I could not believe my own eyes. Dr. Penney quickly took a pair of scissors from his bag and began to snip at the corset laces. Even before he had finished severing the last lace did Mary's stomach balloon up out of the corset and she did scream in agony. Once he had the corset free of her, he moved at her pelvis to guide her into better light so that he might further examine her. A glance was all he needed for his diagnosis. Dr. Penney turned to Marie, "Fresh sheets! Hot water! Whiskey and string!" he ordered, and old Marie rushed forthwith from the room, almost knocking down our monsieur and some of the others gathered outside the door. The physician turned his gray, wrinkled face to me, "Her water's broken and she's dilated. Probably lost her mucus plug sometime last night. Should be delivering directly."

So astounded was I that I knew not what to say, what to tink. What more could these Irish women bring down on this house, I wondered? And then I remembered the monsieur's fine Persian rug in the hall. I hurried to open the door a crack, just enough to peek through. I called aloud to Sonnier. "Get all that glass up from the hall before someone cuts himself. And take the carpet out back and see if you can get the oil out of it before it's ruined!

The delivery proved to be most difficult, primarily because Mary Dunnigan refused to cooperate with Dr. Penney's instructions. When he would implore her to contract herself, she would ignore him and dig her fingers into the divan, scream and try to cross her legs. I tell you it was as if she wanted to keep the child—her dark secret—buried deep inside her, never to let it lose in the light of day. At long last, Marie and I could subdue her legs and Dr. Penney was forced to reach inside her and extract the infant. And once the baby was at long last delivered, we three were so overcome with exhaustion we could scarcely attend the mother and crying child. A cursory look did the old physician give the infant as he tied off the cord and severed it. He spun around and handed the newborn to me.

"Looks a little premature but healthy enough. Clean him up and get him under covers before he gets chilled. You," he said to Marie, "light that lamp and hold it over here so I can attend to the mother." And as old Dr. Penney and Marie labored to stem the flow of Mary Dunnigan's bleeding and deliver the placenta, I did bathe and bundle the little boy child, although I suppose I was in such a state of shock by the whole affair that I remember almost nothing of it.

I am told that beyond the library, outside in the great hall, it was the baby's own cry that heralded news of what was going on behind the closed library door. The men servants, I am also told, scattered like they'd just been confronted by a spirit. Mon. Isaacson dropped his head and retreated quietly into the front parlor, where he closed the door behind him and took to strong drink. Molly Connelley and Miriam, alone, were left keeping vigil beside the door. And as I bundled the infant in a bed sheet, I grew aware of concern in Dr. Penney's tone.

"Give me the infant!" he demanded of me. I passed him the child and he leaned over Mary to show it to her. "See, my dear. You have a precious baby boy. Now you must listen to me. You must feed the baby," he coaxed her, but Mary Dunnigan recoiled at his suggestion. "Listen to me, young woman! Breast-feeding causes your body to expel the placenta! You must do this, do you understand? We must get all that out of your womb before it makes you very sick. Or you bleed to death."

The old doctor took the infant and guided its little mouth to his mother's breast and as it began to suckle, Mary did at first react most adversely. Yet with Dr. Penney's coaching in his soothing tenor, it was not long before it was obvious how mother and child did bond. Poor, pathetic Mary did cradle her child and weep openly as the little one nursed, all the while Dr. Penney and Marie struggled to free the afterbirth from within her. In time, then, Mary's womb was cleared and her hemorrhaging abridged. Mercifully then did the mother and child soon fade into sleep, as beside them old Marie wadded up a blood-soaked sheet. And as she did, I tell you my heart did sink within my chest, as I saw for the first time that the magnificent, silk damask upholstery on the monsieur's divan was soaked through to the horsehair in Mary Dunnigan's gore.

The arrival of a child is a time for joy, for celebration. This I believe, not only with my heart, but my mind, as well. Yet that May Day morn, there would be no joy, no cause for celebration over the birth of Mary Dunnigan's son. To the contrary, the house grew uncharacteristically quiet that day. What little talking the staff did, they did in brief whispers. As soon as I could steal away from the library, I made rounds, where I told each of the servants, in terms most imperative, that our monsieur was fully capable of dealing with what had transpired under his roof; that it was no concern of theirs. They were, I told them, to go about their business as if nothing had happened and under no circumstances were they to gossip about any of this in front of the neighbors. Then I returned to the library with a drawer from an old bureau.

This I gave to Marie with instructions she should pad it with a blanket to make a crib for the child. On the divan, Mary was dead to the world for all practical purposes. Dr. Penney did inquire as to where Mon. Isaacson was to be found, and I showed him across the hall to the front parlor.

As we entered the room, I closed the door behind us and stepped across the room to slide the great doors to the music room shut, lest some inquisitive one be lurking about with designs on eavesdropping. Dr. Penney poured himself of a glass of bourbon whiskey from monsieur's liquor cabinet, and drank it down before saying a word. "Damnedest thing I believe I ever saw," he seemed to tell the air. "Bound herself up like that thinking no one would ever know she was in a family way. Almost worked too, didn't it? She's a tall woman and it doesn't look like she gained more than ten pounds. Guess she just didn't reckon on the baby ever coming out. Not the wisest thing to do, binding herself up in a corset while she was pregnant. Still, I don't see that she's done herself any life-threatening harm. She must have been in pain these past few months, but she should be better in a few days." Then he turned to monsieur. "I take it, Hiam, the woman is unmarried?" Monsieur merely nodded his head whilst I took a seat nearby. "The father would be that boy that died of malaria out by the canal?" Again, did the monsieur nod his head.

"Undoubtedly," he replied quietly, almost in a whisper.

"Shame. A crying shame, that's what it is. What will become of her?" he asked of Mon. Isaacson. "You know you can't let her stay here. Not after all that's gone on around here this morning?"

Master did look up with surprise to the physician. What would you have me do? Put a mother and child out on the street?"

"No! Certainly not. In a day or so she can be moved from your library. I suggest you have one of the nunneries come around and pick them up then. Let those two be their problem."

For the first time in hours, I remembered the evening's dinner plans. "Dr. Penney, you can't expect that woman to remain in the library! Monsieur is expecting guests this evening." I explained, but master did hold up his hand to me.
"No. We shall cancel this evening's plans."

"Cancel? At this late hour? What will you tell the Goldstein's? No monsieur, it's too late for that," I insisted.

"Not to worry, I'll take care of it. I'll just have to tell them what has happened. And Doctor, do you really think bringing the nuns into all this would be in Miss Dunnigan's best interest."

"Of course I do!" exploded old Dr. Penney. "My heavens man! What else can you do? That's an unmarried woman in there with a bastard child," he said, bending over toward master and pointing in the direction of the library door. "You can't have someone like that living under your roof. People will talk. People will start to wonder who the father is. They'll wonder if it's you! Once word gets out about what took place here this morning, they'll be wondering about your role in all this anyway, I imagine. Folks are like that: they gossip sometimes.

They imagine the worst. No, it just won't do. You need to get that woman and her child out of your house with all haste."

Mon. Isaacson then took to studying his hands, and when he did, my heart fairly sank. He always studies his hands when he's going over tings in his mind. What could there be for him to 'tink over, I wondered? Surely this had been the last straw. Master's great Irish experiment had been an unfortunate failure. That much must be evident, even to him. What could there possibly be for him to tink over? Then and there I did determine that I, myself, would visit old Mother Superior before the sun had set on that day. If master was hesitant about Mary Dunnigan's future, I was not. I could not—I would not—sit idly by and watch these Irish women destroy my master's good name.

Once Dr. Penney had gone, I turned to Mon. Isaacson. "Monsieur," said I, "You know we cannot leave that woman in the library. Even if there's no company coming tonight we can't leave her there. Besides which, I do fear she has ruined the upholstery on the divan."

"The divan can be reupholstered," he sighed. "I hardly think Miss Dunnigan is in any condition to be climbing stairs right now."

"No, but I'll have her put in a chair. The stable hands are strong mens. They can carry her to her room. In a chair," I said, and then left the room. I knew the divan could be reupholstered. That was not the point, though.

I returned to the library where I ordered Marie to go and fetch Mary's gown. "Let's get her dressed. She can't stay here in the monsieur's library like this. And on your way back, go by the coach house and have Clyde send his two strongest boys to carry her up to her room." I could tell by her expression that Marie had reservations about my orders, but she obeyed me without protest, like the trained and loyal retainer that she was. Old Marie was from the old school, you see. She was not like those Irish women bringing all this trouble on our house. By the time she returned, I had the baby bundled up and sleeping in the drawer and a nice, solid, high back chair drawn up close to the divan.

I jerked the sheet off Mary and shook her to rouse her. "Come Miss Dunnigan," I said to her. "Help us to get your gown over you. It's time we were getting you back to your own room. We had managed to get the gown over her head and her arms through the sleeves when there came a knocking at the door. It was the groomsmen sent to carry Mary upstairs. "Attendre un minute, plait," I called to them.

Together Marie and I swung Mary's' legs from the divan, turned her around and lifted her to her feet. As Marie held on to her, I saw to it her gown was pulled down around her, before further draping her in the sheet. Slowly, ever so cautiously we guided her into the waiting armchair. Once she was seated, I called for the groomsmen. It was obvious they would have rather be anywhere than in the room with Mary, but one obediently took the back of the chair whilst the other took the two front legs. Gently did they lean the chair backwards, then lifted it up and bore it on out of the room, up the grand stairs and down the rear balcony to her room in the servant's wing. Old Marie followed behind, bearing the baby boy fast asleep in the drawer.

Once we had Mary Dunnigan in her own bed and settled, I eventually returned to the library to check on the divan. I had been right. It was ruined. It might as well be thrown out in the street, I thought. A fine, modern lamp shattered; an expensive Persian carpet oil stained; and now this—monsieur's elegant divan soiled with the blood of a bastard's birth! Old Mother Superior would be receiving a visit from me, all right. Just as soon as the monsieur had left for the bank, I would be leaving for the convent. That I did promise myself.

The trouble was, Mon. Isaacson had been so consumed by the morning's unfortunate affair that he had sent word to the bank he would not be coming in that day. He had barricaded himself in his library, as he so often did when he had matters to tink through. This I knew, because when I came with the groomsmen to take away the soiled divan, I caught him sitting at his desk staring out the window. As soon as we did enter the room, he made like he was busy with paper work on his desk. "Veuillez m' excuser, monsieur," I said, trying to sound as cheerful as possible under the circumstances. "We are here to take out the divan.

He looked up from his papers. "Where are you taking that?"

"Out, sir. I fear it is ruined. And we wouldn't want it to cause flies, would we?"

Old Marie had worked over the couch for some time, rubbing in a special paste of ash, vinegar and clear water, and had succeeded in taking out much of the stain, but too much discoloration remained. Monsieur said not a word, he just returned to the papers he only pretended to study, as the boys effortlessly hoisted the couch up and bore it out of the library. At the rear gallery, I instructed them to take it out back and break it up and send for someone to carry it away. "And when you are through, one of you come to my chambers. I shall have a message for you to deliver," I told them.

Upstairs in my room, I took my place at my desk and took out a sheet of writing paper. Taking quill in hand, I then did write a note to old Mother Superior, explaining all that had transpired that very morning—of how Mary Dunnigan had sought to deceive us by binding herself up so we would not see she was bastard-pregnant. I told of how she had gone into labor, doing much irreparable damage to master's residence, and causing him to incur the expense of old Dr. Penney's services. In conclusion, I implored her to come without delay and retrieve the mother and ill-gotten child from Mon. Isaacson's respected home, before his reputation should be further tarnished. I was sealing the envelope when the older of the grooms did tap at my door.

"Here. Take this and deliver it into the hands of the Mother Superior at the Sisters of the Poor. Tell no one of this, do you understand?" I questioned him, then put a shiny new penny into his hands. And as the groom hurried away, I sighed to myself: maybe at long last this was the incident that would get these Irish women out of this house.

For once and for always.

Saturday, 22 July 1837

Old Mother Superior arrived in a huff late that same afternoon. As I opened the door to her knock, I was greeted by the expression of no quarter she wore upon her face. Her stiff back told me there would be hell for Mary Dunnigan to pay for such a transgression against God and Mon. Hiam Isaacson. Not a word had she to say to me, as I stepped aside to allow her into the great hall. I motioned to the library door and she followed silently behind, her chin held high in the air. I knocked. No response came from within. I knocked again and then eased the door ajar. "Je vous demande pardon, monsieur."

It was not yet sundown that Friday afternoon, but already was master preparing for his Sabbath. In his hand he held his prayer book, upon his head he wore his yarmulke and he stood frozen in the act of draping his prayer shawl around his shoulders. Mon. Isaacson was obviously about to leave for the synagogue. After services, he would return home on foot, where, as usual, he would find his dinner set out and waiting for him in the dining room. He reacted with some annoyance when he saw Mother Superior follow me into the room.

"What is the meaning of this?" he demanded. "Can you not see I am about to leave for services?" How I wished I had asked the old nun not to come until after the Sabbath, but in my anger over the day's happenings, it had slipped my mind, so upset had I been that monsieur had been forced to cancel his Seder dinner with Miss Myna and her parents. But Mother Superior was there, and there could be no turning back then.

Forgive us, monsieur. Mother Superior has come calling about Mary Dunnigan." The nun was not nearly so timid as I was, however.

"I came as soon as I got the word, sir," she declared most curtly. "Please accept my apology for all the inconvenience Miss Dunnigan has caused you. And rest assured I shall see to it she and that…child!…are removed from your home first thing tomorrow." There came a long, most uncomfortable pause as the monsieur did study Mother Superior through squinted eyes, before hiking up his prayer shawl around his neck.

"You will do nothing of the kind," he responded softly but coldly.

"Beg your pardon, sir?" she asked in disbelief.

"I said you'll do nothing of the kind. Show up here tomorrow morning and you shall be turned away. Miss Dunnigan is in no condition to be moved around like some animal. And if and when she decides to leave this house, it will be of her own volition. Do I make myself clear?" He pitched a choleric look upon me, "Ladies?"

Mother Superior turned to me as if she could not believe her own ears, as if she had been most grievously affronted. The look upon her face did implore me to intervene. "Monsieur, you can't be imagining you'll let that woman stay here?" I said hesitantly.

"I think my position is clear enough. You would both do well to remember this is my house and I—and I alone! —decide who is or is not welcome in it. If Miss Dunnigan wishes to leave, she is free to go. Otherwise, I will not tolerate either of you making her uncomfortable for being here." Then again, he did look directly, intently at me. "She has as much right as anyone to be here, in my home. Now, if you will excuse me, I must be off."

"But sir!" Mother Superior persisted. "We are talking about an illegitimate child here. It's not right, your having to harbor a wayward mother and child under your roof. And the child! This is a human being, sir. This child can't be left to grow up a... To..." The old nun struggled to find the right words. "To grow up without benefit of a surname. The little one must be taken away now, while it's still young enough to be put out for adoption. Into a fine, Catholic home that can give him sustenance and a good name!"

"Sister, none of us have any right to make such a decision. Whatsoever. That child has been freeborn to Miss Dunnigan, and any and all decisions about its future are hers and hers alone. Not yours. Not mine. Not even the Catholic Church's. Now, enough said, already!" With that, master did make his way from the room, only to be stopped at the door by Mother Superior's further query.

"Mr. Isaacson, please. According to our faith, Miss Dunnigan's soul is in peril. It is imperative that she confesses her sin. Won't you allow a priest to come for that purpose? At lease? Or do you also dictate how and when one attends to the will of their God?" Master gripped the doorknob so hard I saw his knuckles turn white. Slowly did he revolve around to the Mother Superior, his face flushed with anger.

"Madam, what Mary Dunnigan—or anyone else in this house—does in the exercise of religion is of no concern to me. If she wishes to give confession, you may rest assured one of my servants will summon the proper clergy for her. Now, I bid you a good day. Miss Maneau will show you the way out." And with that, he turned and departed from the room.

Old Mother Superior peered at me with a look on her face like she had just argued with a demon. "Never have I been spoken down to like that! That... Man!" she managed to say through teeth gritted in ire. "My child, you must intercede—" But I could not let her finish.

"Mother Superior, I do appreciate your concern. And I share your views on Miss Dunnigan. But I do know our monsieur. It would be better if we gave him a few days to calm down. Let him tink a little clearer. However, I will approach Miss Dunnigan about confession. You may send a priest around on Monday during the day. While monsieur is by the bank."

She could do nothing more than wobble her head in agreement. "I suppose you're right. Still, we need to get the child to Maison l'Infants while there's still time to adopt him out. It'll do no good to let him get so big he'll just spend the rest of his life in the orphanage, without a name to call his own."

I gently took the old nun by the arm and guided her toward the door. I too shared her frustration, perhaps even more so. Just a few hours earlier and I had been convinced today's incident would at long last get these Irish women out of the house. How wrong I felt I had been. I bid Mother Superior Godspeed at the door and watched as she made her way down the walk. She who so loved a crusade would be forced to sit this one out.

Thus it was, that, much to my own dejection, I was to stand helplessly by and watch old Dr. Penney visit Mary and her child each morning, to check on their progress. Such was monsieur's wish. Just as it had been Monsieur's wish that Molly Connelley be taken off her regular chores and charged with making sure mother and child were comfortable at all times. Just as it had been Monsieur's wish that he should visit Mary's room twice each day, to comfort her, to assure her she and her bastard had a home under his roof for as long as they wanted.

I suppose no life ever truly escapes the trying times, but it did seem to me my trials and tribulations now were most overwhelming. How had all this happened? How had it come to pass that I had lost control of the house that had been my life's work? My destiny, no less. How had it come to pass that I had lost the affection of the one who had given me life in the first place, even if he was never to own up to it? During these days, I kept my profile most low and did work most resolutely to see that the household did run smoothly. But I labored, as well, to avoid his presence; sometimes at night I would fall asleep on my pillow dreaming of my old neighborhood in Kingstown.

One week to the day following the child's birth, however, monsieur did summon me to his library, just after one of his visits to check on Mary Dunnigan. It was with dread and trepidation that I entered that room, but there I found him sitting in his reading chair, perusing the day's newspaper. The air smelled of his cigar smoke and for the first time do I remember finding it repugnant to my senses, so low had monsieur fallen in my estimation.

"You wished to see me?" I asked as softly as I could.

He looked up to me and answered as casually as if nothing had ever happened in this house, as if Mary Dunnigan had never driven that wedge between us. "Oh, there you are. See here, I want you to prepare the yellow guest room for Miss Dunnigan. See to it her things are moved in there and put away. And then I want you to go into town and buy a proper crib for the little one. It's disgraceful, that infant sleeping in an old drawer like that."

For the longest have I sat here at my desk, trying to remember whether I said any ting to monsieur. I don't recall I did; I don't believe I was capable of responding, so shocked was I. I must have been repulsed at the very idea of Mon. Hiam Isaacson moving such a woman into his house-proper. Yet, at the same time, I tink I knew I was defeated. I remember feeling I could not be long for staying in this house under such conditions. What I do recall clearly, however, is finding Molly Connelley in the upstairs hall. "Come along, Miss Connelley," I charged her. "Monsieur wants that we should pack up Miss Dunnigan's room and move her tings into the front guest suite." But she pulled up short, even as I continued down the hall.

I turned back to her, inquiring by my manner as to what her problem could be, that she could not follow along beside me. I fear she'll be a havin' none o' that, I'm a tellin' you, ma'am," I heard Molly say, almost defiantly and I tilted my head to the side, more confused than ever. "Mr. Isaacson's done gone and proposed marriage to her! Got her in a real state, he has. I just left the poor soul a cryin' her eyes out."

"Marriage?" I gasped, feeling myself grow suddenly light-headed, grasping at the wall for support.

"That he did. And Mary? She would've turned him down flat, right then and there. Only he told her to take her time and think it over. Now she don't know what she's to do. She can't be a stayin' on here and she's got no wheres to go. It's breakin' me heart, all this is!" And Molly began to sob.

That same evening, after taking dinner in my chamber, I was sitting at my vanity brushing my hair when there came a tapping at my door. "Entrer dans," said I, trying to be pleasant, even brave, knowing full well there was only one person who could be knocking at my door at that hour. Monsieur entered my chambers and stood behind me where he could see my face in the looking glass.

"When I left this morning, I gave orders for you to move Miss Dunnigan and her things into the yellow guest room," he said, matter-of-factually.

"Yes," I answered softly. "I heard you. I went into town this afternoon and found a lovely crib for the baby. It has a canopy with mosquito netting and all. It's to be delivered tomorrow morning."

"Fine. Now maybe you can explain why you disobeyed me and did not move Mary's.... Miss Dunnigan's things."

It tore at my heartstrings to realize monsieur knew well how much torment this Mary Dunnigan caused me, but that he did not care. Or at least he cared more for her serenity than for mine. All too often there comes a time when one must come to grips with the fact that their discord means little to another, and to continue battling over it is futile. All too often does there come a time when the best one can do is change tactics and try to reason with the other. This was one of those times. Monsieur Isaacson had to be cognizant of my feelings in this whole, sordid matter and to further express them would have only had the reverse effect from what I sought. Thus, did I resort to reason. I laid my brush gently upon the table, and breathed an audible sigh as I considered his reflection in my mirror.

"Monsieur, you know I mean you no disrespect" I carefully wrapped my approach in humility. "You know I would never intentionally show you any impertinence. But you are a mon of commerce. You are a mon accustomed to having others do your bidding, without questioning. Please forgive me, then. but when it comes to matters of the emotions and not of the reasoning... Well, sometimes I tink you get in a hurry and get carried away. Don't tink tings through like you ought. I know you mean well, but what kind of woman do you tink you would make Miss Dunnigan feel like if you moved her under your roof without benefit of marriage. Or even being of kin to her?"

"You live in my house, don't you?"

"Indeed, I do. But folks tink differently of me. My blood's not pure like Miss Dunnigan's. I'm not white like—"

"Don't say that!" he discharged. "I never want to hear you say that again. Did I ever treat your mother…? Have I ever treated you like anything but…" He could not finish his sentence.

"As you wish, monsieur. I'll not speak of it again," I answered. (And how I did so want to ask of him if, indeed, he had treated my mother and me all that differently from the others of our color—drug screaming and kicking to this land; but I held my tongue and focused, instead, on the issue of Mary Dunningan moving into the house, as I continued on.) "But you do put too much pressure on Miss Dunnigan right now. Give her some breathing room. Leave her to her room out back for right now. Let her tink tings through in her mind, get used to that new child of hers. Lots has happened to her lately. Give her the time to adjust."

He looked away from my reflection, down to the floor and I could feel the disappointment weighing him down. "I suppose you're right," he sighed. "I haven't thought this through very well, have I? I've just never been very good at this sort of thing." Then he did kiss me atop my head before silently retreating from my quarters. I took up my brush and continued with my hair. And as I looked myself in the eye in my mirror, I vowed either Mary Dunnigan and her ill-gotten Irish infant would leave this house, or I would. If it be war, so be it. Might the better side win out.

Sunday, 23 July 1837

Over the course of the next three weeks, Mon. Isaacson did remain most reserved, almost despondent. He came and went, going about his business with little acknowledgment of anyone else. He rarely visited Mary Dunnigan's room. One of Mme. Laveau's zombies cadavre had about as much soul, as much free will to him as Mon. Isaacson did. But the days went by, one-by-one, and I worried little about it; time has a way of taking care of matters of the heart and I was willing to bide my time, if it meant getting those Irish intruders out of my house.

Then came that morn, some weeks later, when old Marie was in her kitchen, working the morning's bread dough. She was standing, leaning over the worktable in the center of the room, directly across from the opened window on the sidewall. In the courtyard just outside the window, beside the banana shoots growing taller by the day, Mary Dunnigan sat holding her little boy baby. Marie thought not much of it, it was such a pleasant spring day, that she envied Mary being able to get out in it and enjoy it. Soon it would be too hot and sticky and rainy for anyone to enjoy the outdoors, so she thought nothing much about Mary taking time out from her chores to enjoy a breath of fresh air with the little one. That is to say, until the monsieur did appear on the scene. Marie wondered to herself what he was doing home from work of a weekday. From her vantage point, then, she did observe him approach and inquire of Mary as to how the little one was doing.

"Fine," she replied. "I've given him a name, have you heard?"

"No, I haven't. What is it?"

"Thomas. Thomas O'Kelley. After his grandfather on his...on Rory's side."

"Well. That's a fine name, Mary. A fine name indeed."

Then there was a lull in the conversation, and Marie was forced to stand on her toes to peek through the window to see what was happening outside in the courtyard. There, monsieur, she noticed, motioned to Mary if it would be all right for him to sit beside her on the wrought iron bench. "Of course," she replied as she slid down to give a proper distance between the two of them. Mon. Isaacson, Marie said, sat for the longest leaning forward with his elbows on his legs, his hands clasped out in front of him like they were in prayer.

Only after a while was it that he spoke, then almost timidly. "I was wondering if you have had time to think over...you know. What I proposed... What we talked about in your room that day."

"I have, indeed," Mary answered. Then there was another long pause before master broke the silence with a nervous little laugh.

"I don't mean to pressure you, Miss Dunnigan," he said, then his voice turned serious: "It just tears me up to think of you and the little one there trying to go through life with no..." Quickly did he turn to face Mary. "I would be a good husband and a good father. You must know that. And I could give little

Thomas a good name! A good name and all the privileges that go with it. He'd never have to want for anything. Neither of you would.

"I know that," Mary sighed. "I know that. I've thought of little else these last weeks.

"And?" he asked. "Have you reached any conclusions?"

Mary adjusted the sleeping child in her arms and looked up to the sky before responding. "The Doctor tells me I won't be a havin' anymore wee ones. On account of me womb bein' so scarred up from me bindin' me self up like I did," Marie heard her say, and it amazed the old cook that Mary would dare broach a subject so intimate with a mon—especially a mon such as Mon. Isaacson. Still, he did not seem to mind. "Doesn't it bother you to think you'd be a marryin' someone who couldn't bear ye none o' your own children?"

Monsieur, I'm told, hesitated not in the least. "Not if I were marrying the woman I loved, it wouldn't. Wouldn't bother me for a minute."

"Little Thomas here would have to be brought up a Catholic, you know. Wouldn't that bother you none?"

Monsieur looked directly at Mary with a most solemn expression on his face as he shook his head. "Surely all that can be broached in time."

"Perhaps. But where would you have us to be married? We couldn't be married in the Church without you a convertin'."

"No. Nor could we be married in the synagogue without your conversion, and that would take a long time. We could be married by a civil servant, though. A justice or a judge. Or, if it's important to you, I could go through the conversion process. As long as I could keep going to synagogue after we were married."

Mary studied her sleeping baby as she thought monsieur's response over in her mind. "No," she finally said. "I wouldn't want that. T'would be like tryin' to deceive God Himself." She turned to monsieur. "I suppose the only thing for a pair like us would be to be married by a judge after all."

According to Marie, the monsieur did raise his eyes up slowly from the ground, looking to Mary like he was not sure he had heard her right. "Then you mean you'll marry me?"

"Aye. I suppose I will," Mary affirmed.

Poor old Marie; a bolt of lightning out of the clear, blue sky could not have startled her any more than Mary's response. "Lawd have mercy!" she breathed out to herself as she pitched her hands up in the air, dropping her ball of dough on the floor. Quickly did she chase after it as it rolled to the hearth. And as she snatched it up and carefully dusted it off, she smelled a peculiar odor and felt a peculiar heat on the back of her legs. Looking over her shoulder she discovered that, In her haste, she had managed to drag her long skirt into a pile of coals on the hearth and set the back of her dress afire.

From the butler's pantry, I heard her bellowing and Sonnier and I did exchange startled glances. "What now!" I remember I exclaimed in utter exasperation.

Quickly we rushed out into the courtyard, where, along with the rest of the staff, we witnessed Marie running around in circles as flames leapt up the back of her dress, all the while our monsieur chased after her, beating at the flames with his coat. Finally, master did catch hold of Marie, and what do you tink? He shoved her down into the fish pond, flat on her backside. "Eoooooo!" she hollered, and instantly master pulled her to her feet, where he went about picking at the back of her skirt—like no gentleman of manners should—to make sure the fire was out.

Finding no harm done, only Marie's skirt and pride being scorched, he threw back his head and laughed out heartily and long. "By damn it's turned out to be a hell of a morning around here! Marie! Go buy yourself a new dress and put it to my account. But before you do, fix up the finest lunch you have ever made," he commanded and he took Mary by the hand and coaxed her up from the bench. "My fiancée, Mary Dunnigan, and her fine son here will be taking lunch with me in the dining room today!" he announced, for the entire household to hear.

Strutting like a peacock, Mon. Isaacson did take his bride-to-be arm-in-arm and led her off toward the main house. How clearly do I remember telling myself that I would have my tings packed and be on the boat for Jamaica long before that wedding could take place, when to my shock what do you tink? Sonnier did twist the stem off one of the crystal goblets he stood holding! The goblet's bowl shattered in his left hand and blood gushed forth like wine spilling out onto the ground. "Oh no, Sonnier! You've cut yourself wide open!" I cried. He gave the gaping wound not the slightest bit of attention, though. He merely stared straight ahead at master for the longest, hatred burning in his eyes like I had never seen before.

"You jist better hope that's all I cuts open 'round here today," he hissed, then stormed back into the pantry, leaving monsieur, Mary and me appalled at all the blood spilled on the gallery floor.

"Good Heavens, Miss Maneau!" monsieur exclaimed. "See to it that mess is cleaned up."   And that was it. That was all he had to say to me. He merely turned from me and ushered his beloved Mary and her child into the great house. Humiliated and abandoned, I called out for one of the footmen to come wash down the gallery, then hurried up the outside stairs to my room, tinking all the way that Mary Dunnigan had won, that she had defeated me. From me had she had stolen my responsibility; my home; even my birthright.

And yet, never in my life had I been more wrong than I was that spring morning.

Monday, 24 July 1837

Less than a month had it been since Mary Dunnigan had shaken this house to its very foundation with the birth of her bastard-child. It had been little more than a year since she first came into this happy home, and tings had just grown shakier, and shakier, more and more unsteady, ever since her arrival. Now, at last I had been forced to flee to my chamber where I might hide the shame of my tears from the others. There, I sought out the peace slumber so often yields, that welcoming refuge from the distresses visited upon me by a day still young. But sleep was not to come; I tossed and turned upon my daybed, until I finally got up and spent the next while pacing my floor, going over my options in my head. I did not truly wish to return to Jamaica: I had no family there, only a few outgrown friends from my childhood and youth.

Moreover, I would not have my Etienne there, either. It was bad enough for me to be separated from him by those few miles down the Mississippi, but to be an ocean voyage away! I was not sure but what that would be more than I could bear. And where would I live, once I got there? In my mother's house in Kingston? Such would be a logical place, but would monsieur give me the run of it? It was all too overwhelming. I needed a cool head to aid me in my plotting. This I understood. I had to get a note to Etienne, beseeching him to come to my aid and help me make out a plan of retreat, in light of Mary Dunnigan's siege of this house. Accordingly, I did seat myself before my writing table, where I took up pen to put to paper, even as that Molly Connelley came scratching at my door.

"Miss Maneau? You in there?" she asked through the closed door.

"Oui, what is it?"

Molly quietly turned the knob and opened my door. Hastily I did avert my face to the opened window, there to deny her the sight of my red and swollen eyes. I was most rankled that she would enter my room without first receiving invitation, but she was all too common I reminded myself. Not that I was in any position to confront her, with my eyes still vinegary from their tears.

"What is it, Miss Connelley," I demanded, as disagreeably as I could.

"Beggin' your pardon, ma'am," she squeaked in that faux-unassuming tone she could employ so adeptly to her advantage. "It's Mr. Isaacson what's sent me. He's asked you to go to the butler's pantry. Sonnier won't have nothin' to do with Dr. Penney puttin' a stitch in his cut, and his hand keeps a seepin' blood in his white glove. Mr. Isaacson'll be a needin' you to wait the table."

I felt my eyes stinging like Molly had pitched warm ocean water in them and I forced my gaze straight-ahead. I could not even trust the strength of my own voice; I just nodded my head and waved her on with the front of my hand. It seemed for all eternity that I sat at my desk, staring out the open window, before I was to hear the door close behind the Irish wench. I rose from the chair and went to my dresser, where I took pitcher in hand and poured myself a bowl of cool water. There I anointed my face with the soothing waters, praying it would wash away the stigma left by my tears. Deep, deep breaths did I take, until, at last feeling calmer, I lifted my chin and went forth from my quarters to serve my monsieur—my monsieur and his would-be Irish bride.

I went down the outside stairs to avoid passing by the dining salon, lest that pair be in there: the less I might have to set my eyes upon them the better. With each step I took downward, I resolved not to let my heart be troubled. After all, the time for tears was gone. "It is finished," my mind kept whispering to me, over and over again. And to be sure, with all my heart and soul I did believe my mission in this home had at last come to an end. Soon I would be leaving this place, I was certain, but for now it was my duty to wait upon monsieur's table.

In the pantry, old Marie had come from the kitchen to platter the fine lunch of roast shank of lamb and fresh vegetables. Sonnier sat alone in the corner of the room, pressing a clean white rag against his wound. "Sonnier, let me see how bad you've cut yourself," I said, but he jerked his hand away from my reach.

"Jist don't you worry yo'self none on Sonnier's count, mam'oselle. He be awright," he pouted.

"I know you'll be all right," I humored him. "Never's a grown mon died from a little cut on his hand. Still, I don't see why you don't let the doctor put a stitch in it to stop the bleeding."

Sonnier's sympathy, it was obvious, was all spent on himself that noonday. He was in no mood to be humored. "Like I say, you jist don't go worryin' yo'self none 'bout Sonnier. Mast Isaacson in there," he lifted a belligerent chin toward the dining room door, "got's hisself a pretty white woman! He ain't worried 'bout Sonnier. Hell no! Sonnier kin sit out here 'n bleed' to death! Mast won't care none. An' y'all don't need to be worrin' none neither." Old Marie and I exchanged glances. He was a most complicated mon, this Sonnier. It could be so difficult to understand him at times.

"Missy, you best get this tray on in there 'fore the massah's stomach starts to growlin'," the old cook told me. And as I took the tray and leaned into the swinging door to pass through, I heard Marie lash out at Sonnier. "Chile, I don't know what's got into you. Talking to mam'oselle like that! Don't you know she gots 'da power to gets you sold back down the river? And you hands is too damned soft to go cuttin no cane, Mister Big Britches."

Whatever smile may have come to my lips on hearing old Marie scolding Sonnier, quickly soured with my stomach, once I was confronted by the sight of the monsieur sitting at the head of, not the little table by the fireplace, but the great table itself. Prominently positioned on his right hand was Mary Dunnigan. In the chair beside her, the infant slept in a wicker basket. I tell you, the anger that welled up inside of me, seeing that woman sitting at the great table, caused me to fear that my trembling would rattle the serving dishes on the tray. But I gritted my teeth and persevered, as I knew I must. I stepped behind monsieur and positioned myself to offer the tray to Mary. She hesitated at first, then awkwardly took up the serving forks and dished herself, with some difficulty, a tiny portion of lamb. I adjusted the tray before her to present the pot of mint jelly, old Marie's specialty that monsieur loved almost as much as her spicy rice dish. Mary took the spoon, then hesitated again, looking up to me for guidance. For once I had no difficulty forcing a smile. "Would mademoiselle care for some mint with her lamb?" I asked in a most delicate timbre, making sure I subtly emphasized the word mademoiselle.

She gently replaced the spoon and shook her head. And as I turned to attend to monsieur, I could not believe what I was to hear. "Thank you," Mary Dunnigan did utter to me. Instantly, I wheeled around to her and dropped my chin, as I peered at her in disbelief. This woman was so unschooled in the social graces that she would actually thank a servant for doing her job! Hiam Isaacson could dress her up and take her to the opera; he could make her the queen of his elegant home; he could even give her bastard an undeserved name; but even Mon. Hiam Isaacson could not make pumpkins to grow upon gourd vines. He could never make Mary Dunnigan into any ting more than what she was: an Irish peasant girl, common as the day is long, and not fit to untie his shoes for him come the night. As I turned back to him, the whole while I offered him the tray I could not wipe the smirk off my face, so sweet can satisfaction be at times.

As soon as monsieur had been served, I hastened back to the shelter of the pantry. There I did listen to the deafening silence emanating from the dining room. For all of his joy in the morning, lunch with his beloved Mary had been as lively as a funeral. Even in the pantry, Sonnier continued to sit in sullen silence, nursing his wounds. I remember asking myself when was it that a house as robust as this had once been, had so suddenly turned inward on itself. When was it that we had become a camp of prisoners, held captive by our own worst fears? Quickly did I have my answer. My mind murmured it to me: ever since Mary Dunnigan first set foot upon this property. Strangely enough, that realization gave me pleasure in listening to the hush flowing from the room next door.

The baby's cry finally and abruptly broke the silence, however. As soon as I did hear its bawling, I returned to the dining room, to see if the table was ready for the clearing. Standing beside the hall door, I was to witness Mary with child in arms, rocking him slowly to soothe his fussing.

"He's ready for a changin' I expect," the mother mused aloud.

Monsieur dropped his napkin beside his plate. "And I'm afraid I'm late for the office. Will you excuse me, dearest?"

How that word—dearest—burned me. Could it be I was truly nothing more to this mon than the servant-daughter of some Negress who had shared his bed? Was I nothing more to him than someone to do his bidding? How dare he! How dare he use that term of affection he so often showered upon me with that homespun Irish woman. I watched in sheer disgust as monsieur did rise from the table and move to Mary's side. No sooner had she lain the child in its basket than he tried to offer her a little kiss on the cheek; and no sooner did his lips touch her cheek, than she instinctively jerked away. It was an awkward moment for both and he resorted to kissing the top of her head before leaving the room—in silence.

I slipped through the swinging door, back into the pantry. "They're through Sonnier," I announced, "Where's the clearing tray?"

Much to my surprise, Sonnier checked and found his wound had at last stopped bleeding. He rose to his feet and sighed, "No need for you to go clearin' no table. Sonnier 'bout to take care of things round here."

Together we entered the dining salon, Sonnier bearing the big, silver, clearing tray while I toted the stand. We both stopped short, however, for much to our astonishment what were we to find but Mary Dunnigan crouched down on the floor, her baby laying on master's fine, Aubuisson rug whilst she changed his diaper. Every muscle in Sonnier's body did go rigid with rage. I too was incensed, but I counseled myself that this was, henceforth, Mary's home and, therefore none of my concern. I snapped the stand open and took the tray from Sonnier. Still he stood erect, moving not an inch, so I took it upon myself to commence clearing the table. No sooner did I have my hands full of dishes, though, than I was to witness our steward crossing the room to pull the hall door closed, where he latched it behind him.

"Sonnier, why are you locking that door?" I asked, puzzled at his behavior.

He offered me not a word, not so much as a glance. He merely crossed the room and stood towering over Mary Dunnigan, still crouched down on the floor. Then, in one fell swoop, Sonnier did take the great table and flip it over. Never in my life will I ever forget the horrible sound of that crash, as the luncheon dishes shattered upon the floor and the heavy table flipped over the chairs on the far side of it. I stood, dumbfounded, looking at master's broken china and crystal, at his beautiful table wrecked in a heap atop overturned chairs. Then I looked to Sonnier, hoping to find some explanation for what he had just done. Instead, I found him glaring down at poor Mary, an insane rage burning in his eyes, all the while the infant wailed. "Sonnier, mon Dieu! You'll be sent to the cane fields for sure this time!" I wailed, even as he reached down and in the blimk of an eye grabbed a fist full of Mary Dunnigan's hair and lifted her to her feet by it. Never shall I ever forget the look of terror on that woman's face, as Sonnier pulled her head back by the hair and stuck his face in hers.

"Who 'da hell you think you are, you 'hoe!" he snarled and then slung poor Mary by the hair, sending her crashing into the wall. "You think you kin jist come in dis fine home...come in dis house an' squeeze out that bassard! Like it ain't no shame put on the mast'?"

My heart did stop—literally, I felt it stop, as I saw Sonnier slip his foot under the child and send it sailing across the room. Both Mary and I screamed in unison as the baby bounced and rolled across the floor and I rushed forward to scoop him up in my arms. "Sonnier! Stop this! Stop this now before I call for monsieur!" I screamed, and no sooner had the words escaped my mouth than he did begin to bang at the door, demanding to be let in.

The baby was shrieking so loudly that I could barely hear myself tink, but I remember being relieved and hoping its crying only indicated the tiny ting was not badly injured. Within my chest, my heart had begun to beat so hard I could actually hear its reverberation in my ears; and my breathing came like I had just out run one of monsier's fancy race horses. I dared not take my eyes off Sonnier, though, as I watched him standing there, still glaring at Mary, his breathing as labored as mine. His shoulders rose and fell in great swells with every breath he took. And then I saw it. I saw it in his eyes. They changed. In an instant I could see the change. Some ting snapped. It was in horror that I watched as he flipped open the knife box on the sideboard beside Mary. "Oh Sonnier no!" I cried when I saw him take out a sterling silver carving knife. "For God's sake, no! Somebody help me! Somebody help me! Please! Please!"

I scrambled to his side and grabbed at the hand with which he held the knife, but he wheeled around and with his free hand did backhand me with all his might. He sent me spinning, stumbling and falling and trying to tink, through the excruciating pain, of a way to land without injuring the infant. I tucked the baby up under my left arm and put out my right hand to steady me, as I landed on my knees. No sooner had I hit the floor, though, than I was back on my feet and heading for the pantry door, looking back over my shoulder at the mad mon menacing poor Mary Dunnigan. Sonnier had her by the hair again and she screamed in terror as he held the knife above her. And then it happened. In an flash it happened and I guess I knew, at that very moment in time, that world I knew would never be the same again.

"You bitch-dog, you," Sonnier screamed at Mary, just as monsieur and Clyde kicked through the door. "You ain't shamin' my mast' no mo!"

And with that he plunged the knife deep into the poor girl's chest. In panic, I fumbled behind me, blindly trying to find the pantry door, unable to take my eyes away from Mary. No sooner had the blade entered her chest than her eyes opened wide in horror; her expression did beseech of me as to whether this was not just some bad dream, nothing more. Then, even before Sonnier twisted at the handle, I did notice a subtle sense of serenity come over poor Mary's face, a benign acceptance of what was to come registering in her stare. Sonnier just stood there, holding her up by the handle of the knife, his arm trembling under the weight of her body so rapidly going limp.

It was not until that point that I did notice monsieur and Clyde standing beside the door, the lock to which they had broken. They both appeared as frozen in time as Lott's wife, turned into a pillar of salt by the ghastliness of what had just been witnessed. Clyde came to his senses first:

"Sonnier," he said in a firm steady voice, holding out an upturned palm before him. "You be lettin' her go, now. You hear, boy?" And as he did step closer and closer to him, Sonnier jerked the knife from poor Mary's chest and began to menace Clyde with it.

At once did Mary collapse to the floor, blood beginning to spout fourth from her wound with every beat of her poor, pitiful heart. Terror seized me as I saw Sonnier look toward the pantry door where I stood, but he quickly looked back to the hall door: behind me, the pantry was filled with the staff peering in panic at the scene of carnage there in that genteel dining salon. Sonnier brandished the knife in such a way as to menace monsieur and Clyde away from the door. And as they stepped aside, he bolted out of the room, out into the hall where he fled through the front door. A commotion was to be heard outside in the street as the wild man ran out into the road, waving a bloody knife at the passers-by, before charging like a mad dog, blindly, insanely on down Josephine Street.

Back in the dining salon, no sooner had the monster fled than I felt my knees buckle under me, even as monsieur did rush to Mary's side. Marie and one of the grooms each grabbed me by an arm to keep me from falling, and it was at that moment that I heard Mary utter her last words. "Oh, sir. Take care of me baby, won't you? He's got no one but you," she begged of monsieur. And then she went limp and all the color drained from her face. Gray as a winter sky did she turn.

I ceased to read, I could not help myself. I felt as if I'd been sucker punched in the gut. Apparently—Aunt Alice, who'd read the story before—was the only one in the room not dumbstruck. She sat with her glasses atop the pile of needlework in her lap, her head tilted back, her eyes closed. Silence had overtaken the library until at length Susan almost whispered. "Ghastly. Unbelievable."

Without ever opening her eyes, Aunt Alice came to life. "Sometimes it just seems like it rains hardest on folks that need a little sunshine the most. Didn't I tell y'all kids you wouldn't like what you'd read?"

"Sure wasn't prepared for something this depressing, though," I let her know.

"Nineteen," Pamela breathed out. "Isn't that what he said?"

"Who?" I asked.

"Patrick O'Bannion. Isn't that how old he said Rory was when we first started reading?"

"Yeah. He did. Come to think of it."

"First him, then her. How sad. They were just teenagers and already dead."

My Aunt slipped on her bifocals and pulled them down to the end of her nose to peer over them. "My granny probably put it best. She'd always say that the ones God loves the best always die young. That's what she'd say."

I could have taken issue with my dear Aunt on that. It seems to me that we mortal beings are demonstrably ill-equipped to discern and understand and God's will, much less to nurture it, at least here on earth. Pretty words; clever adages, nothing more. Just something to fill the void the inexplicable always leaves in our consciousness, nothing more. God as we understand Him didn't love those two Irish kids any more than any of His other creations. It was absurd to say He took them to Himself because they were special to Him, but then, very little on this earth has much to do with the Devine's wishes, I've always thought. Nonetheless, the atmosphere hung much too heavy to interject theology into it, so I quickly returned to the text before anyone could add anything more.

As I stared ahead at the blood splattered walls, the blood-soaked carpet, I felt myself growing light-headed and I feared I would faint. I remember tinking the room was too quiet. Nothing was to be heard but the crying of the baby and the ticking of the clock out in the hall. The entire staff was gathered just behind me and yet the room was so quiet. Pandemonium should have prevailed, but the room was deathly still. And then I looked to monsieur and I understood. There he sat on legs bent back under him, covered in blood and cradling Mary's lifeless body in his arms. His eyes told me that, like the rest of us, he was in shock. I handed the baby to old Marie and pulled myself from the groom's grip, that I might crawl across the room to him. I had wished the monsieur ill and God, it seemed, had seen fit to grant my wish. Now I could tell from the look on his face that he had no one to turn to but me. I waded across the magnificent carpet, soaked through to the boards below in crimson and when I reached my master I did cradle his head in my arms. I rested my cheek atop his head and I looked up to Clyde.

"God have mercy, Clyde! Go! Run! Get Dr. Penney!"

My words, it seemed, brought him to life and Clyde bolted from the room like a mon half his age. As he hurried forth, I was reminded that this was the third time in recent months that I had been forced to issue such a command to a member of my staff in Mary Dunnigan's behalf. I looked back across the room and found the younger groom who had held me to keep me from falling.

"You! Take a horse and go fetch the sheriff here!" He too hurried into action and as I cradled my monsieur's head even more tightly I was to hear the silence finally broken. Pandemonium, at long last, reigned.

Four hours later and I did pray that all the commotion would come to an end, that peace and quiet would again prevail.

In the front salon, the good Dr. Penney sat off to himself, looking for all the world like he was a mon who had seen more than his share of suffering in this world. I sat on the settee beside Mon. Isaacson, whose mind had already gone, the light in his eyes having been replaced by a distant and empty stare. Through the open windows came the murmur of the crowd gathered outside the front gate, whispering and wondering to each other what had precipitated the rampage that had taken place within our noble walls. Before us, the sheriff held court, questioning Clyde and me about Sonnier and the possible reasons for his crime. I tried as best I could to attend to Sheriff's words, but my mind was dulled by all I had beheld. I recall glancing into the music room and there seeing Marie, Molly Connelley, Mordecai, the two grooms and the footmen assembled, waiting for their turn at interrogation. Old Marie and Molly did sob quietly, while the men-folk could do nothing more than shake their heads and rub at their faces with their hands. Would they ever be the same after witnessing what they had witnessed, I asked myself. Would monsieur? Would I?

The undertaker did at that time appear in the doorway, shown into the room by our footman. He clutched his top hat in his white-gloved hands and nodded to the sheriff as he entered the room, then immediately loped to monsieur's side. His voice was deep and resonate, and the words dripped off his tongue like sweet syrup off a corn cake. "Mr. Isaacson please accept my condolences that such an unfortunate event should have taken place inside your fine home," he said, as he offered monsieur his hand.

For his part, monsieur absently accepted the hand and looked up to the undertaker to inquire, "Who are you?"

"Forgive me, sir. Harold Hightower, undertaker. At your service. Now, if I may be given the run of your Negro kitchen, or one of your service buildings, and a couple of your female slaves, I can have the deceased removed to there. I'll need to bleed the body out. Flush out the veins and get the openings closed up. Then the womenfolk can bathe and dress it. I can put a little fluid-wash over her until we can find out which agency will be responsible for the burial. At any rate, I'll strive to have all this inconvenience out of your house just as soon as humanly possible."

Monsieur did merely look upon the undertaker with a look of disorientation and this vile creature at once repulsed me, speaking so freely in front of one of monsieur's standing of matters so indelicate as the disposition of Mary Dunnigan's remains. "That will never do," I spoke up, and he turned to me with an astonished look on his face as I rose and directed him toward the doorway, away from monsieur's ear. "See to it that Miss Dunnigan is taken to your parlor and prepared for a proper burial, sir."

"Forgive me, miss," he gasped as he threw his hand upon his breast. "I was led to believe it was no more than one of your servants—an Irish maid—who has been dispatched."

"Miss Dunnigan was in service to this house, yes. But even the memory of a cane field slave deserves a measure of human respect. You are not to haul that body out of this house in a pine box in the back of some buckboard. For all the world to see. Do you understand that? Either take Miss Dunnigan to your parlor and get her ready for a proper burial, or I shall summon your competitor. I don't recall having summoned you in the first place."

"Again, you must pardon me, Miss..."

"Maneau."

"Mademoiselle Maneau. But am I to understand that you would have me to embalm the body?"

"Certainly not. There's no need for such vulgar measures. Miss Dunnigan is not to be returned to Ireland for burial or anything of the like. But neither will she have a pauper's dismissal. Mon. Isaacson will compensate you for your service, don't concern yourself on that account. Your charge is to render a decorous, dignified internment for the poor soul.

"As you wish, mademoiselle. But of course."

"I shall call upon you tomorrow of the morning to select a coffin for her." Mr. Hightower did appear even more perplexed than ever. He did look back to monsieur, but the vacant stare he encountered led him to bow his head to me.

"Yes, mademoiselle. Your wish is my command. Permit me to take my leave and I shall return with the hearse."

"One other thing, Mon. Hightower. There are no slaves in this household."

"But of course. But of course." The undertaker then did smile and bow to me, and as he turned to leave, I caught the haughty little shrug of his shoulders he gave the sheriff.

It was then that I motioned for the younger groom to come to me, and as he approached I laid my hand on his shoulder to guide him down where I could whisper in his ear, and in so doing I noticed my hands were caked in dried blood. It was then that I realized why the flies had been annoying me so, my hands and arms and the front of my dress were covered in Mary Dunnigan's blood.

"Take one of the horses and ride hard and fast. Down the river to Mon. DuBoisblanc," I instructed the boy. "Let Mon. Etienne know what has taken place here and bid him to come right away. But be discreet boy. Speak only when away from the ear of Madam DuBoisblanc. Involve me in none of this, do you understand? " The good and obedient boy he was, the young groom merely nodded and unobtrusively slipped out of the room and hurried on along to the coach house.

I turned next to the Sheriff. "By your leave, your honor. But both Mon. Isaacson and I are soiled with blood and the flies are after us, I am afraid. Kindly allow us to go wash." He nodded his consent and I rose from the settee and motioned for Mordecai to come forward and assist with monsieur. Together were he and Dr. Penney able to coax him from the couch and his valet did slowly, gently guide him from the room, up the stairs to his own chambers. " Marie, Molly," I ordered, "See to it we have fresh water and touailles in our rooms."

In my chambers, I stood before my dressing mirror and was repulsed at my reflection. Not only were my hands and arms covered in blood, my cheeks were smudged and even my hair was matted with Mary's gore. I had torn off my soiled dress and dropped it to the floor and stood examining my bloody hands, when Mariam tapped at the door and let herself in. "Fresh water, mam'oselle," she said as she placed the pitcher on my dressing stand, then turned to face me. "Here, let Mariam hep gets you all cleaned up again."

She filled the bowl with water and took a cake of lilac soap and lathered up a washcloth. Softly, gently did she bathe at my face, my hands, my arms. The blood would mix with the rinse water when it would wash off me into the basin; and each time the cloth would turn bright red, Marie would rinse it until, alas, the basin could hold no more water. She took the bowl from the stand and stepped through the front windows, onto the gallery, where an audible gasp went up from the throng gathered down in the street when she pitched the bloody water off the gallery, onto the ground below. Back into my room she came, where she poured a fresh basin of water and washed at the blood caked in my hair. "Mariam, my dress is ruined. Please see to it that it's burnt up."

"Oui, mam'oselle," she said. "Anything else you wants."

"No. Nothing now. I must get back downstairs to the sheriff, I suspect."

Once I had washed and changed my clothes, I did make my way back down the staircase. At the top of the stairs, however, I did view the undertaker in the hall below, talking to the sheriff. Through the opened front door, I could see his fancy black hearse and matched black team parked in front of the house, the drapes inside the compartment drawn together in anticipation of receiving Mary's body.

As I descended the staircase, I was to observe two men in the dining salon wrapping, her body in a maroon, velvet blanket. I could not help myself; I became petrified and could not take my eyes off the spectacle. As I watched the men wrap and lift her body and place it in the wicker carrying-coffin, the younger of the two broke out in a most indecorous chuckle.

"J.B., what's ailing you?" the other demanded of his amused colleague.

"Ah, shoot, Henry," he replied, "I was just thinkin'. This here's gotta be the darnedest pickup we ever been on."

"How's that?"

"Hell's bells, just looks at us. Here we are in this fancy house owned by some old Jew, loadin' up a dead Irish girl, who done gone and got herself killed by some lunatic nigger. Now if that don't just beat it all..." The one called Henry happened to notice me, there on the stairs, as they arranged the body in the wicker container. I could tell by the look on his face and his gruff manner with his underling, that he was embarrassed to the core.

"Ah! Behave yourself, now!" he chided.

Once the casket lid was lowered and latched, the two labored to lift it up, then bore it on out of the dining room, shuffling as they did to make it through the door. The irreverent, young one looked up to see me for the first time, there on the stairs, as he struggled with his load, and I did offer him up a casting of the evil-eye. Long and hard did I glare at him, moving my lips as if in chant: if there's one ting that can paralyze a white liver, it is fear of the darker people's spiritual power. On down the great hall the pair struggled with their load, fleeing in terror, my impotent but menacing gaze, leaving behind them sticky, bloody footprints down the length of the passage.

As they stepped out onto the porch, the crowd that had gathered outside parted like the Red Sea, gentlemen removing their hats, and everyone stepping aside in respect to the departed. And yet, it was only when they bore that casket across the threshold that I did turn to God in torment and beg for His forgiveness. Looking at the bloody footprints left down the length of the great hall, it did at last occur to me that finally had my prayers been answered: Mary Dunnigan was leaving this house, never to return.

Friday, 2 September, 1837

Word came today from Mme. Laveau, inquiring as to whether I have finished my writing as yet. I know I have neglected this daybook since my last entry, but the truth of the matter is the reliving of Mary Dunnigan's demise has left me spent. Now, as I sit at my writing desk and again face this undertaking, I find my emotions torn asunder: on the one hand, I can now see the light at the end of the tunnel in all this drudgery. Yet on the other hand, that light is a far piece away and the road leading to it is rocky still. And how I dread the dredging up of what all took place here after poor Mary's murder.

Who, exactly, is it Mme. Laveau expects will be reading writing as dismal as mine? I do wonder. Or will the purging of all this horror onto the pages of this daybook be the end of it? Will there be no one else to read all this, to experience the awfulness I have seen of late? But I do wander too much, I know. I must persevere ever onward if I am to finish the course.

The morning after the murder found me on my knees in the dining salon, helping the footmen with the cleanup. Molly Connelley was in too much a state to be of much help, and old Marie had taken it upon herself to attend to the infant, along with her kitchen duties. So I made do the best I could. The night before, the grooms had mucked up most of the congealed blood from the floor. First ting that morning, monsieur's fine Aubuisson carpet, blood soaked and ruined, had been hauled out into the courtyard, where it was cut up in pieces and burnt out at the street side.

The great dining table had been removed to the front porch for the cabinetmaker to haul away to his shop, to repair the chips, dints and scratches Sonnier's rage had inflicted upon it. Back in the dining room, the boys continued scrubbing at the stubborn bloodstain on the wood floor, whilst I did wipe gently at the splatters that desecrated the silk wall murals.

"Those damned stains are still visible in the dining room, you know." We had gotten ourselves so engrossed in the drama playing out in Amanda Maneau's diary that we had forgotten Aunt Alice cuddled in her wingback working her needlepoint, something she could attend to for hours on end. "I can show you if you want to see it."

T.K. and Susan looked at each other. Susan seemed to hesitate and he looked to me for direction, I suppose. After all, it was a peculiar sort of thing for my aunt—slightly eccentric though she was—to ask; would someone like to take a tour of a gory murder site. Having pretty much grown up in the house, I was familiar with that dark stain on the dining room floor; the one that wouldn't come up no matter how hard you scrubbed at it. I was also aware that it had a sideshow allure about it, the sort that appeals to our more gruesome sides. On several occasions my brothers and I had proudly showed the big, circular spot to our little friends, embellishing upon the event that precipitated it to the extent it quickly became the place where a slave had cut off a white woman's head. There really was not that much to it, I knew; still, I was not sure how to guide T.K., what to suggest. Eventually, I took the middle road and shrugged my shoulders. "It's just a dark spot on the floor."

And so, while Susan waited behind, T.K. and I followed Aunt Alice into the dining room, where she spun the rheostat to the chandelier and flooded the room with bright light. She tugged back a corner of her carpet to reveal the deep, black stain permeating the carefully finished wide pine flooring.

"We had the floors refinished as part of our renovations, but they were never able to get that stain out. Said it had penetrated too deep in the wood grain. And look here," she said, pointing to a sprinkling of brownish splatter marks on the wall murals. "It's a lot harder to see than the floor, but you can still see where her blood splattered on the wall. Isn't that something! Guess we really should've had all this replaced, but it just seemed like we'd be tinkering with the house's history if we did."

T.K. looked up from the floor and sucked a breath of air deep down in his lungs. "Kind of makes it all so real, doesn't it?" he mused.

"It does at that," I agreed.

"My maid won't stay in this house after dark, you know. Thinks she's seen Mary Dunnigan's ghost in here looking for her baby. Few others swear they've seen something. Your mama, Bodie, swears she saw something once. Me? I been living here near seventy-three years now and I've never seen nor heard a thing. Go figure."

Once we returned to the library, T.K. plopped down beside Susan on the sofa and took up Amanda Maneau's journal. Yet for a moment he just seemed to survey it; then he turned to me. "Would you mind? My eyes are getting tired." I took the old volume in one hand as I fumbled to slip my reading glasses on with the other. One of the cruelties of middle age is that one often cannot fully see what is closest at hand. What a wonderful thing it would be, I thought to myself, to see again through young eyes.

Eventually, my dependable old peeps found the place where T.K. had left off, though, and I began to read aloud.

And as I sat on my knees, scrubbing on the murals, a shadow did suddenly come across the wall. I looked up to see my Etienne standing above me. He must have ridden all through the night to come to me. Like a flash in the pan, I was off the floor and in his arms, the groomsmen notwithstanding.

I could not help it, all that I had been bottling up inside for monsieur's sake, suddenly spilled out there in my Etienne's arms. And as I wept, I managed to sob the sad story to him—of how I had wanted Mary Dunnigan out of this house and how God had seen fit to favor my wish; of how I was then forced to witness the very life drain out of that girl's chest as Sonnier plunged and twisted the knife inside her. Of an instant, there in Etienne's arms, truth chilled me like a cold wind blowing up from the Gulf in the dead of winter and I was forced to accept that it had not been monsieur's actions, but my own petty jealousy that had done us in. We were truly cursed—cursed by my own selfishness, by my jealousy over Mary's coming between my unrequited father and me. For the rest of our lives would we each and all be haunted by the specter of what had taken place that day in that room. And the blame was none other than my own.

In his own strangely strong, but gentle way, Etienne sought to assure me all would be well. He took me by the hand and led me from the horrible dining salon, out to the front parlor where he could help me find my composure and wrestle control of the direction of the household from oblivion. Once I was over my crying jack, he patted me gently on my hands and inquired of monsieur's state of being. "He's taken to his bed in grief. Not more than an hour before he'd proposed marriage to pitiful Mary Dunnigan. And she had accepted! Now this!"

"Has the poor girl no family in Louisiana?"

"None. She came here alone from Ireland. I tink she has a mother and sisters over there, but we'll have to inquire of

Molly Connelley about that. They must be notified, don't you tink?"

"But of course they must, but there is time aplenty for that. What disposition has been made of her remains?"

"They removed her to the undertaker's parlor yesterday. We must notify the Church so they can make arrangements for a Christian burial, no?"

"Oui, oui. Allow me to handle all that. The Church has tombs for the disposing of the indigent. I'll make those arrangements, you needn't bother yourself about that."

"No, Etienne. She mustn't be sent to an pauper's grave! Monsieur would have none of that. She must be buried in a proper vault. And in a good cemetery, too. You must go to the undertaker and assure him monsieur will be responsible for the burial fees. Ask him to find a place for her in the wall at Lafayette No. One."

"You're speaking of the little tombs? The ones they call the 'ovens'?"

"Oui. The wall vaults that look like the baker's ovens. One that's up off the ground but not on the top. That should be a proper place to put her, don't you agree?"

"But of course. By your leave, I shall go to take care of all this without delay."

"Yes, by all means. Do see to it all this has been arranged and return to me as soon as you can. Monsieur will wish to see you and he'll be most pleased that you've taken care of that pitiful girl's final arrangements."

"Try not to worry yourself, Amanda. I shall return as soon as I can."

Then, it was with a kiss that my Etienne hurried out to his steed waiting in the street and rode away in a cloud of dust to attend to Mary Dunnigan's burial.

Sometime later that afternoon there came a knocking at the front door. Monsieur had made his way downstairs and we were seated in his Library, where I was telling him of Etienne's gracious gesture in making Mary's arrangements, when the abrupt knockin echoed through the great hall. Immediately did I jump from my seat and rush out into the hall to the front door, where I expected to find my Etienne. Rather, as I lugged the door open, I was almost struck upon the head by the cane of old man Duffosat, as he sought to whack rudely at the door once again. Startled I jumped back, in a most ungracious manner, to avoid being struck. Aloud I gasped. Monsieur, in an instant, was at my side, but old Mon. Duffosat pushed the door fully ajar and waltzed into the hall as if he'd been issued invitation.

"I've come for my nigger!" he roared.

I flinched, I could not help it. How I did hate a milky heart that could so freely utter a word so demeaning to so many. I did bite at my tongue to keep from asking where he had left his conscience, only to have the monsieur intervened on my behalf.

"What is the meaning of this," he demanded. "Striking at my door with your cane like that. Can't you see the knocker? You almost hit—"

"What've you done with my property?" the disgusting old creature interrupted, his face red as a crimson tide, the veins swelling out on his neck. "I've come to retrieve what is rightfully mine."

So taken aback was Mon. Isaacson at the old mon's anger, that he took a step backwards to give himself some breathing space. Then it was my turn to intervene. "If you're talking about Sonnier, no one knows where he's run off to." I was ignored, as again he bore down in my master's face.
"I tell you, if anything happens to my nigger you'll be paying me for him. That's my personal property that was left in your bailment. You'll be legally responsible if anything happens to him."

"I'll be responsible for nothing of the kind. There are no slaves in this house, you know that!" monsieur shouted back, the anger growing in his voice.

Old mon Duffosat fairly trembled with rage, as he glared with the eyes of a mad dog at my master, before he was finally able to speak. "That's right," he drawled out in a condescending tongue. "You free all your slaves, don't you?" In an instant he reached across and grabbed me by the front of my dress and jerked me toward him. "Like this one's free! Free to come and go as long as she's home in your bed at night!"

With lightning speed monsieur drew his fist up to strike the old fiend, when suddenly from out of nowhere, Etienne grabbed Mon. Duffosat by the hand that clung to my frock. In all the confusion, neither monsieur nor I had noticed Etienne hurrying up the front steps to our aid. He trembled as he dug his thumb deep and hard into the soft side of the mon's wrist, causing him to howl like the animal he was and let go his hold on me. And no sooner had he let me go, than Etienne grabbed him by his collar and pulled him out onto the front gallery. There, as the passers-by in the street gawked, he did slap the old mon hard across the face with his glove and spoke out loudly enough for all to be witnesses.

"Sir! You have affronted a good and decent woman. I call you to account! Prove yourself a gentleman and name your second." The old mon's eyes popped open so wide I did fear they would fall out on the ground as he stumbled backwards, trying to flee Etienne like he would a charging bull.

"A duel?" he gasped in disbelief. "You're challenging me to a duel?"

"That I am, sir. In front of all these witnesses," he motioned to the passers-by in the street.

"Now be a gentleman and name your second. Or will you be a coward instead?"

Farther backwards did the old mon advance, down the porch steps, down the walkway, one step at a time.

"I'm an old fellow, sir. I've no intentions to duel with you."

"You were capable enough to manhandle a lady, were you not? You should be capable enough to handle yourself in a duel. Will it be pistols or blades?"

"Sir, you take me wrong! I've merely come for what is legally mine. Namely, my nigger man-servant, Sonnier."

"If it's Sonnier you've come for, he's not here. And no one knows where he's gone. Now will you name your second, sir."

" DuBoisblanc," he pled, "you, yourself, are a slave owner. Surely you can understand—" But my Etienne did interrupt him.

"I am nothing of the kind. My brother, the Marquis DuBoisblanc, owns those on the plantation I manage. Not I. And insofar as your property goes, that is your affair and none of mine. Nor this household," he said, pointing back to the house as he spoke. "Were I you, sir, and held so much in store by my claim to possession of another man, I'd scurry about to find Sonnier and ferry him up North where some abolitionist will pay you the price of his freedom. If the long arm of the law snatches him before you can, I fear your investment will be devalued to the penny. The man has committed murder on a white woman, sir. Or have you not heard."

Old mon Duffosat then looked beyond Etienne to monsieur, standing on the gallery beside me. He shook his fist at him and bellowed, "I'll sue you, Isaacson. If anything happens to my property I'll sue you, you damned thieving Jew!"

Etienne bounded down the walkway toward the old mon, shooing him off with the wave of his arms like he would a stray dog in the yard. "Go on and get out of here," he shouted. "You've bothered these good people enough. You've no claim against them. Name your second like a proper gentleman, or get on that horse of yours and ride away from here like the coward you are!" And as Etienne neared him, old Duffosat quickly spun and fled to his waiting horse, the witnesses in the street mocking his cowardice, as he did. He struggled, comically, to mount his gelding and was barely in the saddle before he was spurring the animal on. Etienne returned to the gallery and motioned for us to retreat back inside.

"Enough nuisance for one day. Let's go inside and allow me to pour us all a little drink to calm our nerves."

It was to the front salon that we retired. There, Etienne poured us each a strong drink: bourbon whiskey for monsieur and he; sherry for me. And as we sipped, he told us of the arrangements he had made for poor Mary Dunnigan. Monsieur did listen most intently, nodding his head in appreciation of all my love had accomplished that day. Once Etienne was finished, however, master did announce one change he preferred in the plans. And as he spoke, it was painfully evident how heavily this tragedy was bearing down on him. His hand shook almost uncontrollably each time he lifted his glass to his lips. "I've been thinking about a place to put her away and I don't think I want to put her in one of those ovens. Too many people of questionable repute get shoved into those walls. No, I have a fine, big plot in the new cemetery at Metairie. I think I'd rather she be buried there, instead."

Automatically I did speak up. "Monsieur," said I, then thought better of what I was about to say. I was about to question the propriety of laying a common house servant to rest amid people of such importance as they who owned the plots surrounding master's. Indeed, the new cemetery at Metairie was to be one of the more exclusive gardens of repose in the entire nation. But, I had intruded enough in all this matter and muddle. I quickly realized it was time for me to remember my position in this house. "Are you... If this will ease your mind, by all means..." I stumbled and stammered. "We can send a message to the undertaker. Instruct him to make the necessary changes."

Monsieur did seem pleased with my suggestion. He requested I send one of the footmen with the message right away. Then he rose, wearily, and excused himself. He was tired, he said, and the row with old fool Duffosat had taken away much of his energy. He retreated to his quarters for a little rest, whilst Etienne and I lingered in the parlor, relishing our time alone together.

Time has such a way of getting lost when I am with the one I do so love. Perhaps then, more than ever, I needed the comfort, the reassurance only my Etienne could give me. For some while, we remained in the front parlor, talking about this and that, tings both pressing and unimportant. Sometimes we would just sit for spells in silence, needing no words to enhance the satisfaction we found in each other, only the touch of the other's hand. It was during just such a lull that a racket quickly arose from the rear of the property. We looked at each other, puzzled at what such a commotion could be this time of the late afternoon, when much to our stupefaction Molly Connelley did come running down the length of the great hall as fast as she could. At the door to the parlor, she tried to stop but the rug skidded out from under her and she fell with a great thud flat of her back, her dress shamefully hiked up over her ankles. Quickly, she gulped to replenish the air knocked from her lungs and scrambled to cover her exposed legs. To her feet did she struggle, wheezing all the while, "Out back! Out back! Hurry!"

As fast as our own legs would take us, Etienne and I were off the settee and dashing down the hall, overtaking Molly about midway. Out the back door we raced, where we were greeted with the sight of a large assembly of rogues, gathered out in the street beyond the back gate. Every one of them seemed animated, angry yet joyful. So odd and confusing was the scene. At first I thought it had some ting to do with the Hermann's estate, since they were all congregated around the big oak tree across the street. I strove without success to find a face in the crowd I could recognize, until a horrified Mrs. Hermann and Miss Myna Goldstein suddenly appeared out of the crowd. They fumbled at the gate like a pair struggling to flee a burning house and Clyde quickly rushed to get the gate opened and let them in.

By now, the entire staff had once again assembled in the courtyard to see what all the commotion could be. Miss Myna and Mrs. Hermann came running toward Etienne and me, and I could almost smell their fear. My own heart raced inside my chest until I feared I would grow light-headed. "Get Mr. Isaacson! Get Mr. Issacson!" I heard Mrs. Hermann screaming. "They're going to hang that poor man, that band of vigilantes!"

No sooner had she said that than a cry went up from the crowd, and as I looked up to the street, I saw Sonnier, by then astride a horse, a noose drawn around his neck. He looked to the house and his eyes were opened wide in unbounded terror. His mouth gulped at the air, as would that of a fish out of water, when suddenly he did find his voice. It was a pitiful, high-pitched shrill that came from within him. "Mast' Isaacson! Hep me Mast' Isaacson!" he screamed, almost like a woman would.

I tell you the fear in his eyes and in his voice did almost cause me to retch up the contents of my stomach. A time or two more did Sonnier scream his pleas to monsieur—much to the delight of the bunch of scalawags, I might add—when in an instant the horse was pulled from beneath him. Up high in the tree, up above the crowd his body swung, helpless with his hands tied behind his back. His feet kicked wildly at the air, trying to find some foothold on which to stand for what seemed an eternity. Then suddenly the kicking slowed, finally stopped. He hung still for a second or so, then began what would be several minutes of the most violent convulsing imaginable, as there was no broken neck to put him out of his misery and he merely writhed in agony. And the more tormented his jerking became, the more the crowd would cheer and look to the house for approval. Miss Myna and Mrs. Hermann hid their eyes in each other's shoulders and even I had to turn my face away, burying it Etienne's chest. Oh, but mon Dieu! How the cheers and jeers of that crowd still ring in my ears. And as the cheering grew louder, I sought to bury my face deeper into my love's chest, when suddenly he pulled away from me.

"Clyde, no!" I heard him shout and he took off for the gate. I turned to see Clyde scurrying through the back gate, running head-on into the crazed mob, Etienne chasing him every step of the way. Both of our grooms made to rush the gate as well but were rebuffed by Etienne. Into the crowd he chased after Clyde, emerging instantly and manhandling the coachman all the way back into the courtyard. Clyde was outmatched by my love, but he was incensed that he had been restrained from intervention.

"Leave me 'lone! Ya jist cain't let 'em dance at the end of a rope like that! Ain't right. I don't care whut he done!" But Etienne persisted, insisting to Clyde that that murderous bunch would just as soon hang him as Sonnier. He slammed the back gate shut and locked it, then turned to the assembled staff and took charge of the situation.

"Everyone go into the house right now! You hear me. Now! Everyone!" And as I turned to flee to the great house with the others, something on the upstairs balcony did catch my eye. There, on his knees, holding onto the column and clutching at his chest was monsieur, his eyes fixed on the depravity taking place down in the street below. At that very instant, seeing such a great and strong man reduced to his knees in front of all the world, I knew he would never be the same again. Anger welled up inside me and I could no longer control myself. I stopped and turned back to the street scene so quickly that Miss Myna and Mrs. Hermann almost collided with me. There, hanging from that very tree Mary and Rory had spent so much time beneath, Sonnier was still going through his death throes. Myna and Mrs. Hermann studied me with concern before taking my arms.

"Come Mr. Isaacson," said Mrs. Hermann. "Let us do go on into the house."

But the anger was still growing within me and I stood my ground. And as I looked directly ahead at the dying Sonnier, I gritted my teeth. "Must be a powerful potion," I cried out for all to hear, "the putting together a Christisn conscience with a white face! White magic, that's what it is! It's what's given the world most of its troubles!"

Neither Miss Myna nor Mrs. Hermann said a ting. They merely took me by my arms and turned me away from that horrid scene and led me to the house. Yet despite their guidance, I did oncemore pull myself free of their grips. Up the back stairs I rushed to monsieur, Mordecai following in after me. Gently we did get him to his feet and led him inside to his bed.

It was for more than an hour that he lay upon his bed, gazing blankly at the ceiling overhead, before his eyes finally fell closed and he mercifully drifted into sleep. We—Etienne,

Mordecai and I—sat with monsieur until it was decided that Dr. Penney should again be summoned.

"Let him sleep," the physician told us, "He's seen enough suffering these past two days to last a lifetime. When he wakes, if he's too uneasy you can give him two tablespoons of this every four hours." He placed a bottle of his elixir on master's shaving stand. "It'll make him groggy, but it'll calm him down some." Mordecai was given charge of sitting up with monsieur as Etienne and I saw Dr. Penney down the stairs.

The silence in which we descended was misleading, for my mind was anything but quiet. Over and over in it the picture of what had transpired that afternoon kept reappearing. Over and over in my mind would the roar of the crowd drown out even the ticking of the old grandfather clock. Never have I considered myself a delicate woman, like those so gentle of manner they seek refuge within the confines of the convent, there to be sheltered from the cruelties of the world. Still, I tink mine must have been a protected life, for Sonnier's death, like that of Mary Dunnigan, I found to be all too confusing, too detestable, too disgusting, to make any sense out of it. I quickly found myself wondering aloud to the two fine men who accompanied me, "What manner of animals are these people? That they would actually tink we could delight in seeing poor Sonnier lynched before our eyes!" It was without hesitation that old Dr. Penney offered an answer to my query, perhaps because it has been such a aggregation of life he has had to witness in his many years on this earth.

"The lowest of the low," he voiced. "Provincial. Ignorant. Uneducated. People like that act out of the basest of instinct, not higher reasoning. No Miss Maneau, it's times like this that make me wonder if the Almighty didn't set us loose on this world before He'd worked out all our little defects."

At the front door, the doctor bid us to call him if master's state deteriorated. Then he trudged on down the steps and disappeared into the dark at the end of the walkway. By ten o'clock of that same evening, he would be back. He would return to attend to monsieur as he wandered up and down the hall, squeezing Mary Dunnigan's little infant to his chest and wailing in gut-wrenching sobs like one would expect to hear coming up out of a dungeon.

Or the bowels of hell, itself.

This then is the story—the one Mme. Laveau did enjoin me to reduce to writing. Truly, it is the story of the catastrophes that have brought such misfortune upon this noble house and those of us who reside within it. It is at once the story of those Irish knuckles that came knocking at the rear hall door; from all the way across the ocean did they come to knock at our door. But in a larger sense, it is more—much more—than that. And as such, I suppose it is nothing less than the story of the purulent heart that beats within this young nation. How easy is it to look for some particular one on whose shoulders to place the blame, but such must always be a futile search. Blame is not to be laid upon Mary Dunnigan and Rory O'Kelley for their lack of restraint in their love for one another. Blame is not to be put upon Mon. Isaacson for his feelings for one too young to ever be his. Blame is not even to be heaped upon Sonnier for his insanity. No, to be sure, if condemnation is to be rendered, it must be doled out, equally, among us all, for we are all responsible for permitting our own intolerance to infect the souls others.

Only now do I understand all this; only now do I fully see that if we humans are to ever find our way out of the wilderness, we must first learn that the way to wisdom—though a straight and narrow course—is a many forked path. And now that this story has been spelled out; now that the festering boil blighting this fair house has been lanced, may the wound at long last be healed. At long last, may God once again grant us His peace and deliver us from all this trial and tribulation.

Mlle. Amanda Maneau
Nouvelle Orleans, Louisiana

    As I finished reading that last entry, I stuck my finger in the journal to save my place and peered around the room. T.K. a Susan seemed misplaced in their own minds. For the second time that night, the echo of the old grandfather's clock struck me, so resounding was the silence. Tick, tock; tick tock. It was an almost eerie quiet that settled down over the house. It was Susan I noticed, lifting her head to peer around the room. As she leaned in close to her fiancee, he lifted his arm around her shoulders and gave her a slight smile. Then the silence overtook the room once again, not unlike the calm after a storm.

More as an instinct to insulate myself against the unsettling hush than anything else, I suppose, I opened the journal to where I had left off and thumbed ahead a few pages, discovering as I did there were a few entries still unread. Pamela, however, broke the silence about then. "So the walker family line actually goes back to Hiam Isaacson," my wife mused. "I would have thought it would been the other way around. I'd have thought you Isaacsons were his direct descendants."

"So did I," T.K. responded with a slight snicker.

"Well, anyone who wants to figure out the Walker tribe's geneology needs only follow the chain of title to this house," Aunt Alice chimed in. "I'll bet good money you could count the number of families living in the same house as long as ours has on your fingers. Never have to count a toe in the process."

"How so?" I asked.

"Simple. Hiam Isaacson built this house. Now he and that Maneau woman down in Jamaica begat Amanda Maneau, who took title to the place after Isaacson moved up north. Amanda and Etienne Duboisblanc begat Maurice Maneau, who took title after his mama died. Now he and his wife had two daughters, don't you see? The oldest was named Lizbeth and she married Charles Walker. That's where the change in our family name happens.. Charles Walker was your great grandaddy, Bodie. Lizbeth inherited the place from her parents, and from there on down you just follow the Walker name. Only three surnames have ever been attached to the deed to this house: Isaacson, Maneau and Walker."

"Well, I'm still trying to come to terms with having the Isaacson name, but none of the DNA," T.K. interjected. "I wonder what the rest of my family is going to think when I tell them about all this. That we descend from poor Irish immigrants, not some pillar of the Jewish community in America."

"Well, I think it's fascinating," Pamela said. "To think our boys are come from English Jews, African Americans, and French nobility on their father's side. Where but in New Orleans?"

"Don't forget to tell the boys about their being at least one bastard thrown in there, too."

"Aunt Alice" I chasten, realizing my tenor sounded very much like hers when she would correct me as a child.

"Well now, I'm just saying..."

"It does seem like both of our families descended from red-blooded, American mongrels, doesn't it?" T.K. posed. "I wonder if my grandmother has known we're genealogical orphans all along?" He looked to me and asked, "So is that all she wrote?"

Saturday, 14 1837

Even as I had last put my pen to page and signed thereon my signature, I had been tinking to myself how relieved I was that this heavy task was at long last off my shoulders. I admonished myself that once my signature was dry, I was to install this daybook randomly among monsieur's sizable collection of books in the library, then see to it my time and attention were fully occupied: no ting good would come of my sitting about, listening to the clock tick and waiting for Mme. Laveau's portent to come true. All through the writing of this account of so much misfortune, Mon. Isaacson's condition did gradually appear to improve. Now was not the time, however, to sit at his bedside in anticipation of his resurrection to former glory, which might, or might not, come to pass. So, it was that I threw myself into the running of this household—that and the managing of monsieur's business affairs, which was no inconsequential undertaking. To the contrary, many were his associates and collaborators who were growing most disquieted over his lengthy absence from the theatre of commerce.

And so it was that the very morning after I had signed the daybook and inserted it among the monsieur's other books, I found myself overseeing the grooms who, although I had assured them of extra wages for their services, were, nonetheless, most downcast at again being relegated to housework. It could not be helped, though, so short-handed were we with Mary Dunnigan and Sonnier and now even Molly Connelley all gone. Even I had been forced to don an apron and lift my hands in deference to a presentable house. Thus, was I to be found that sunny morning out in the courtyard stubbornly scouring at the remains of bloody footprints left behind on one of the great hall carpets. My arms somewhat ached from all of the rubbing I had done, with every concoction for the removing of stain old Marie and I could imagine. Sweat did trickle down my face, and as I used the back of my hand to push a wayward curl of my hair from out of my face, what should my eyes behold but Mme. Laveau, herself, standing at the back gate, clutching at the iron bars. I perceived a certain radiance about her, there that morning, all dressed up in a loud frock over petticoat, white apron and her hair bound up with the seven-knotted tignon. She smiled a wide, toothy grin and called to me.

"I woke up this morning sensing you'd finished the writin'. Now you be bringing the book to me."

Without a word (I was rather annoyed at her intrusion, so occupied was I with the stain on the hall carpet)I dropped my scrub brush and wiped my hands on my apron. I pushed my hair again out of my face, before turning to the house. When I returned from the library with the volume, the old mamaloi was still there, still clutching at the bars to the back gate. As I approached her, I did open the gate from between us and presented the daybook to her. She took it as reverently as she would have accepted a newborn infant and gently stroked the cover. Once she opened it, I was surprised to see her examine the pages, not with her eyes, but with her hands, which she delicately ran over each leaf. "Mmmm," and "I see," she would mumble from time to time, as if she were reading with her hands. I was left to wonder if Mme. Laveau, for all her power and influence in this community, might not be unschooled in the art of reading and writing.

Once she had taken her time and caressed each page, she withdrew a fist of oak leaves from her apron pocket. She nodded over her shoulder, implying the leaves came from the great oak across the back street. Three of the leaves did she select before discarding the others, then grasping the selected leaves in her fingers, she stroked them across the cover of the daybook three quick times, in three separate sets, before crumbling them and tossing them aside. "Back to the earth," she explained. "Always back to the earth. It must be."

Then it was that she did the strangest ting. She did reach into her other pocket and extract a handful of dirt, which she handed to me. "Hold this, baby," she instructed me. And as I accepted the dirt in my cupped hands she did stab it with her thumb and mark three crosses on the book's cover.

"This be powerful earth," she told me. "Come from Mary Dunnigan's grave, no less." I looked at the dirt in my hand most uneasily and she did read my mind and held out her palm for me to pour the soil back into. "All of it," she commanded, and I did brush my palm carefully over hers so as to get all of Mary's grave dirt back into her hand. Then the old priestess closed her hand around the soil, crossed herself with the fist, and then in the wink of an eye did toss the dirt over her shoulder.

As she clapped her hands clean, she looked intently at me though squinted eyes. "Now tell me, Chile, did you learn nothin' writin' this account?"

"To the contrary, woman. I learned much," I replied. "Much about other people. And much about myself."

"Gooood, then. Fiiine! Now you do as Mme.. Laveau tells you do, you hear? You make a solemn novena to St. Jude and on the tenth day you'll see. All the bad luck be gone off this house by then. You believe Mme. Laveau on this, chile."

I nodded, "I do."

"Gooood. Fiiine. Now, Chile, also. You move on and leave the dead to their graves and forgive all the others who had their hands in all these dark doings. Those two you scribbled about in this book be like two seagulls trying to build 'em a nest in the middle of a hurricane: some t'ings this old world just won't allow no matter what. No, you move on chile. Always be moving on. That way, you can forgive yourself your own fault in it. Then it was without so much as another word that she did turn and slowly walked away from me, down the street, singing under her breath all the way. Near the corner, two ladies fitted out in their finest recognized her face and stepped into the gutter to give her wide berth. Mme. Laveau did laugh heartily at their squeals as she deliberately spooked the horse of a passing carriage with a mere flip of her wrist, before sauntering on, merrily down the way.

Faithful to her command, the next morning I did cause a Solemn Nine-Day Novena to be made. Early and bright that first morning of the novena, young Patrick O'Bannion did accompany me to Mass and afterwards Clyde did drive us to the riverfront where we put him on a sailing ship over to Galveston in that new place they call Texas. Several days before, he had come upon me in the herb garden where I was forced to pull up weeds like a common yard worker. There, on my hands and knees, with hands grimy from the sticky soil, he let it be known the painting I had commissioned was at last finished. In his manner, I could read that he was most eager that I come and see what he had created, but I asked that he be patient and let me finish my weeding and make myself more presentable before viewing his masterpiece. He nodded his consent, but immediately fell to his knees to help me along with the weeds, so anxious was he that I see his work.

When at last I reported to the loft over the coach house, I found the young mon most nervous and his painting turned ceremoniously facing the wall. Unprepared was I for a canvass so large, being taller in height by far than I am in heeled shoes, and surely no less than three feet in width if it is an inch. "You said I could paint on any subject I wisht, so long as I give it me best, did you, no?" he asked of me, apprehensively.

"Indeed, mon, I did. "

He inhaled deeply through flared nostrils and then turned to the canvass. "Very well. Here goes, then." Gingerly did he turn the painting around to face me and as I took in my first eyeful of it, I tell you it almost took the breath right out of my lungs. I heard myself gasp out loud and did cover my mouth with my kerchief.

"You don't like it, then!" Patrick reacted in distress, misreading my reaction, as he had.

"Au contraire, mon ami!" I exclaimed. "C'est magnifique! It's...beautiful. It's...like the image in a mirror!" Try as I might, I could not find the words to describe how spellbinding the painting was. Spellbinding, yet eldritch, at the same time, for before me was the most realistic of oil paintings I had ever seen in my life. To be sure, at first I was not certain it was not some ghostly apparition rather than a painting; so life-like, so haunting was Patrick's portrait of Mary Dunnigan, dressed to the hilt in that opera gown and necklace monsieur had given her. "No, an image in the mirror couldn't be any more realistic," I exhaled. "And the dress? The necklace? How did you know?" I asked, puzzled as to how the mon could have so faithfully reproduced tings I was sure he'd never seen before.

"I'd sketched her before in that same dress and necklace," he explained. "So Rory would have something pretty to remind 'em o' her, out by that canal. Only I ne'er got it to the lad in time." From a stack of charcoal sketches piled on the floor, he extracted the drawing of Mary. "See, here it is. I worked from this."

I studied his sketch and marveled at the faithful reproduction he had made of her in charcoal pencil. "Still," I heard myself saying. "The colors? How could you remember the color of her gown and the way the light would fall on her hair? Without her here to sit for you? Young Patrick was clearly embarrassed by my praise. No doubt praise was some ting with which he had little experience. "You, ma'am, are a musician. Ye hear tones and rhythms I could never hear. I'm an artist, though. It's colors and textures and patterns that stay around in me head," he explained, most plausibly.

"Moi oui, Patrick O'Bannion. Some ting deep down tells me monsieur will want this painting hanging at the head of the great stairs. Oui, young mon, you've certainly earned yourself the price of passage to Texas. If that's what you want." I looked from the picture to the young mon, squinting as I looked him in the eyes. "And are you sure that's what you want. Are you not sure you wouldn't rather stay in New Orleans a while longer? You know, Monsieur Isaacson and I are not without contacts in this community. For an artist of your talents we could surely get work.

But he dropped his head. "I thank ye for your generosity, ma'am. And I thank ye for pullin' me outta that canal afore twas too late. But if's it's all the same with ye, I think it's time this Irishman was a getting' himself on to some other place."

"And will you find the future any brighter in that place Texas than New Orleans?" It was a question I had to ask him, although I was not prepared for his answer.

"No. That I won't. For sure I won't. On that account, I've no

illusions. But at least the pain won't be so bad, with nothin' to remind me ever' time I turn a corner."
So it was we said little to one another, that first morning of the novena, as Clyde pulled the landau up beside the ship, all rigged and ready to take the boy to a new and untried future. He stepped down from the carriage and Clyde handed him his little valise containing a single change of clothes and his art kit. "Patrick O'Bannion," I called to him, and he did look up to me there in the carriage. "Don't you go ruining your hands so you can't paint any more, working that land you crave.

God's given you a talent to use, monsieur. You go on and use it now. Do you hear me?

He bestowed a shy little smile upon me, along with a wave of his hand and turned for the gangway. Midway up did he stop, quickly, and turn back to me.

"I won't be forgettin' ye, Missus Maneau," he called out. And as quickly, then, did he turn and disappear up the walkway into the ship, leaving me feeling low the whole way home. For the first time in my life did I understand a most significant aspect of my being: I do so hate the good byes. Sometimes it seems I've spent the better part of my life saying goodbye.

No, no ting so unsettles me as much as change and there is no greater change to be had on this earth than the bidding of farewell. Such was a lesson I would soon come to appreciate all the more, for you see, on the tenth day—the day after the novena—as I returned home from my morning

Mass, I was most delightedly surprised to be greeted by my Etienne waiting in the front salon.

"I wasn't expecting you," I gasped as he rose to take me in his arms.

"Nor was I expecting to be here this morning," he told me as he did kiss my hands. " Mon. Isaacson issued me an urgent summons."

Concern rose up inside me. "Is any ting the matter?

"He's foreclosed on the plantation.

"Oh no. That mustn't be. I'll speak to him—" But my Etienne cut me off short by putting his finger to my lips.

"No. It's quite all right. My brother's mismanagement of the property has brought it to this sad state. It's far, far better that it is out of his hands now."

"But what shall you do?" I cried. "Return to France? You've a family to care for."

"I'm afraid that all depends on you?" he said with a puzzling little smile upon his face.

"On me? But however so?"

"You shall see. Go to him, to MonsieurIsaacson. He waits for you in l'bibliotheque."

All the way out of the parlor, across the hall to the library I did look back over my shoulder, questioningly, at my Etienne, as he shooed me along with little waves of his hands. At the door, I tapped and entered upon master's command. As I stepped into the room, marveled to see him seated in his club chair, presentably dressed and for all outward appearances as fully in command of himself as he had ever been, as he played with Mary Dunnigan's infant son upon his lap.

"Monsieur, you are up and about. C'est merveilleux," I declared.

"Amanda! I've been expecting you," he sang as he motioned for me to be seated. "Have you seen Etienne?"

"Oui, monsieur. He told me you wished an audience with me," I replied as I took my seat.

Mon. Hiam Isaacson made goo-goo eyes at the little infant, which only now do I recognize as having been exceedingly humorous. At that time, I was so confused and so concerned by Etienne's mysterious behavior, that I failed to be fully cognizant of how funny it was—a grown mon of such position and earnestness making funny faces at a baby.

"What did Etienne tell you of our conversation?
"Only that you had taken away the plantation and he has no way to provide for his wife and children now."

"And is that all he told you on that matter?"

"Oui. It is."

"I see. Then let me clarify this for you. Perfecting my lien on the plantation only makes good business sense. It has nothing whatsoever to do with Etienne. Had he been left to his own talents by that no-account brother of his, there would be no need for me to have to take such drastic measures. I can assure you that the only reason I've not moved to foreclose earlier has been in deference to your alliance with him. Insomuch as his not being able to take care of his family, however, don't worry your head over that. Etienne did marry well, even if Mme.. Duboisblanc is as homely as an alligator. The family will not suffer.

"Let me also say this: I have requested that Etienne continue on in the management of the property and he has consented to do so."

"Merci monsieur. Merci You do relieve my anxiety."

"There's no need to thank me. Etienne DuBoisblanc is an astute planter and a gentleman of commerce. It only makes good business sense for us to engage his talents. To keep the land profitable. Indeed, you are a woman of some means, yourself. You would be well-advised to rely on Etienne to manage your estate, as well."

Once again, confusion clouded my mind. Monsieur, and monsieur alone, had always tended my affairs. Why now would he be suggesting I look to Etienne to conserve my estate, I wondered? "I don't tink I understand, monsieur?"

Master did beam a most warm smile at me. "Amanda, it is high time you had a life of your own. Your own family! This house and the plantation are to be placed in your name. Etienne will oversee and shelter his family there, but there is no reason the two of you shouldn't have your own home and—in time—a family here in the city. That is if you agree to be his consort."

"Wait. I don't understand," Susan blurted out. "He's a married man! And Isaacson is telling her to go share her to go shack up with him?"

"Oh honey, don't try to understand how the men did things back then. You'll come closer to figuring out the mystery of the Holy Trinity than you will their notion of love and marriage," Aunt Alice insisted.

"But he was married with a family! It's hard enough to accept them carrying on in this house like they did. But setting up house and talking about having children? While he's got a wife and kids on the plantation? Crazy! This is just crazy. I just don't get it."

Pamela and I understood the mores of nineteenth century New Orleans. The Quadroon Balls they held back then for eligible *married* Anglo/Franco men to find a mistress are still part of the lore of the city, but we were content to sit back and let Aunt Alice explain it.

"See, what you don't understand is upper crust men in those days took a wife to improve their financial and social positions. That and breeding: producing good offspring—sound of mind and body. That sort of stuff. Love just didn't figure into marriage in those days. For love and affection and... You know... S.E.X. For all that they took themselves a mistress. Raised a family with her, too. Legal marriages and de facto marriages. That's the way it was. Don't make a damned bit of sense to us today, but that was just how it was. That's what old Hiam Isaacson was putting Amanda Maneau up to. Let Duboisblanc take her as a mistress and worry about her from there on out."

Susan looked over at T.K. "If you know what's good for you, you won't go getting any ideas about that business."

"I'd want another family like I'd want a root canal," he said as I took up reading where we left off.

"But monsieur? If Etienne and I are to be together here, in this house, where will you be? It wouldn't be seemly for the three of us to share the same roof," I asked, more perplexed than ever, as he grew serious.

I fear I have kept you at my beck-and-call too long now. You are entitled to your own separate happiness. Just as I am. No, over the next several months, I will be liquidating much of my Louisiana holdings. Island properties too. I plan to relocate to New York City. And I will be taking this little one with me. It's time—past time—for each of us to make a new and better life for ourselves."

"But why? Why New York? Why can you not stay here? Etienne and I can find a place of our own. You've no need to abandon your fine home."

"New York has been at the forefront of my plans for some time now, I am afraid. All that's kept me in this city has been that cursed canal, but now my associates are eager to buy me out. So you see, it's the logical time for this move.

There are opportunities for me and the little one in the great city that are just unavailable in New Orleans."

"But you're sure? About the little one? I fear it will be a tremendous responsibility."

"Indeed it will be. But a responsibility I vowed to his dying mother I'd undertake."

"Still this is all so much to grasp in such a short span."

He broke out in a most genuine snort of laughter. "One thing at a time, Amanda. One thing at a time."

My master did cradle the baby up against his shoulder as he rose up from his chair. Across the room, to the door he marched and there he swung it open wide. He called to Etienne and motioned with a sweep of his arm for him to enter the room, then announced he perceived we had much to talk about. Ever so gently did he close the door behind him, leaving Etienne and me alone together.

I tink the monsieur knew his going to New York would force me into Etienne's waiting arms. Oh, of course I tink he did truly want to leave New Orleans , to start life anew somewhere else: too many's the ghosts, too many's the reminders at every turn, not to haunt him if he stayed behind here. I know he was a mon of his word, so I always knew he would keep his promise to Mary to watch over her child. Still, I do believe the idea of starting over anew , of building a good life for the little one did appeal to him, as well. It gave him some ting new and fresh to live for. And I also reckon monsieur realized that his leaving Louisiana would, for me, open the door to a new life with the mon I loved. At least I would like to believe so, for such would be a grand gesture, a most magnificent sacrifice on his part. It would be equivalent to my ultimate emancipation.

Sitting here today, going over all this, putting in down on these pages, I find a smile has grown upon my face: Mme. Laveau had assured me that on the day after my novena, all the bad luck would be lifted from off this house. That she had done. What I had expected, though, was that tings would return to they way they always had been.

What I knew now is tings will never be the same again. Ever.

A.Maneau
Nouvelle Orleans, Louisiana

December 19, 1864

It has been twenty-seven years since I last set eyes upon this daybook, set pen upon one of its pages. I had forgotten where I had placed it, in and amongst the many volumes in this library, and it has taken me some time to find it. For reasons I cannot quite put into words upon this page, was it important to me that I find this book and record therein one, perhaps, final entry. So much has transpired since last I wrote herein that I ask myself again where shall I begin?

How the years have flown by. My beloved Etienne sleeps in St. Louis Cemetery, dead these six years now from a most difficult outbreak of the yellow fever, which took with it nearly half the population of this city. He shares his crypt with Mme. Duboisblanc and their only son, victims of the cruel fever themselves.

Our son, Maurice Maneau, stands as a mon in his own right, now, married and a father himself. He oversees operations on my plantation as Marquis upon the demise of his uncle in France who departed this life without male issue. What there is to oversee, that is, what with this cruelest of wars dragging on and on. He did come with his wife, and two daughters to take shelter with me in the great house when the countryside was overrun by the troops of the northern aggressors. Our fields were burnt, and all our livestock carted off. Even the old DuBoisblanc home is now infested with Yankee vermin. We pray that now that all of Louisiana is under federal occupation, perhaps this spring he may return and again plant crops in the DuBoisblanc soil.

But, then, one can only hope, I suppose.

These, then, are the days of our winter, which find me with pen in hand once again. Sometime ago did the winds change so they now blow down from the north, heavy and damp like a wet blanket. The heavens have gone gray and the sun seldom does show her face anymore. I dress in layers against the cold and damp, my greatcoat pulled tight around my shoulders, even when I am inside the great house—which now stands shuttered against the outside world. Like a freedwoman most refined, there is a time to be bejeweled and gowned elegantly, and there is a time to cloak oneself in dark clothes and stand aside in the shadows. This is a time for monsieur's beloved mansion to retire away and not call attention to herself. To do otherwise, in this day and age, would be to invite ruination.

The Negro kitchen is now our home. You see, there has been no coal to be had in the city in over a year, now—not a single piece for my master's modern grates. And what little fuel there is to keep the chill off us comes from the tearing up of the floorboards in the carriage house. Long ago were our horses procured by the vile northerners, and even monsieur's fine Fisher landau is now the personal carriage of the insufferable Yankee, Gen. Butler. So, you see, it is no great loss if we burn the whole of the coach house, as long as it keeps the cold at bay.

With the great house closed and the kitchen our refuge, Maurice and his wife have taken quarters back in Marie's old room. There the bricks of the chimney stack stay warm through most of the night. My grandchildren and I sleep before the fireplace in the kitchen proper. Our sides away from the fire quickly grow cold, causing us to constantly roll over in our sleep, all the night long, like great roasts on a split before the fire.

With no staff at hand, no house to oversee, I find too much of my time is spent watching the winter rain on the windowpanes. How like tears the raindrops do seem, as they form, then make their long journey down the glass, only to be consumed by the dark, cold ground below. Or else I waste my while rocking before the fire, my gaze inexorably drawn into it, all the while tinking, remembering, going over in my mind the way tings used to be. No ting is as sure as change, but mon

Dieu, mon Dieu! How I do hate tings always changing the way they do.

The privation all of New Orleans—not just we—now endures is beyond description. With my accounts in foreign banks now lost, we are forced to make do with the most meager of sustenance and are happy for it. And tragically enough, we are most probably better off than many in other parts of the world. Oft times do I find myself wondering about young Patrick O'Bannion, immigrating to Texas, as full of hope as the day he first stepped off the boat here in New Orleans. Often do I wonder about him in that strange, untried new place, but always rest assured he is undoubtedly far better off that the rest of his kind, starving amid that infamous potato famine in Ireland. At such times, I do thank my God most heartily for what little we have. At least we still have the roof over our heads and the great house has not been looted nor burnt like the property of so many others. At least we live and are healthy: old Marie and Clyde have both passed now, and Molly Connelley's health has been ruined giving birth to no less than eleven children, all fathered by a drunkard, killed at the Battle of Vicksburg, at that.

Just this very morning—for reasons I shall reveal hereafter—I found myself drawn to Mary Dunnigan's old chambers. Only a day or so after her demise had I seen to it that the room was locked up and no one has set foot therein for, lo', these many years now. It was with some difficulty that I was finally able to break the lock with a prying bar I found out in the coach house, the key to the lock having long ago been misplaced. As I entered the room, I found it exactly as it had been on the day of her death, nothing in the least disturbed. It was a fine powdering of dust that covered every ting, along with cobwebs and the smell of mold—all the little tings that make a tomb a home. Still tacked on the wall above the bureau did I find an arrangement of Patrick O'Bannion's sketches of the riverfront, of St. Patrick's Church, of the old tree across the back street. And there, still lying atop the chiffonier, was a little dish of corset laces, snipped in two by Dr. Penney's scissors.

Some ting lying in the window overlooking the back street did catch my eye; there upon the sill, dust-covered and forgotten, lay the lovely medallion monsieur had given Mary all those many years ago. I made for the window and took seat upon the dusty sill, where I took up the medallion in my hands. With my breath I blew away the dust and examined it there in the light of the window. It was an indeed exceptionally fine piece, and as I rubbed at the bejeweled bird with my thumb, I was taken unawares when the bird moved, causing the case to flip open, revealing a picture compartment within. Therein, fitted carefully in place, was that oil-on-porcelain portrait of Rory O'Kelley, the unmistakable work of Patrick O'Bannion's gifted hand, painted as a Christmas present for Mary so many years ago!

How I did marvel at the miniature, at the fine detail of workmanship. Surely many of the strokes had required Patrick's brush to be pared down to a single hair. Moreover did I marvel at how handsome Rory had been, his image having long ago dimmed in my memory. I tink I understood for the first time how Mary did fall so in love with that freckled-face boy. Cobwebs I brushed from the window with my hand, and I wiped at the dusty pane with my sleeve.

There from the second floor vantage point, I noticed, as I gazed out at the panorama, that with the trees bare for the winter one could just make out the New Basin Canal making its bend into the business area. The morning sun reflected dimly off its murky waters and I shuddered as I was reminded that Rory rested in a watery grave beneath that very canal. And just a short way up from that bend, Mary now slept beneath the most magnificent monument, on the most prominent corner of the most prominent cemetery in the city, overlooking, of all tings, the New Basin Canal.

O' irony—surely you must be the cruelest of them all.

It was a goodly while that I stood there, staring out Mary's window at that canal of such misfortune. And whilst I did so, it crossed my mind that all the while they were building on that girl's monument, master did near drive me insane with his almost daily letters from New York, charging me to make sure this was done and tell so-and-so not to forget such-and-such. I tell you I did relish the day I wrote to him and told him the monument was finished and most magnificent. I wrote suggesting he come down and see it for himself. It was a suggestion that was to go unanswered, for once Mon. Hiam Isaacson had left New Orleans, never was he to set eyes upon the city again.

From Mary's chamber window, across the far side of the canal my attention came to focus on the white tented encampment of the Union troops under Gen. Butler's command. I did note that from this distance it looked not much different from the squalid Irish workers' camps, scattered up and down the canal the whole time it was being dug. Mon Dieu, how I do despise that canal, even as I despise this hideous war that so tears us apart. Up from the window I did rise, slipping the medallion into my pocket as I did, vowing under my breath that once the war was ended and mail routes were again reliable, that I should send it to Mary's son in New York.

Once I had risen and made my way out of the room, there on the balcony I struggled to get the door pulled shut. As soon as this war is ended, and workers are again to be had for the hiring, I told myself, I shall see to it that door is bricked and mortared over, leaving Mary's room a shrine forever sealed.

With the door adequately pulled to, I turned to make my way back into the kitchen house, noticing for the first time as I did, how dust-covered I had become, there in that room. I paused to brush the dust from off me, but it proved to be a most futile attempt and all the while I beat at my dress I found myself wondering would tings never be the way they used to be.

I suspect that this most barbarous of wars is rapidly drawing to a close, however. And yet I do fear that war's end will bring with it times more terrible than those we now endure. Along with her campaigns, the South's spirit has been routed, to the extent folks now look for somewhere—anywhere—to place the blame—anywhere but on their own, misguided haughtiness, that is. Perhaps the fear that so overtakes my heart from time-to-time can best be explained in terms of an unfortunate incident encountered when last my family and I ventured into town. With no fields to tend, no livestock to nurture, my son does prowl the property looking for little projects to occupy his time and mind. For that reason, he determined we were in need of a new file to sharpen the ground implements in anticipation of the spring garden.

Together, the four of us journeyed downtown, and while Maurice whiled his time away at the smith-shop, my daughter-in-law and I did take the opportunity to peruse the empty store windows on Canal Street. There we tarried for a moment, before the window of no less than Miss Julia's dress shop which I had for years patronized, when suddenly, the owner herself did fly through the door, whilst screaming like a crazy woman. "Shooo! Scat! Y'all nigras are driving off my business. Go on! Get! Go on while you still can!" she shouted at us, all the while the passers-by gawked at us like we were a band of gypsies intent on robbing the poor woman. I tell you I was astonished. Dumbstruck. For nearly as long as I have lived in this city, have I been a patroness of that very store. Always! Many has been the time I have loitered by those windows looking for some ting to capture my eye, some ting to purchase.

Many are the years in which I have been one of Miss Julia's better customers. Always have I abided by the rules of the game. Never have I ever been guilty to setting foot inside that store—or any store—without my hair bound up in the tignon. Never, never have I been guilty of being seen in public in extravagant dress. Never in my wildest imagination would I have done anything to cause the proprietress embarrassment. Then to be so ill-treated by those who have taken my money for so many years wounds my nerves. And so it is that I do fear that we of darker pigment are to be made the bearers of the blame for all the South's misfortune, the brunt of a proud peoples' anger, no matter how unwarranted, how misdirected.

God help us if my worst of fears should come to pass. I would that I could avail myself of the monsieur's counsel in this matter. But then, I doubt the South land, as an independent nation, is not long to exist, so overtaken are her defenses. Perhaps there is no better omen of the fall to come, than the letter that came today, postmarked New York, N.Y., March 19, 1862. It does grieve my very soul that it has taken more than two years for this letter to arrive, but at long last it has reached its destination. How I do thank God that it has found its way into my hands, for the letter comes from no less than monsieur's attorney in the great city. In the letter, I am advised that on the evening of 20 February, 1862, whilst surrounded by his loving son, Thomas, and his loyal staff, my master did enter into eternal rest. He shall be missed; he shall be sorely missed, and I do fear that tings won't ever be the same without him.

How I do regret, even though we wrote to one another on an almost weekly basis, until the war interrupted the mail lines, that I was never to set eyes upon him again, after that blustery January morning when I saw the baby and him off at the train station. Now he is gone, and I shall never have the opportunity to see him, to touch him; to sense his aroma; to enjoy the sounds of his voice; ever again. Now he is of the past, and the past, like the future, is nonexistent in the here and now. Left lingering behind like I am, I am left to wonder: if I can call to mind the times of my father, all the little nooks and crannies where his memory resides, what can he remember of me? Is there not some part of him left behind that is aware of my continued existence? If I listen carefully, can I hear his voice in the gentle autumn breeze? Can I discern his laughter in the thunder rolling up from the Gulf in summer? If I gaze deeply enough into the winter hearth, might I find his joy there among the glowing embers, his anguish in the rains of May? Or does that essential core of his being (which is or was his soul) lie molding and decaying with his body in the grave? And if his soul was at last set free, has it so dispersed in the vastness of the universe as to be impotent forever more, much like a sugar cube in the Mississippi; or a spray of perfume on the wind? Is there nothing but fading memories of him, left behind to accompany me along this march of time?

I am advised by his counsel that all his worldly possessions he did leave to his only child, Thomas Kelley Isaacson, which is only befitting. Monsieur did years ago provide for me by the gifts of his controlling interest in the Canal Bank, the Duboisblanc Plantation and this house. A most generous gesture that was, for when monsieur departed New Orleans that January morn, the only worldly possessions he took with him were his wardrobe and Patrick O'Bannion's portrait of Mary Dunnigan. All else he left behind for me. I would, however, have given this house and all the considerable fortune he has bestowed upon me for some ting far, far less costly; some ting far, far more priceless: to be recognized for what I truly am: his one and only child. It is, and always has been, monsieur's good name that I consider my one, true birthright.

Shalom, havir! Yih' yeh b'seder. Let not my love for you keep you too close to this place. Go on and soar on high with the angels. Now is the universe your home.

A.M.D.
New Orleans, Louisiana, C.S.A.

PART THREE

...OF DESTINATIONS DISCOVERED

I can't tell you why but I knew there were no more entries in the journal once I finished that last date. Still, I licked at my thumb and turned a few pages, then flipped through the remaining ones, magazine-style. Sure enough the rest of the sheets were blank.

"Well, that's all she wrote, folks. Sorry," I told the room.

Once again, the old house on Carondelet Street grew silent as the four of us became lost in our thoughts, all the while Aunt Alice stabbed the needlepoint and peered over her glasses as she would draw out a long thread. Eventually, Susan asked if it was the same clock offering the only sounds in the house that had been in the hall in Hiam Isaacson's days. Aunt Alice nodded in the affirmative, cleared her throat. then inquired, "So was I wrong to tell you boys about that journal? To let you read it?"

I shrugged and said it wasn't wrong; T.K. added, "You were right, though, Mrs. Monroe. It wasn't the story I was expecting." Susan seemed concerned and asked if he was all right. "Me? I'm okay. Little confused. Slightly embarrassed."

My aunt sat her needlework aside and pulled her glasses down low on her nose to peer over them. "Why would you be embarrassed?"

"Why wouldn't I be? My grandmother donates a painting to the art museum that's supposed to be a portrait of *Catherine Isaacson*... There's even a little plaque beside it that says just that. Last night at the ball, much ado was made about how *Catherine Isaacson* was a daughter of old New Orleans. Now I find out *Catherine Isaacson* never even existed. The woman in that painting may in fact be my great-great-great grandmother, but she surely wasn't anyone named *Catherine Isaacson*. And I don't think you could exactly call her a daughter of the old south."

"Do you think we should ask the museum to change the name?" Susan asked.

"We're acquaintances of the curator. We could set up a meeting with him if you'd like," Pamela volunteered.

But T.K. just shook his head no. "Let's keep it under wraps until I can meet with our lawyers. We may need to change the title but the last thing we want is to make a big deal out of it. Let's let the lawyers handle it. You know, not cause a lot of attention."

Aunt Alice returned to her needlepoint, asking without ever looking up from it, "Does it bother you to find out you're not Jewish after all?" "Oh, I'm a Jew alright. No doubt about that. You're Jewish when you're born to a Jewish mother. My mother is definitely Jewish. It's just the man I always thought was the founder of family in America isn't. Wasn't. At least not the biological founder."

"How does that leave you feeling?" I asked. "Surprised is about all. I'm not about to change my name or anything like that, if that's what you mean." And then T.K. said the most peculiar thing. "But what about you? Don't take this wrong, but as southerners does it bother you to find out your roots go all the way back to Africa?"

It was a fair question and I thought about it for a bit. "I had no idea in God's green earth who Amanda Maneau was until we read this book," I finally began. "I'm a little like you, T.K. Little surprised to find out she's my ancestor. But to answer your question: no. Doesn't bother me that she was part black. We've all known there was a Negro line in the family. Our state government made sure everyone knew that."

"Really? How so?" Susan asked.

"A person's race is listed on the birth certificate. Anyone as little as $1/32^{nd}$ black would be classified as Negro. The lunacy of the whole thing is my birth certificate says I am white, but my father's says he's black. But I've known about that crap for a long time now. So no, it's no big surprise. What is surprising to me is finding out I'm a descendant of Hiam Isaacson and you're not.

"Yeah, but still," T.K. mused, "You have to admit it's a bit ironic: we read an old journal and found out you've got Jewish blood and I've got Irish blood."

I couldn't let it go at that. I couldn't stop myself from adding, "And you know what makes it all the more amusing? You ended up with all my great-great-great grandfather's money, and all I ended up with is a dubious claim to a bankrupt French title. How's that for irony?"

A few minutes later, we ventured past the front gate, and made our way down Josephine Street beside the Pontchartrain Hotel, just as a fine harvest moon made its debut over St. Charles Avenue. We shook hands and bid each other farewell at the corner:

a few blocks toward downtown a streetcar came swaying along the tracks like a palm tree in the wind. Pamela and I scurried across the Avenue and hopped aboard, taking one of the backwards facing seats. T.K. and Susan still stood on the corner in the fading light, watching as the car rocked on down the line. I leaned out the open window to return their wave and that was it.

Our family paths have never crossed again since that balmy day in October, in that exceptional old house on Carondelet Street.

END

here is the deepest secret nobody knows (here is the root of the root and the bud of the bud and the sky of the sky of a tree called life; which grows higher than soul can hope or mind can hide) and this is the wonder that's keeping the stars apart: i carry your heart (i carry it in my heart)

e e cummings

...the Jefferson/Orleans Parish line, Interstate 10 takes a left turn as ...enters New Orleans proper. Few speeding down the highway ...day are aware that this section of the interstate was built over ...at had once been the course of the New Basin Canal. Fewer still ...e aware of the role which poor Irish immigrants played in ...nstructing that waterway through some of the more treacherous ...amp land in North America, nor of the price they paid in doing so. ...aths by yellow fever, malaria, dysentery, poisonous snakes and ...igators were so prevalent that the use of slave labor was quickly ...termined to be too costly to be practical. The solution, therefore, ...s to send to Ireland for impoverished Irishmen willing to risk their ...es toiling in such hostile conditions for meager wages. They came ... shiploads to die in great numbers.

...fying, yet gut wrenching and heartbreaking, what Pumphrey has ...itten is a book of fiction based on a little known American ...ocaust. The stories of the Irishmen who dug the canal have been ... but lost to history, the only acknowledgement of their existence ...ng a small monument at the foot of West End Boulevard ...rlooking Lake Pontchartrain. It reads:

"In memory of the Irish immigrants who dug the
New Basin Canal, 1832-1838, this Celtic cross
carved in Ireland has been erected by the Irish
Cultural Society of New Orleans"

...CHAEL PUMPHREY is a former longtime New Orleans resident. ...ding master's degrees in Architecture and Preservation Studies ...m Tulane University, he specialized in historic preservation, city ...nning and cultural resources ...nagment. Today, he is retired, ...ng high in the Sierra Madre ...untains on the shores of ...utiful Lake Chapala in western ...xico.

$24.00

ISBN 978-0-9828700-3-7

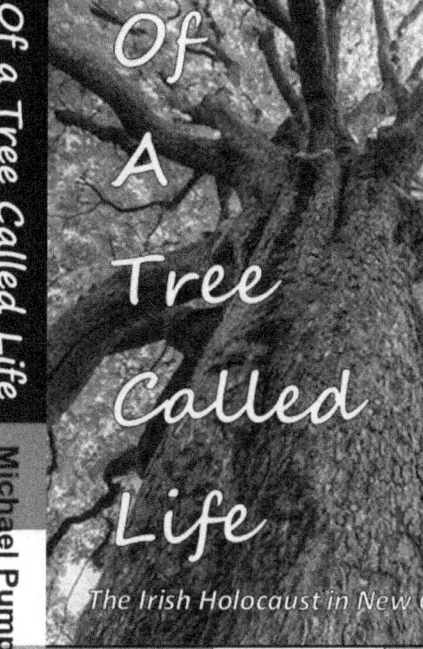

Of A Tree Called Life

Michael Pumphrey

The Irish Holocaust in New Orleans

Michael Pumphrey

www.ingramcontent.com/pod-product-compliance
Lightning Source LLC
Chambersburg PA
CBHW031307150426
43191CB00005B/113